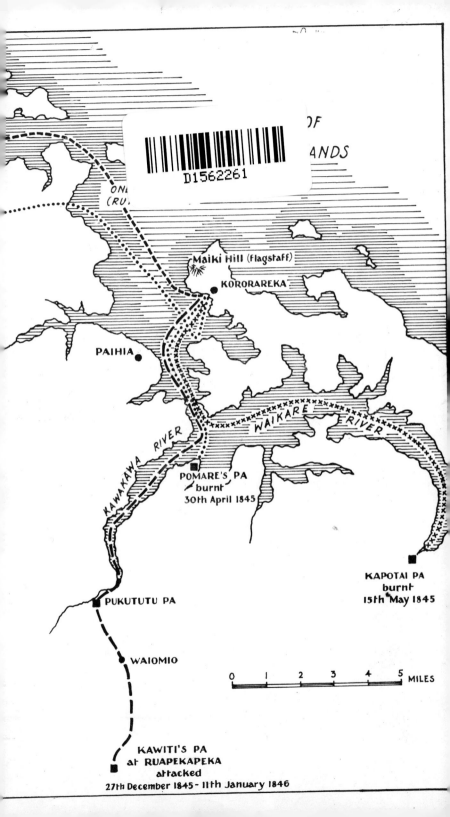

OF
ISLANDS

D1562261

ONE
(RU

Maiki Hill (Flagstaff)
● KORORAREKA

● PAIHIA

WAIKARE RIVER

KAWAKAWA RIVER

POMARE'S PA
burnt
30th April 1845

KAPOTAI PA
burnt
15th May 1845

■ PUKUTUTU PA

● WAIOMIO

0 1 2 3 4 5 MILES

■ KAWITI'S PA
at RUAPEKAPEKA
attacked
27th December 1845 - 11th January 1846

To Face the Daring Maoris

To Face the Daring Maoris

Soldiers' impressions of the
First Maori War
1845–47

by

Michael Barthorp

When first we landed on that shore to fight we went straightway
To face the dareing Maories all on the 8th of May

PRIVATE ALEXANDER WHISKER,
58th Regiment

HODDER AND STOUGHTON
LONDON SYDNEY AUCKLAND TORONTO

British Library Cataloguing in Publication Data

Barthorp, Michael
   To face the daring Maoris.
   1. New Zealand – History – 1843–1870
   2. New Zealand – History, Military
   3. Great Britain. Army – History
   I. Title
   993.102'1   DU420

ISBN 0 340 22719 2

Hodder and Stoughton Editorial Office: 47 Bedford Square, London WC1B 3DP

Contents

Illustrations

The author wishes to thank the following for permission to use their photographs:
Royal Anglian Regiment: 1; Mrs E. J. G. Clark: 2; Rev R. Hattaway (photograph by D. Roberts): 3; Lieut S. H. Speight, R.N.Z.N. (photograph by D. Buttimore): 4; L. M. Lennard (photograph by D. Buttimore): 5; Hocken Library, University of Otago: 6, 8, 9, 10, 11, 12, 19, 24, 26, 28, 29; Alexander Turnbull Library, Wellington: 7, 13, 15, 16, 17, 18, 21, 22, 23, 25; Auckland Institute and Museum: 14, 20; Auckland City Art Gallery, Partridge Collection (photograph by Alexander Turnbull Library): 27.

Maps

Acknowledgments

DURING THE COURSE OF SOME RESEARCH INTO THE DRESS WORN by British troops in the field during the many colonial wars of the last century, I was put in touch with Mr Peter Coates of the New Zealand Broadcasting Corporation, who had produced a television documentary on the First Maori War. Mr Coates very kindly drew my attention to the existence of some accounts written by British officers and men who had fought in the campaign. Copies of these documents were generously made available to me and, using this material, I wrote a short article called 'Baptism of Fire in New Zealand' for the *Journal of the Society for Army Historical Research*. This caught the eye of a New Zealand member of the Society, Mr John Kitt of Auckland. Although my original interest had been solely one of military costume, Mr. Kitt's enthusiasm and never-failing kindness in providing me with further information inspired me to attempt the whole story of this campaign, as seen through the eyes of its participants. Without his aid, this book could hardly have been written, for, not only has he been assiduous in sending me books, cuttings, copies of documents and photographs, he has put me in touch with descendants of men who fought in New Zealand, who have also been most generous with their help. Among these I must list, with gratitude, the Reverend R. Hattaway of East Tamaki, Auckland, Mr Keith Slattery of Auckland, and the Speight family, also of Auckland. In addition, Mr J. Bryant Haigh, the New Zealand military historian, has given me much valuable information and filled in many useful details. I am also most grateful to the staffs of the Alexander Turnbull Library, Wellington and the Auckland War Memorial and Museum for providing me with copies of documents in their possession and for permission to make use of them in the book. I am further indebted to the Alexander Turnbull Library and to Miss Janice Eskett of the Hocken Library, University of Otago, for their assistance with the selection and provision of illustrations.

In England I have been much encouraged and helped by members of the Bridge family, whose forbear plays a leading role in the story: Mr Cyprian J. Bridge, Mr Christopher Bridge, the Dean of Guildford, and Mrs E. J. G. Clark, who very kindly lent me two portraits of her great-grandfather. I am grateful to Captain A. M. McKillop R.N. for filling in some details of the naval career of one of his ancestors who appears in these pages. Major Donald Baxter, Curator of the Museum of The Northamptonshire Regiment, has been most generous in making available documents in his possession, and Major J. Hughes M.B.E., Headquarters Scots Guards, provided me with the answer to a point which I had been unable to find elsewhere. I must also acknowledge the helpful and courteous service given by the staffs of the National Army Museum, the Ministry of Defence (Army) Library and the Public Record Office.

Finally I must offer my thanks to Miss Sheila Watson and Miss Margaret Body for believing that the project was worth undertaking, and for their help and friendliness in bringing it to fruition, and to my wife and family for their patience and encouragement.

Jersey, C.I., 1977.   M.J.B.

1

Redcoats and Rebels

THE ENGLISH-SPEAKING WORLD HAS, THROUGH COUNTLESS books, films and television series, become thoroughly familiar with the frontier campaigns fought by the United States Army against the Indian tribes of the West. Custer and Geronimo are almost household names; 'Cavalry and Indians' has long since replaced 'French and English' as a children's game. Yet few people today are aware that the British Army has a much longer and indeed more varied tradition of similar campaigning. Since the Battle of Waterloo, the British regular found himself crossing swords with foes as equally fierce as the American Indians, in actions just as dramatic as the Little Big Horn. In mountains and jungle, veldt and desert, the redcoat encountered Afghans and Burmese, Zulus and Fuzzy-Wuzzies, enduring much hardship and danger, even defeat and disaster, but gaining little reward or recognition, and certainly not achieving posthumous fame on the scale accorded to his counterpart in the U.S. Cavalry.

Among the British soldier's most formidable opponents were the Maoris of New Zealand, but the first campaign against them, which took place in the North Island from 1845-7, four years after the establishment of that country as a British colony, is now an almost forgotten episode. Its purpose, in British eyes, was to subdue certain rebellious tribes who had revolted against the Crown. To the rebels, it was a struggle over land and against what they saw as Government oppression. The spark that ignited hostilities was the felling, not once but several times, of a flagstaff bearing the symbol of that oppression, hence the name by which the fighting is sometimes known—the Flagstaff War.

The British garrison in New Zealand in the early 1840s was tiny, barely a hundred men. To fight a campaign, reinforcements had to be summoned from the garrison in New South Wales, where the troops were mainly employed guarding convicts or hunting bush-rangers. One regiment and parts of two others were all that could be spared, a force supplemented by a handful of artillery, some colonial militia, and the invaluable support of other Maoris loyal to the Crown. Fortunately there were, in New Zealand waters, ships of the Royal Navy, and later of the Honourable East India Company's fleet, which provided not only a measure of mobility and some logistical backing for the land forces, but also parties of seamen and marines, with ships' guns, to fight on land. The war was thus very much a joint service operation.

Compared with the wars of this century, the First Maori War seems little more than a punitive expedition. Yet to the men engaged, it was far from that and such punishment as was going often fell more on them than on their enemy. The terrain was atrocious—forest, hills, bush and swamp—with few communications other than the merest footpaths, and the weather usually vile. They fought in red coats, were armed with the weapons of Waterloo, and for artillery support, which was to prove vital in the campaign, they were largely dependent on naval guns, which had to be manhandled, on shipboard carriages, through the undergrowth. There was no transport to speak of, little shelter, infrequent rations, and no medical facilities other than what could be provided by a few regimental surgeons working in impossible conditions. As for the force commander, he was a man in whom none, other than himself, had any confidence. Ignorant of the country and his enemy, he arrived after the campaign opened, superseded two more competent and experienced officers, and proved stubborn, careless of his men's lives, and reluctant to listen to those more knowledgeable than he. Above all, there was the enemy. Savage and ferocious, not averse to cannibalism, yet possessing an often chivalrous, even sporting attitude to their opponents, the Maoris were doughty warriors. Strong, agile and cunning, they had a marvellous talent for fortifying their strongholds, or *pas*, which they defended with firearms of the most modern type, supplied by American and European traders. Savages they may have been in many ways, but many had been converted to Christianity by missionaries and their aptitude for warfare moved a British officer to the opinion that a European must have had the direction of them. Out-numbered, out-gunned and usually out-manoeuvred, the British soldier and sailor could only fall back on their traditional courage, endurance, good humour and, it must be said, their 'grog'—when they could get it. Somehow these characteristics saw the campaign through to a successful conclusion.

It is not the purpose of this book to recount a straight-forward history of this campaign, but rather to portray what life was like in this distant colony in its early years during the struggles with the Maoris, through the eyes of some of the first British soldiers to serve there, using the accounts they made of their experiences. The British soldier of the mid-nineteenth century, officer or man, was not, as a rule, as greatly gifted with the pen as with the sword. Obviously the officers were educated men, if hardly intellectuals, but in the rank and file, about two in three men were illiterate. Nevertheless, from the ranks of one regiment alone, there have survived six accounts of this period in New Zealand. What makes them even more valuable is that the authors represent a cross-section of military rank, and also of differing social standing and backgrounds, so that we can read narratives of the same events which, while generally corroborating each other as to fact, vary in interpretation. Thus, at one end of the spectrum, we have a field officer, aged thirty-seven, who received his first commission in 1825, and at the other a twenty-six-year-old Irish private, soldier servant to a company commander.

All were members of the 58th (Rutlandshire) Regiment of Foot, which had been despatched from England to New South Wales by detachments between 1843–5 as guards on convict ships. The Regiment provided the first reinforcements for New Zealand when trouble with the Maoris seemed imminent. The first companies to arrive were later joined by the rest of the Regiment, which was engaged in all the actions of the war, and subsequently formed part of the permanent garrison of the colony, remaining there until 1858, when it returned home. After so long a period, many soldiers came to regard New Zealand as their home and, during the fourteen years the Regiment served in the garrison, some thousand men of the 58th took their discharge there and remained as settlers.

It is this group that has provided the majority of the diarists, whose accounts form the meat of this story and which have been preserved in various collections in New Zealand. Robert Hattaway, one of the first of the 58th to land at Auckland, reached the rank of Colour and Pay Sergeant, and after his discharge received a commission in the New Zealand Militia. He was clearly a man of some education and kept a diary throughout the campaign, which he later made use of to write his 'Reminiscences of the Northern War', published in the *Auckland Weekly News* in 1899; his record is now in the Alexander Turnbull Library, Wellington. Corporal John Mitchell, a native of Stamford in Lincolnshire, enlisted at Uppingham in 1841 and kept a record of his service from the day he joined until he was wounded at the Battle of Ohaeawai in 1845. He subsequently became a Captain in the New Zealand Militia. Parts of his account, which deal with his early service, appear to have been written some time after their occurrence, but from his arrival in New Zealand it reads as though he kept it up fairly regularly, possibly during lulls in the operations; it was transcribed by his daughter and is now, together with a letter written to his family from Auckland and dated 19th March 1848, in the Museum of The Northamptonshire Regiment, of which the 58th became the 2nd Battalion in 1881, when the numbered regiments of infantry were reorganised on a territorial basis. Private Alexander Whisker, who was born on 22nd July 1819 at Markethill, County Armagh, kept a 'Memorandum Book' of his experiences from the date he sailed for Australia on 8th October 1844; this is now in the Auckland Institute and Museum. Like Mitchell's account, the early part is written as a consecutive narrative but later, from 1st January 1846, entries appear almost daily. After his discharge in New Zealand on 1st January 1850, there are a few spasmodic entries about his life and family, interspersed with a large number of songs and ballads, mainly Scots or Irish. Whisker was clearly a man with some talent for rhyming, for his book contains a 'song' describing the actions of the war, extracts from which form some of the chapter headings in this book. Of all the accounts, Whisker's is perhaps the most spontaneous and typical of the British soldier of the period, having little or no punctuation, some delightfully phonetic spelling, and demonstrating the soldier's fondness for loot and liquor. Major Cyprian Bridge, who came from a Suffolk family with a considerable naval and military tradition, commanded the 58th during the initial operations before the arrival of the Regiment's commanding officer, Lieutenant-Colonel R. H. Wynyard, and kept a daily 'Journal of Events on Expedition to New Zealand commencing 4th April 1845', now in the Alexander Turnbull Library, Wellington. His journal shows his to be a most capable regimental officer, conscientious, careful and attentive to his men's welfare, and although it is a brisk, factual record (if somewhat unconventionally punctuated), it sometimes reveals his inner feelings as when, for example, he expresses his forebodings about a forthcoming assault or vents his wrath on the shortcomings of a superior.

The other two accounts are of a rather different order, being the recollections of two old soldiers related later in life to other writers, and thus lacking the immediacy of the other four. Corporal William Free, another Irishman, lived until 1919, dying at the age of ninety-three; he also remained in New Zealand and achieved commissioned rank in the local forces. He gave a graphic description of the assault on Ohaeawai to the New Zealand historian, James Cowan, whose book, *The New Zealand Wars*, was published in 1922. The story of Private, later Sergeant, Joseph Hinton appeared in a book called *Told from the Ranks* by E. Milton Small, published in 1898. Hinton on his own admission did not learn to read or write until after his return to England in 1850, when he was taught to do so by his wife, so his account was clearly told from memory and he is inaccurate on certain details. His narrative was no doubt considerably edited by Small, but it is of interest in that it deals with the subsidiary operations of the war in the south of the North Island, which the other accounts do not feature, and records an incident famous in the annals of the 58th, the bravery of a drummer boy, William Allen, at the action of Boulcott's Farm. This incident is also referred to by Mitchell in his letter, mentioned above.

Supplementing the memoirs of individual officers and men and, incidentally, providing a check on the accuracy of their writings, is the regimental record of events, or 'Digest of Service', maintained by the 58th which is now kept at the Regimental Museum in Northampton. This contains copies of despatches and orders written during the campaign and other important regimental details. In the Public Record Office are the Muster Rolls, which serve to verify the existence of the soldiers with whom this book is concerned but unfortunately not all the records of men of the 58th at this period are complete.

Like many men of the time, particularly soldiers, there were among the 58th those who were fond of sketching to while away their leisure hours. Cyprian Bridge was one, Lieutenant George Hyde Page another, and Lance Sergeant John Williams a third; their water colours made during the campaign have also been preserved in New Zealand and some illustrate these pages. Though no great works of art, any more than Whisker's 'song' is great verse, they nevertheless give a contemporary view of the terrain, the Maori *pas*, the support given by the Royal Navy ashore and afloat, and the way soldiers were dressed and accoutred for the field.

The extracts from the different accounts appear as nearly as possible in the form in which they were written, although some additional punctuation has been inserted; where any spelling is particularly eccentric, or the meaning of a remark is unclear, some explanation is given as a footnote.

2

The Old Black Cuffs

'That best of all instruments, British infantry'.
The Duke of Wellington.

IN THE YEAR 1755 IT WAS DECIDED TO INCREASE THE STRENGTH
of the British Army by the raising of new regiments of foot.
The formation of one of these was entrusted to Colonel Robert
Anstruther, who chose to have the red coats of his new regiment faced with black, an unusual and sombre facing colour
compared with the more popular blues, yellows and greens of
other regiments, but one which featured prominently in his
own coat of arms. Two years later the regiment was ranked as
58th of the Line and sailed to the New World where, after
facing its first action at the taking of the French fortress of
Louisburg, it earned the commendation of General James
Wolfe as 'the best trained battalion in America', and fought
under him at the capture of Quebec. From 1779–83 it formed
part of the garrison during the great siege of Gibraltar, during
which, in 1782, it acquired a titular link with the county of
Rutland, and in 1801, while serving in the division commanded by Sir John Moore, it held the right of the line at the
Battle of Alexandria in Egypt. As the Napoleonic Wars continued it fought in the Mediterranean, the Peninsula campaign
and the American War of 1814 but arrived back in Europe too
late for Waterloo. In the years that followed, apart from an
uneventful stay in Ceylon, the Regiment soldiered peacefully
in the British Isles, the only flicker of excitement to disturb its
routine existence being the Chartist Riots of 1842. The next
year a detachment of the Regiment embarked for New South
Wales as guards aboard a ship carrying convicts to the penal
colonies, to be followed at intervals by the remainder in a total
of nineteen ships on similar duties, until the departure of the
last party in January 1845.

In the early 1840s a regiment of the Line had changed little since the previous century. It had, as a rule, but one battalion, composed of a number of companies, which varied between eight to ten, split into two wings. Presiding over all was its Colonel, who frequently was little more than a figurehead, often being a general officer of advancing years. The destinies of the 58th at this time were, theoretically, in the hands of General Frederick Maitland who, after a not particularly distinguished career, was appointed at the age of seventy to the colonelcy of a regiment in which he had never served, a position he held until deprived of it by death in 1848 at the age of eighty-five. It seems unlikely that he could have exercised much influence on the Regiment for good or ill, and even doubtful whether he was aware of its departure for the Antipodes. The executive command of a battalion was in the hands of its lieutenant-colonel. Since 1842 command of the 58th had been vested in Lieutenant-Colonel R. H. Wynyard, an officer of twenty-eight years' service and the son of a major-general.[1] He was aided by two majors, who each commanded a wing of the battalion; in his absence the senior major would assume command of the whole battalion. The senior major of the 58th, Cyprian Bridge, will appear frequently in this story, so something must be said of his background.

He was born in Canada on 7th June 1807, the eldest son of Lieutenant (subsequently Lieutenant-Colonel) Cyprian Bridge, an officer of the Royal Artillery, and Elizabeth Powell Goddard, whose father had emigrated to Canada in 1790. The Bridges, who were a Suffolk family from Harwich, traced their descent from one John Bridge, of Ramsey and Dovercourt, who held the appointment of Deputy Commissioner for the Suppression of Pirates in 1565 and again in 1577. The Christian name of Cyprian, which has appeared in every generation of the family until the present day, was first borne by a grandson of John Bridge. Until the second half of the eighteenth century the Bridges had pursued various callings in Suffolk as grocers, clothiers, brewers and tallow chandlers, but the sixth Cyprian in line entered H.M. Packet Service, which carried the mails from Harwich to the Continent, and became the captain of his own ship, *The Prince of Orange*. He

---

[1] For details of his, and other 58th officers' service, see Appendix 1.

founded a naval and military tradition in the family for, of his eight sons, three became officers of the Royal Navy, while four entered the Army, amongst whom was the father of the Cyprian with which this story is primarily concerned. The latter received an ensigncy in the 58th Foot on 8th April 1825, progressing to lieutenant on 31st January 1828. Six months later he went with his regiment to Ceylon where, in 1836, he married Sophia Anne Walker. She bore him seven children, all of whom died in infancy, and three years after the regiment returned to England she herself died in 1842. Bridge had become a captain on 16th December 1836 and, on the 30th December 1842, he purchased the vacant majority in the regiment created by Wynyard's accession to the command. On 8th August 1843, at the age of thirty-six and now senior major of his regiment, he was married again to Louisa, daughter of General M. L. Bowen, with whom he sailed nine months later, to New South Wales in command of the headquarters of the 58th, since Colonel Wynyard was not to leave England until later.

The regimental staff officers included an adjutant, a quartermaster, a paymaster, a surgeon and two assistant surgeons. The adjutant, as the lieutenant-colonel's chief staff officer, was responsible for the drill and discipline of the battalion and was often, in the nineteenth century, a man promoted from the ranks, as was the quartermaster. The adjutant of the 58th at this period had attained his position through somewhat romantic circumstances. Of Scottish descent, John M'Lerie was born at Brompton in Kent in 1809. As a youth he took up labouring but at the age of seventeen he enlisted at Glasgow in the 3rd Foot Guards, shortly to be renamed Scots Fusilier Guards. He must have been a promising soldier, for a year later was promoted corporal and, in 1833, he reached the rank of sergeant. On 10th June 1840 he was on duty in London on Constitution Hill, along which Queen Victoria and the Prince Consort were due to pass in an open carriage. As the royal party approached a man named Edward Oxford drew a pistol and fired at the Queen. The shot missed and Oxford was immediately arrested, due to the quick action of M'Lerie who happened to be close by. As a reward, he was appointed Ensign and Adjutant of the 58th, his commission being backdated to 28th December 1838. He was promoted lieutenant in 1841.

The paymaster of the 58th was one of the few officers to have seen active service. Thomas Richardson Timbrell had served in the final battles of the Peninsula War in 1813–14, first as a volunteer with the 94th Regiment and then as an ensign in the 87th. In 1830 he was appointed quartermaster of the 58th and twelve years later he became its paymaster.

The regimental staff were assisted by a number of non-commissioned-officers. Responsible to the adjutant were Sergeant-Major William Moir, No. 1364, the senior N.C.O. of the regiment and the Orderly Room Clerk, Sergeant George Brown, No. 1091. In the quatermaster's department was a quartermaster-sergeant and an armourer-sergeant, whose task was the serviceability of the regiment's weapons. Finally there were the paymaster-, schoolmaster-, and hospital-sergeants and the bandmaster, whose duties are self-evident.

The establishment of the 58th had been increased from eight to ten companies in 1825 and on its departure for Australia the authorised total strength of the regiment was 1118 officers and men.[2] Each company was numbered consecutively, although No. 1, or right flank company was traditionally known as the Grenadiers, despite the grenade not having been used since the early eighteenth century, and contained the tallest and strongest men, while No. 10, or left flank company was designated Light Infantry, whose men were selected for quickness and agility. The two flank companies were regarded as the elite of the regiment, the remainder forming the battalion, or centre, companies, Nos. 2–9.

A company was 110 strong, including officers, and was divided into two sub-divisions, each being further divided into two sections. The company was commanded by a captain, who was assisted by two subalterns, lieutenants or ensigns, each having a responsibility for a sub-division. It had ten non-commissioned-officers, five sergeants and five corporals, the senior sergeant of the company being appointed the colour-sergeant, who combined the duties of the present-day company-sergeant-major and company-quartermaster-sergeant. In each company there were two drummers, who could play drum, fife or bugle and whose main task was to

[2] Colonel 1; Lt-Colonel 1; Majors 2; Captains 10; Lieutenants 12; Ensigns 8; Staff officers 6; Sergeants 58; Corporals 50; Drummers 20; Privates 950.

sound the signals by which the routine and movements of the company were regulated; they could also be massed with the other company drummers under a sergeant ranking as Drum-Major to play as a corps of drums. A drummer was a combatant soldier whose task in action was to relay the commands of his captain by drum beat or bugle call. Two men of the company were trained as bandsmen and, although held on the strength of their respective companies, they wore white coats instead of red and performed with the other bandsmen in a regimental band twenty strong. On active service their instruments were usually set aside in favour of stretchers on which the wounded were borne to the surgeon. Finally one man per company was trained as a pioneer who, under a corporal, provided a pioneer section of ten, equipped with saws, axes, spades and picks to carry out minor engineering tasks for the battalion.

A regiment's cohesion and loyalty was symbolised in its colours, two large flags just over six feet square secured to ten-foot pikes; they were carried in peace and war by ensigns, an honour which was frequently rewarded by the bearer's death in action, and escorted by sergeants. The first, or Queen's colour, was the outward and visible sign of the regiment's loyalty to the Crown, while the second, or Regimental colour, embodied the soul or honour of the regiment. These symbols were the sacred possessions of a regiment, providing an inspiration and rallying point for its soldiers, and for which every sacrifice could be demanded to preserve their safey and integrity. The colours taken by the 58th to Australia had been presented in 1841 at Edinburgh. The Queen's colour was the Great Union flag with, in the centre, the regimental number in Roman figures, encircled by the name 'Rutlandshire', and surmounted by a crown. The Regimental colour bore the St George's cross with the Union in the upper canton, the other three being black, the colour of the regiment's facings, and the same design in the centre; the various distinctions, or battle honours, awarded to the regiment for past glories were placed on scrolls on this colour.[3]

During the Napoleonic Wars the social backgrounds of Army officers had become extremely diverse, but with the

[3] See Appendix 1.

ensuing reductions in the size of the Army, the chief source of
officer material again reverted to the aristocracy and the upper
classes which, as far as the Infantry of the Line was concerned,
meant the younger sons of the country gentry or the off-
spring of service officers. In 1840 it was thought that the
internal security of the State depended upon the officering of
the standing army being in the hands of those with a stake in
the country, and that on no account should commissioned
rank fall into the clutches of ambitious adventurers. A young
man of the right class could obtain a commission in two main
ways: he could enter, at the age of thirteen or fourteen, the
Military College at Sandhurst whence, providing he could
endure the rigorous, often brutal, regime and could satisfy his
examiners, he would be rewarded three or four years later with
an ensign's commission; or, and much more customary, he
could purchase an ensigncy. Thereafter, regardless of the
method of entry, all further promotion was by purchase,
irrespective of merit, unless vacancies for the next higher rank
occurred either by an increase in the establishment of the
regiment or the sudden death of the next senior officer. If, for
example, a major created a vacancy, either by his retirement or
by his purchasing a vacant lieutenant-colonelcy in his own or
another regiment, the next senior captain who could raise the
price of a major's commission[4] could take up the vacancy
(providing he had a certain number of years' service), even
though he might be junior to his more impoverished seniors in
the rank of captain. The elevation thus achieved by the fortunate captain of course caused other vacancies down through
the rank structure, so the departure or promotion of the major
benefited not only the captain who succeeded him, but the
lieutenant and the ensign who each paid for their next step up,
furthering their own promotion and increasing the capital
value of their commissions, which they could sell on retirement whenever they wanted. If a new company was raised, or
the junior captain died, the senior subaltern would automati-
cally be promoted into the vacancy without purchase, and
would find himself richer by several hundred pounds.

Under such a system an unpopular senior officer in a regi-

---

[4] The regulation prices for Infantry were: Lt-Colonel £4500; major £3200; Captain
£1800; Lieutenant £700; Ensign £450. In the Cavalry and Foot Guards the prices were
much higher. These sums were frequently, though illegally, exceeded.

ment could virtually be bribed to sell out by those officers, who stood to benefit from his departure, clubbing together to raise a sum, over and above the regulation price. It could also condemn a penniless officer to spending long years in the same rank, while other men young enough to be his sons could purchase their promotion above his head. On the other hand, in an age when there were no pensions from public funds, a system which enabled an officer to realise a capital sum on his retirement by the sale of his commission made such retirement attractive and thereby kept promotion going.

A study of the officers serving in the 58th at the time of the Maori War shows the effect of this system on one regiment. The average speeds of promotion were: ensign to lieutenant, two and three-quarter years; lieutenant to captain, eight and a quarter years, although if three of the captains, who each respectively spent twenty-two, fourteen and a half and thirteen and a quarter years as lieutenants, are discounted, the average for the remainder reduces to four and a half years; captain to major, six years. The lieutenant-colonel assumed command after only one and a half years since obtaining his majority and after a total of twenty-eight years' service. These average speeds of promotion compare favourably with those pertaining to the Army today. A comparison of steps obtained with and without purchase show that out of eight ensigns, only three purchased their first commissions; out of twelve lieutenants, seven purchased their step to that rank; out of ten captains, six; while both majorities and the lieutenant-colonelcy were all purchased. Of all the officers, only one, the second senior captain, had more service than the lieutenant-colonel, and in his case it was only one year. Five of the captains had more service than the senior captain and two of the lieutenants had been overtaken by officers with less service than themselves. Thus although by modern standards the circumstances of these officers disclose some anomalies, particularly in the captain bracket, their overall position was not as iniquitous as some descriptions of the purchase system, with its boy colonels and ancient lieutenants, would suggest.

When in barracks the officers lived in their mess, which was run on the lines and according to the rules of a gentleman's club, with individual bedrooms furnished according to their means, and communal dining and other public rooms, which

could be quite lavishly appointed, depending on the wealth of
the officers. The pay which officers received for the privilege
of serving the Crown was so low that an ensign's four shillings
and sixpence a day was completely swallowed up by the cost
of his breakfast, dinner, wine, servant and laundry; to indulge
in high living, or even to save for his next step, private means
were essential. Every evening the officers would dine formally
together, followed by a game of cards, billiards, or simply an
evening's drinking. Any discussion or study of their profession in the mess was totally deplored. The more rakish young
officers might end the evening with a foray into the local town
in search of loose women,[5] while young ladies of a different
sort could be met when the officers gave a ball to which the
leading notables of the district would be invited with their
daughters. Many a provincial miss, who later found herself
condemned to long years in dusty cantonments abroad, would
look back with nostalgia or regret to these glittering occasions
when her susceptibilities were smitten by the attentions of a
scarlet-coated young officer. When stationed at home a married officer with money would seek to rent a house in the
neighbourhood, but his less wealthy counterpart might be
able to offer his bride nothing better than one, or at best two,
rooms in barracks.

To while away an officer's daytime leisure, which was
plentiful, the usual pursuits of a country gentleman were the
most popular, though again the extent to which he might
hunt or shoot depended entirely on whether he could afford to
do so. A few might sketch, or take up amateur theatricals, but
intellectual diversions were, as a rule, uncommon.

Since an officer's main role was to lead his troops on parade
or in the field, his military duties in barracks were not onerous.
Once a newly-joined ensign had learned his drill, which he did
alongside the new recruits under a non-commissioned-officer,
and had mastered the intricacies of the drill manuals, there was
little for him to do, other than attend the daily orderly room
where disciplinary charges against soldiers were disposed of,
unless there was a parade or field day which required his
presence. The social divisions of the age caused him to main-

---

[5] According to the anonymous officer-author of *A Few Remarks about the British
Army* (1857), the practice of entertaining prostitutes in the officers' quarters was
common.

tain his distance from his soldiers, and the daily routine of the men's lives was left to the non-commissioned-officers. The British officer, as a French observer noted, 'had joined the army to fight, not to perform the wearisome duties of an accountant or jailor'.[6] Only the regimental staff officers, the adjutant, quartermaster and so on, immersed themselves in the administration of the barracks. There were of course some officers who took an interest in the training and welfare of their men, but generally it was not until a regiment proceeded on active service that the company officer found himself in close proximity with the men under his command.

The common soldier stood low in the social esteem of Victorian England and consequently his profession was not greatly sought after. Wellington's oft-quoted remarks about soldiers being 'the scum of the earth' and 'enlisting for drink' probably contributed to this, but life was so hard for the lower classes, both in town and country alike, particularly in the former, that many honest men were driven to enlist from necessity; few joined for adventure and the glamour of a red coat. Writing in 1846, an infantry N.C.O. recorded that 67 per cent of men enlisting were 'labourers and mechanics out of employ, who merely seek for support,' while 13 per cent joined because they considered 'a soldier's life an easy one'. Criminals and bad characters only counted for 8 per cent and 7 per cent were 'discontented and restless' with their civilian occupations. The remaining 5 per cent were 'respectable persons [i.e. not of the labouring classes] induced by misfortune or imprudence', 'perverse sons', 'ambitious' (only 0.8 per cent), and others.[7]

One of the soldiers of the 58th who will be met often in this story, John Mitchell, No. 1466, a native of Stamford in Lincolnshire, fell into the 'discontented' category. He wrote:

At the age of twenty I held a responsible position in Mr R. Hunt's brewery in St Martins, Stamford at a weekly salary

[6] Halévy, *A History of the English People in the 19th Century*, quoted in the Marquess of Anglesey, *A History of the British Cavalry, 1816–1919* (London, 1973), Vol. 1, page 152.

[7] J. MacMullen, *Camp and Barrack Room; or the British Army as it is, by a late Staff Sergeant of the 13th Light Infantry (1846)*. MacMullen's researches were based on a group of 120 men. See Anglesey, op. cit., page 115.

of 11/- without any prospect of an increase. One evening about the 4th June 1841 I was talking with the book Keeper a Mr Wilford (who was a cripple) about our prospects in life and he said, 'If I were fit for a soldier I would enlist tomorrow'. After further talk we parted, he to his books and I to think the matter over, the result being my mind was made up to leave the service in which I was so wretchedly paid & take service under the Queen, taking care to let no one know of my design, not even my dearly beloved Father & Sister Mary.

On the 21st June 1841, I called to see Sister Mary, she had one little child named John Thomas after Father & myself. I kissed her & the baby & took my farewell leaving her in tears. Shortly after, I met poor Father, he gave me 'Good Morning' & asked where I was going. I told him on business connected with the Brewery. 'How is it you are walking?' I said, 'It was such a fine morning I preferred walking to riding & I am not going far. Good bye Father'. [I] shook hands & that was the last I saw of my dear old Father.

Mitchell enlisted in Rutlandshire, the county to which the 58th was affiliated, and thus it might be thought that there was a permanent regimental presence in the county and that its recruits came predominantly from within its borders. This was not the case. At this time no regiment had any home or base of its own and it recruited throughout the British Isles. In 1840 the 58th had recruiting parties in Kent, Sussex and Berkshire; in 1841 in Scotland, from Aberdeen to Stranraer, Westmorland, Lancashire, the east and south Midlands and East Anglia; between 1842 and 1844 the main recruiting effort was in Ireland, where, as can be seen from the names in the Muster Rolls, many were enlisted, with detached parties in London, Somerset, Kent, Wiltshire and Yorkshire. These recruiting parties were based, in the main, on the county towns rather than the increasingly large manufacturing cities, so it can be assumed that the men recruited were chiefly from agricultural backgrounds. These produced a better type of soldier than the appalling stews of the urban areas, into which the rural peasantry were, in the 1840s, increasingly drawn as a result of the repeal of the Corn Laws.

Between 1829–46 enlistment was theoretically for life,[8] although after fifteen years' service a free discharge could be obtained and after sixteen, a man could also receive a bonus of six months' pay. A soldier with less than fifteen years' service could only obtain his discharge by purchasing it for twenty pounds, a sum for which it might take a man ten years or more to save, unless he could raise it from a relative. Thus many men took to maiming themselves or to crime to obtain their discharges.

When Mitchell decided to enlist he had no particular regiment in mind and found himself in the 58th, which was then stationed in Dublin, through sheer chance:

I intended making for Scotland, but on reaching a town called Uppingham I met a soldier of the 58th Regt on the recruiting service whom I knew came from a village near Stamford. I told him I would enlist, with that he gave me the Queen's shilling & took me to a magistrate who swore me in, from thence to a Doctor who examined me & passed me, the soldier then took me to his billet. Next day I was marched off to Leicester with seven other recruits, remained there three days, then to Coventry where we underwent another examination by Doctors, three of the seven being rejected. Then on to Liverpool [where] I was billeted at a Public House, the people being very kind to me. Orders were sent to the Liverpool Office to forward recruits for the Regt to Dublin. In due course we were taken on board, steamers landed in Dublin & marched to Richmond Barracks. My first night in a barrack-room to describe it would take too long, only how strange it all seemed to me. Next morning again examined & measured, fitted with Regimental clothing & attended drill from 7 to 8. I had to thank a friend whom I made much older than myself who pointed out how I should think & what to avoid. I had now entered on the duties of a soldier, my turn for guard came every five days.

A barracks usually consisted of a number of great stone-built, prison-like blocks constructed round a square. The typi-

---

[8] In 1847 the maximum length of engagement for Infantry was ten years with re-enlistment permitted for a further eleven.

cal room in which a recruit found himself was a long, dark, smoke-filled cavern, with single beds, each with a palliasse, straw bolster and two blankets, placed side by side down each wall, sometimes as little as nine inches apart, containing anything from twenty to forty men. The average allowance for air for a soldier in barracks was estimated at 400 cubic feet. For a convict it was 1000. At one end, divided only by a blanket slung across a rope, might be quartered a couple of the married men, their wives and children. These were the fortunate ones, the 7 per cent of the rank and file of a regiment whose marriages were officially authorised and thereby permitted to live in barracks. This is not to say that other men were forbidden to wed; they could do so, but their married state was not recognised by the Army and no provision of any sort was made for their wives. In these ill-lit, unventilated rooms, for the few windows were seldom opened, the soldiers lived, slept and ate—at a communal dining table down the centre of the room. The daily ration consisted of three-quarters of a pound of beef and one pound of bread, usually more black than brown, for which the soldier was stopped sixpence a day out of his pay; anything else the men had to buy for themselves. There were no cooks and no facilities for cooking other than boiling, which the men took turns to do in coppers provided for each room.

The private soldier's basic pay was one shilling per day, plus one penny beer money. On enlistment he received a bounty, which he soon found he had to use to pay for most of his kit; thereafter this had to be maintained out of his daily pay. When this was added to the sums deducted for his rations and his laundry, he had left, out of his shilling, perhaps between one penny and at best threepence per day to spend or save. When John Mitchell was promoted corporal he found that he was receiving eightpence per day clear, after paying for his rations. The pay of a colour-sergeant was two shillings and tenpence a day while a sergeant-major, the highest non-commissioned rank, received just under four shillings.

Promotion to the non-commissioned ranks went by merit and to a clean, alert man could come quickly. Mitchell found himself made a lance-corporal (i.e. acting rank without pay) after only thirty days in the service. He well recalled the panic he felt when first called upon to drill a squad:

To my surprise the following morning [the] Sergt Major called me to take charge of a squad of raw recruits & put them through the drill. I formed them up but could not find words to go on. Watching my opportunity, after seeing all was clear, told the squad to remain where they were & I bolted off to my barrack room. This was soon discovered, the Sergt Major sent for me & gave me a mild wigging. I told [him] I could not do it as I was only a recruit myself. 'Thats all nonsense,' said he, 'you will have to try', so at it I went & succeeded in a very awkward manner. The Sergt Major having other business to attend to, left me to my own resources. No sooner had he gone when off I bolted once more. When my absence was discovered again, I was brought back & who should be on the parade but the Colonel. He said I was liable to lose my promotion by disobeying orders, so I told him I was ashamed to stand before the squad. 'Oh', said he, 'that is the trouble is it? Come here & we will soon get over that', & directed me where to stand, told me the words of command to give, moved me further away from the squad & [told me] to deliver the word of command with the full power of my voice. From that time I had full confidence in myself & felt pride in my power to give instructions, thanks to my Colonel. In a short time, about six months, I was acknowledged to be one of the best drill instructors in the Regt & promoted to the rank of full corporal.

Just over a year after his enlistment he became a sergeant. The following year he was reduced to the ranks for being absent from parade, but not long after was once again appointed lance-corporal. By 1848 he had made his way to colour-sergeant.

Once a recruit had been instructed how to drill and handle his arms he took his place in the company, where he learned to march, wheel and turn in conformity with his comrades in the innumerable movements which a company, as part of the battalion, was required to perform with great exactness. The soldier's training, with the exception of a little musketry practice, consisted almost entirely of drill, in which the evolutions were endlessly practised to ensure a battalion could manoeuvre like a wall, with as much precision in the face of an enemy, as it did on the barrack square. When a company fell in it always did so in two ranks, the front and rear man in each rank forming a file, with the officers and sergeants arrayed in front, on the flanks and in the rear. The battalion would form either in line, with each company side by side, or in column, with companies one behind the other. The former was the formation most favoured for attack or defence, since it enabled the maximum number of muskets to be brought to bear, while column was preferred for movement.[9] A third formation, the square, was adopted against cavalry, in which the companies doubled up to form four ranks, with the first two kneeling to make a *chevaux de frise* with their bayonets. The fire of a battalion would be delivered either by volleys, fired simultaneously by each company in turn, each wing or the whole battalion, or by independent fire, sometimes called file-firing. The latter would be started by a designated file and continued down the line, the rear-rank men firing after their front-rank comrades.

A line or column would be protected by one or more companies deployed as skirmishers, whose task in attack was to drive in the enemy skirmishers, and in defence to slow down and inflict as much damage on the enemy as possible before it reached the line. A company so employed opened out its files by extending to a given number of paces, usually six, from each other; the men in each file would then work together, one covering the other while he loaded. Once men had learned this technique as a drill, training would progress to teaching the files to skirmish independently, moving from cover to cover, but keeping to the general alignment of the skirmishing line. The task of skirmishing was traditionally that of the light infantry company, but in well-trained regiments all companies received instruction in its skills, particularly since much mid-nineteenth-century campaigning was against savage enemies in close country where the close order of line or column was inappropriate.

Every so often the battalion would emerge from its barracks and march, with band playing, to some open ground for a field day, where it would practise, across broken country, the manoeuvres constantly rehearsed on the square. After expending a

[9] The frontage could be reduced by forming a column of sub-divisions or sections.

quantity of blank ammunition, to the excitement of a crowd of civilian spectators, it would return to barracks, where the officers would hurriedly change out of uniform and depart in search of their afternoon's pleasures, while the soldiers would spend as much time refurbishing their kit as they had taken to prepare it for the morning's entertainment. When not so engaged, the soldier might find himself on any one of a number of guards, from a judge's lodging to a coal dump, guards which became more numerous when troops were deployed in aid of the civil power, as was frequently the case in the 1840s especially in Ireland, or detailed off for the equally numerous duties and fatigues, necessary for the smooth running of the barracks. These not particularly arduous duties left the soldier with a good deal of leisure time, but with little to occupy it other than the raucous jollity of the wet canteen, where drink was supplied by contractors at prices the soldier could afford.

Any tendency to crime among an idle soldiery could only be kept in check by rigid discipline. The ultimate sanction was the death penalty; this could be awarded for a number of offences, from mutiny to sodomy, from striking superiors to ravishing women. Next came imprisonment, for such crimes as desertion, habitual drunkeness and insubordination. However the real bedrock of discipline lay in the ability to award a flogging. By the 1840s these were nothing like so frequent as in earlier times, but all soldiers were kept constantly aware of the lash as a deterrent by the compulsory attendance of all ranks whenever a culprit was 'touched over'. Over the years the maximum number of lashes that could be awarded had gradually been reduced; following a Royal Commission on Military Punishments in 1836, a regimental court-martial was limited to a maximum sentence of 100 lashes, rising to 200 from a general court-martial. In 1846 Private Sutton of the 58th received the maximum award from a district court-martial of 150 lashes for disobedience of orders. A year later the maximum sentence was reduced to fifty from any court, but if an offence was of a sufficiently serious nature, such as being committed on duty, a spell of imprisonment could be added to the flogging. For example, when Drummer Patrick O'Hara was found guilty of drunkenness on guard, he was awarded fifty lashes and twelve months' imprisonment, a sentence which was later commuted to thirty lashes and six months in prison. For lesser crimes there was a host of minor punishments: confinement to barracks, extra drills, loss of grog ration, bread and water diet, forfeiture of pay and so on.

Breaches of discipline by non-commissioned-officers were usually punished by loss of rank, although this did not prevent a basically steady man from working his way up again, sometimes quite quickly. John Mitchell was reduced from sergeant to private twice in 1843, though on the first occasion he did not have to wait long to regain his rank:

> The Sergt Major took ill & had to go to hospital. A Colour Sergt Cooper by name (a conceited fellow) as senior Non-Com became acting Sergt Major in a most dictatorial manner, so much so that I resented his interferring by halting my squad whenever he came & would not put them in motion until he went away. This so nettled him that he made up his mind to injure me. He had to wait. One evening I went to town & did not get back until after Tattoo (soldiers to go to their quarters for the night). I was only a few minutes late & coming along the pathway which was very slippery from frost, I stumbled. He said to the officer of the day who was there to receive the reports of absentees, 'Sir! He is drunk', following it by ordering me under arrest. 'You lie', said I, 'I am not drunk' & as sure as I write this I told the truth. However I lost my temper & threatened to give him a sound thrashing. The guard was called & I was made a prisoner. For this I was tried by Regimental Court Martial & sentenced to be reduced to the rank & pay of private. Captain Laye (of my company) pleaded extenuating circumstances for me but the court martial was approved by the Major, Col Wynyard was away. The Regt was drawn up in three sides of a square, court martial proceedings read by the Adjt, stripes taken off, a few remarks by the Major, finally telling me I was restored to the rank of full Sergt again.

A good officer would keep an eye open for excessive harshness or bullying by non-commissioned-officers, so as to stand between them and any man who undeservedly incurred their wrath. After Mitchell had been reduced the second time, he again fell foul of an ill-natured colour-sergeant, which might

Privates, Grenadier and Battalion companies, 58th Regiment in full dress, c. 1840. In 1844 the 'Albert' shako replaced the bearskin cap and bell-topped shako shown here. (Lithograph after M. A. Hayes)

Major Cyprian Bridge, 58th Regiment, in full dress, c. 1845.

have resulted in his receiving 200 lashes, had not his captain been a man of sense and humanity:

> As private I tried to do my duty faithfully, but the Colour Sergt (George Felter) for some reason took every opportunity (on parade) to find fault with me. The climax was reached on a parade when he was unusually severe. When the parade was dismissed, I followed him with the intention of thrashing him. He ran to his quarters closing the door just in time, calling from his window for an escort to arrest me which was done. The next morning I was escorted to Captain Laye's quarters to answer questions as to the charges brought against me. I did not deny the charges, I told the Capt it was caused by the Sergt being overbearing. He said as the charges stood he was powerless to prevent the serious consequences of a General Court Martial. I was taken back to the guard room & in the meantime the Capt told the Sergt to modify the wording of the charges in order that he (the Capt) could deal with the case. On the second day I was again brought up, the Sergt being present, the Capt addressing me said the alteration in the charges enabled him to deal with them and sentenced me 48 hrs in the cells. I was taken to the cells & had not been there more than an hour when an order came for my release. I was sent for by the Capt, he said, 'Mitchell, I release you & appoint you to be my orderly free from all guards & parades', and directed the Sergt to see that his orders were carried out. I had no more trouble with Sergt Felter.

Despite the hardships of their existence, for most soldiers the barracks became their home, the regiment their family and while they might curse it among themselves, they would defy any outsider to stain its reputation. Furthermore, against all the apparent harshness of the system, there must be set an increasingly humane approach to the soldiers, dating from the early 1840s, with more emphasis on encouraging them to good, rather than discouraging them from evil. This was typified by the institution, from 1836, of badges and extra pay for good conduct. Whatever the defects of the system, and they were many, and notwithstanding the wretched backgrounds from which many of the men came, it was, as the

Duke of Wellington said, 'wonderful that we should have made them the fine fellows they are'; so fine that one Victorian general was sufficiently moved by his memories of the old long-service soldiers, drawn from the rural areas, as to describe them as 'those old Greek gods'.[10]

Their appearance was, of course, greatly enhanced by the uniform, which made a brave show. The 1840s were the era of the coatee, an elegant but impractical garment, cut short at the waist in front with two tails behind, hanging to mid-thigh. Those of the officers and sergeants were scarlet and cut double-breasted, while the rank and file's were red and fastened with a single row of buttons, the holes of which were adorned by horizontal bars of white tape known as lace. The collar and cuffs were of the regimental facing colour, hence the 58th's nickname of 'The Old Black Cuffs', and further embellished with gold lace for officers and white for the men. White linen trousers were worn in summer, and in winter cloth, of a very dark grey shade with a narrow red welt down the seam. At the time the 58th were ordered to Australia, the infantryman's headdress was undergoing a transition. The heavy but handsome black, bell-topped shako of the 1830s was set aside in favour of a cylindrical pattern with peaks in front and behind; a rather curious design, commonly called the 'Albert pot', after its supposed inventor, the Prince Consort.[11] The front was equipped with a gilt or brass plate, which bore the regimental number and insignia, and on top was a worsted ball tuft, of white for the grenadiers, white over red for the centre companies and green for the light infantry. The two flank companies also had other distinguishing features in their dress.

Officers were responsible for the purchase of their entire military wardrobe and, since soldiers only received, as a free issue, one coatee and one pair of cloth trousers each year and a new shako every second year, this finery had to be preserved with care. Therefore all ranks had another uniform for daily work called undress. In essentials this consisted of a forage cap of dark blue cloth, which in the 58th had a black band round it, with a peak for officers and sergeants, and a red shell, or fatigue jacket: a plain, single-breasted garment, cropped short at the waist, with collar and cuffs of the facing colour.

[10] Sir William Butler, *An Autobiography* (London, 1911).
[11] Authorised on 4th December 1843.

Apart from the articles mentioned above as a free issue, to which must be added one pair of boots, all other items of the soldier's kit, including his undress, his white trousers and such things as his shirts, socks, cleaning and eating utensils, were classified as 'Necessaries', and had to be paid for and maintained by the man himself. His accoutrements consisted of two buff-leather shoulder belts, rendered white with pipeclay, one suspending a black leather ammunition pouch and the other a seventeen-inch bayonet, which hung behind the right and left hips respectively; the belts crossed on the chest and were secured there with a rectangular brass plate of regimental design. In addition he had a knapsack, made of leather and black canvas, and a tin canteen, or mess-tin, in a black cover. For some curious reason, while the belts, pouch and breast plate were issued free, the knapsack and mess-tin counted as 'Necessaries' and had to be paid for. When ordered on to field service, he further received a wooden water bottle, a linen haversack, and a blanket, which was strapped, together with his grey greatcoat, to the knapsack. Finally there was his musket. In the 1840s the old flintlock, or 'Brown Bess', which had served the infantry since the previous century, was gradually being replaced by a new model, based on the percussion principle. In 1843 the 58th received one of the earliest types of the new weapon, the 1839 pattern: muzzle-loading, ten pounds in weight, four feet seven inches long, a rate of fire in the hands of a trained man of three rounds per minute, and an effective range not exceeding between 150–200 yards. When fully laden with musket in hand and ammunition in pouch, the soldier's total burden was of the order of seventy pounds.

By contrast the officer had only his sword to carry, captain's and subalterns suspending theirs from a shoulder belt, which bore a gilt plate of more ornate design than the men's, while colonels and majors used a waist belt with slings. When ordered on active service, he would probably purchase a pistol, and would expect some form of transport to carry his kit and such comforts, often extensive, without which he felt he could not survive.[12]

Such were the conditions existing in the British infantry in the 1840s. Though every regiment was a close community

[12] At the landing in the Crimea in 1854, many officers protested vehemently at having to carry their kits on their persons like the common soldiery.

within itself, with no interest or regard for any other, or indeed much sense of being part of the same Army, the military facts of life were much the same at any given period for all regiments. How this strange amalgam of privilege and servitude, brutality and loyalty, squalor and magnificence, would fare under the rigours of a campaign, will be seen in the following pages.

Before they meet the enemy however, something must be said of the characters that will be encountered. Major Cyprian Bridge, Lieutenant M'Lerie and Sergeant-Major Moir have already made their appearance. John Mitchell, once again a corporal, embarked on 3rd October 1844 aboard the *Hyderabad*, carrying 210 convicts 'of the worst class' who were destined for the penal settlement of Norfolk Island, far out in the Pacific. After an eventful voyage, during which the convicts twice tried to seize the ship, the *Hyderabad* sailed into Sydney on 6th March 1845. A younger man than Mitchell was Robert Hattaway, No. 1990, who enlisted at Chatham in 1842 just before his nineteenth birthday. A native of Headcorn in Kent, he attended the church school in the village under the rector, the Reverend Rolfe, and was then sent to a boarding school at Maidstone. It is clear that he came from a rather more superior background than most of his fellow soldiers, his mother being of French Huguenot descent while his father ran a road haulage business, carrying grain, fruit and vegetables between Headcorn, Maidstone and London. From evidence of his later life, it appears that, before enlisting, he had acquired practical knowledge of fruit farming, book-keeping and accountancy, so it seems strange that a youth from a prosperous and settled rural area, with a family business in which he could find employment, should have chosen to enlist. It may have been due to his father encountering financial difficulties but whatever the reason, young Hattaway took the Queen's Shilling and sailed with his regiment for Australia in 1844, never to return to his native Kent.

Among the many Irish in the 58th's ranks was No. 979 Private Alexander Whisker of No. 3 Company, soldier servant to his captain, Charles Thompson. Born on 22nd July 1819 at Markethill, County Armagh, he had enlisted in 1838. He married a girl named Flora Cook, who bore him a daughter, Mary Jean, when the regiment was in Dublin in 1842, and a son, Charles, seven months before he sailed on the *Lord George Seymour* on 21st November 1844 with prisoners for Hobart in Tasmania. Clearly Flora must have been 'on the strength' for she accompanied him to Australia, unlike the unfortunate 'unofficial' wives, who, when a regiment went overseas, were left to fend for themselves, a fate that often meant the workhouse or prostitution. Apart from a fire on board and two 'tremendous storms', the Whiskers' voyage was uneventful, the only excitement being when Captain Thompson shot an albatross; 'the captn got its head stuffed by one of the Prisoners'. After discharging the convicts at Hobart, they reached Sydney on 12th March 1845.

Two more Irishmen who were to make their mark on the other side of the world were 1618 William Free and 1640 Charles Stapp, who both enlisted at the age of seventeen at Dublin in 1842. Stapp had served in the Chartist Riots in Lancashire shortly after joining, and he and Free sailed to Australia as members of the light company in September 1843. Finally there was 2136 Joseph Hinton, who did not enlist until December 1843 when, drawn perhaps by the sight of the 58th men he saw in the streets of Chatham where they awaited the loading of the convict ships, he took the shilling at Brompton Barracks and sailed six months later.

So, month after month, as the ships pulled out down the Thames estuary, the sons of the gentry, with their one-time labourers, artisans, grooms, masons, navvies and ne'er-do-wells sailed away, in many cases for ever, from their homes in the towns and villages of England or the poverty-stricken cabins of Ireland, to the fresh sights and sounds of the Antipodes. There, in the heat and dust of New South Wales or among the great, gaunt prison buildings of Norfolk Island, they resumed the routine they had known in Dublin or Chatham, until the rumours of war came over the Tasman Sea.

3

Outbreak in the
Bay of Islands

'My disobedience and rudeness is no new thing.
I inherit it from my parents—from my ancestors.'
Hone Heke Pokai to Governor Fitzroy.

THE FLAGSTAFF, AN OLD SHIP'S MIZZENMAST, STOOD HIGH ON A
hill, overlooking the scattered buildings of the little settlement
which lay between the wooded foothills and the curve of the
bay. Each day a Union Jack was hoisted to the top of the mast,
a symbol that even this remote corner of the globe was under
the sovereignty and protection of a monarch on the other side
of the world. Sunk deep in the fern-covered ground, its lower
part encased in an iron sleeve, the flagstaff was guarded by a
sentry, while a few yards away the off-duty soldiers of the
picquet rested in a timbered blockhouse. At the foot of the hill
was a small barracks, built within a stockade to house the rest
of the detachment and protected by another blockhouse with
three old ship's guns pointing from the embrasures. Guarding
the defile between the foothills which led to the town, a
redoubt had been constructed and now contained a naval gun,
manned by sailors and marines from the warship in the bay.

At night none of this was visible to the sentry on the hill. As
he paced his beat beside the flagstaff, mindful of his officer's
warning to be particularly on the alert, he would have found
his post in this alien land a lonely and unnerving one. So at the
first light of day, he would have been considerably relieved to
see his officer emerging from the blockhouse, followed by five
sleepy soldiers carrying spades, who were put to work digging
a trench. Suddenly, the surrounding fern surged into life as
hundreds of savage warriors leaped from their hiding places

and charged yelling at the blockhouse. Simultaneously the noise of firing came from the settlement, and as the confused and luckless soldiers stumbled from the blockhouse, they were engulfed by the stabbing, slashing savages. The post was overrun and the warriors threw themselves with axes on the hated flagstaff, hacking at the thick trunk until, with a rending crash, it toppled to the ground as the victors yelled their triumph.

The day that now shed its full light on this suddenly violent scene was 11th March 1845, and as the Maori warriors of Hone Heke Pokai, a chief of the Ngapuhi, trampled upon the loathed symbol of the white man's rule, they could see others of their tribe rampaging into the settlement, overrunning the naval gun position and milling round the lower blockhouse. The flagstaff had been felled before, three times in fact but each time re-erected. Now was the time not only to have it down once and for all, but also to attack and ravage the settlement itself, Kororareka on the Bay of Islands, the most northerly outpost of the white man in the North Island of New Zealand.

The small detachment near the flagstaff on Maiki Hill had been quickly despatched. Although the sailors and marines guarding the naval gun had been driven from their position by Heke's ally, an old chief named Kawiti, they held firm and were soon fighting hand-to-hand with cutlass and bayonet. They forced Kawiti's men back to a gulley and the fighting changed from a close quarter struggle to a fire-fight of musketry, but, with their officer, Acting-Commander Robertson of H.M.S. *Hazard*, severly wounded and the marine N.C.O. killed, they decided to retire towards the houses of the settlement. Meanwhile the troops in the lower blockhouse, supported by the three guns manned by a mixed detachment of civilians and old soldiers, managed to hold their position, though under fire from a third Maori column and from Maiki Hill itself.

As the small garrison of barely one hundred soldiers and sailors struggled to hold the ring, down at the water's edge the women and children of the settlement began to be ferried out to the safety of the ships in the bay, the eighteen-gun sloop *Hazard*, a United States warship, a whaler, a schooner, and a lugger belonging to Selwyn, the first-appointed Bishop of New Zealand. Fortunately the efforts of the attackers remained uncoordinated and, though the defence was in no better case, with Commander Robertson incapacitated by his wounds and control passing into the hands of the reckless Lieutenant Philpotts, R.N., and the inexperienced Lieutenant Barclay of the 96th Regiment, the evacuation proceeded unhindered. Rather desultory fighting still went on through the morning around the three old guns, but on Maiki Hill Heke seemed satisfied with his morning's work and made no effort to reinforce Kawiti down below. At one o'clock the garrison's reserve ammunition, held in a magazine in the stockade, suddenly exploded, setting fire to the nearest buildings. With their ammunition gone and the Maoris holding the high ground round the town, Philpotts decided there was nothing for it but to evacuate the remaining troops to the ships. This he was able to do with comparative ease, for, as the excited Maoris followed up his withdrawal, they quickly became diverted by the plunder and barrels of rum they found in the abandoned houses, and gave themselves up to celebratory pillaging. Fire now raged through the settlement, partly encouraged by the infuriated Philpotts who, as he reached the *Hazard*, ordered its guns to open fire, and partly by the Maoris in retaliation for this bombardment. Curiously they ensured that the two churches, one Anglican, the other Catholic, and the Catholic bishop's house were spared the looting and conflagration. The Maoris had no quarrel with the Church, indeed many of them, including Heke, were converted Christians, and, when the pandemonium died down later in the afternoon and Bishop Selwyn, accompanied by another clergyman, Henry Williams, went ashore to try and restore calm, they were greeted warmly and respectfully. On the other hand, six settlers who were foolhardy enough to return as night fell in search of their belongings, were murdered amid the smouldering remains.

The following morning the crowded ships put out to sea, heading for Auckland, and leaving the smoking little settlement to the Maori looters. Nineteen Europeans had been killed and twenty-nine wounded. Hone Heke Pokai and his confederate Kawiti stood victorious on the land from which the white man had been dispossessed. The flagstaff of the *pakeha* had been humbled, and the anger and frustration that had been building up for years had been appeased.

The Union Jack, as the visible symbol of a British Crown Colony, had only been hoisted at Kororareka and in other parts of New Zealand five years before, but white men had been there for many years. The islands of New Zealand had become known to Europeans following the publication, in 1777, of Captain Cook's journal of his explorations, in which he reported that the Maori inhabitants, though warlike, were intelligent and adaptable, and that the land was fertile. He recommended the place as ideal for settlement by Europeans, mentioning particularly the Bay of Islands. His views received scant attention from the British Government but in the late eighteenth and early nineteenth centuries European and American traders and whalers started to use the Bay of Islands as a base for their activities, obtaining timber and food from the Maoris in exchange for cloth and metal implements and utensils. Soon all sorts of riff-raff, attracted by the easy pickings to be made as middlemen, began to descend upon Kororareka, which before long developed into a shanty town of stores, grog-shops and, when the hardened and brutalised whaler crews demanded diversions ashore, brothels. Maori women were bought up by the middlemen, who in return offered the tribes intoxicants and more dangerous still, firearms.

The Maoris were a tribal people whose lives were governed by a rigid code of conduct, *tapu,* and to whom the prestige, or *mana* of their chiefs and the sanctity of their lands were paramount. The tribal territories covered the whole land, and within its own boundaries a tribe built its dwellings inside strongly fortified villages, known as *pas,* round which it cultivated its crops, chiefly the *kumara* or sweet potato. These localities occupied quite small areas, the rest of the territory being used for fishing and hunting. The tribal land belonged to the tribe as a whole, not to any individual members, and since each tribe's territory adjoined that of another, with the boundaries often in dispute, quarrels over land easily arose. Inevitably the *mana* of one chief would be affronted by the claims of another, revenge for such an insult, or *utu,* would have to be exacted, and a tribal war would ensue. Such wars, of which there were a great number, were bloodthirsty affairs, though hedged round with numerous rituals and courtesies, and often ended in the victors eating the flesh of the vanquished, meat

being a commodity in very short supply. Obviously, to such a
warlike people, the firearms offered by the traders were a great
advance on the primitive clubs, axes and spears of wood and
stone hitherto in use, and the chiefs, though frequently infuriated by the violations of *tapu* committed by the lawless men of
Kororareka, were quick to seize the opportunity presented by
these new weapons to settle old scores with their rivals. By the
1830s Kororareka was sunk in depravity and the Maori population, either through increased tribal fighting or disease
introduced by the Europeans, had become seriously reduced
and, in the Bay of Islands, degraded.

This was the state of affairs that met the appalled gaze of
missionaries from England, sent out to convert the Maoris to
Christianity. Among them was the Reverend Henry Williams,
a former naval officer and a man of great zeal, energy and
sympathy for the Maoris. Impressed by his character and
efforts on their behalf, and suffering from a loss of faith in their
old gods who had not been effective in preventing their mis-
fortunes, many of the Maoris proved willing listeners to Williams and his fellow missionaries and, by 1841, nearly 30,000
had become Christians. For his part, Williams began to urge
that the British Government should assert some proper control over the country. This the Government was reluctant to
do but, when the missionaries' shocking reports were followed
by rumours of French plans to colonise New Zealand, it was
decided, in 1833, to appoint a British Resident, a Mr James
Busby, at Kororareka. However, without force to back his
authority, there was little Busby could do. The Maoris
described him as 'a man-o'-war without guns' and the missionaries complained that floating brothels polluted the bay
over which the British flag flew.

Meanwhile, in Newgate Prison in London, the abductor of a
fifteen-year-old heiress, Edward Gibbon Wakefield, conceived a plan for the settlement in New Zealand of emigrants
from England. In 1837 he formed the New Zealand Association, consisting of an influential committee, who were to press
the Government to sanction his emigration plans, and the
heads of families who were willing to purchase land in New
Zealand on which emigrants of the labouring classes, the
victims of the Industrial Revolution, would work to earn
sufficient money to buy land of their own in due course. The

plans found little favour with the Colonial Office, who thought its details too imprecise and saw in it a threat to the welfare and the very existence of the true inhabitants of the country, the Maoris. Nevertheless Wakefield was undeterred. Reconstituting the Association as a joint stock New Zealand Company, in 1839 he despatched a party, which included his brother and his son, to start negotiations in New Zealand for the purchase of land. Challenged by this act, and perturbed by further reports of French designs on the country and the increasing lawlessness therein, now being further aggravated by land sharks from Sydney attempting to buy up land from the Maoris at minimum prices, the Government realised that some effective control over all these potentially explosive activities would have to be introduced. They appointed Captain William Hobson R.N. as Lieutenant-Governor, with instructions to negotiate the annexation of New Zealand to the Crown, and to supervise the activities of the New Zealand Company, by ensuring that no land could be bought from the Maoris except through the Crown.

On 5th February 1840 Hobson arrived in full naval uniform at the Resident's house at Waitangi, a few miles from Kororareka, to discuss a treaty with a great concourse of Maori chiefs. With the Reverend Williams acting as interpreter, Hobson explained that the Treaty invited the chiefs to cede all their rights and powers of sovereignty to the Queen of England; that they would be guaranteed undisputed possession of all their lands and forests, on the understanding that the Crown should have the sole right to purchase any land which the chiefs were willing to sell; and that for her part the Queen would extend to the Maoris her protection and all the rights and privileges of British subjects.

Six hours' debate followed. Initially the speakers came out strongly against the proposals. Among the chiefs was Hone Heke, the nephew of the great leader of the Ngapuhi, Hongi Hika, who had made his tribe pre-eminent in the north, and who on his death bed had warned his people against selling their land to the white man. Heke however spoke for the treaty, saying that the alternatives to British rule were either the French or 'the rum sellers'. Some of the missionaries doubted his sincerity, but whether he was true or false, all those present were swayed by a powerful speech from Tamati

Waaka Nene, a chief of the Hokianga and a Christian. He spoke of the destructiveness of the inter-tribal wars and how much better it would be for all to live in peace, trading with the white man and secure in his protection. He pleaded with Hobson to preserve the Maoris' customs, to prevent their land being stolen from them, and to stay as 'our friend, our father and our Governor'. His words carried the meeting, and after the treaty had been taken about the country for those who had not been present to hear its terms, 500 chiefs signed it. Many had not, but the number was deemed sufficient to ratify it. On 21st May the country was formerly annexed to the Crown and in due course Hobson established his seat of Government, with a Legislative Council, Supreme Court and County Courts. The place he chose was Auckland, a natural port and strategically placed between the chief concentrations of Maori power.

The New Zealand Company meanwhile had wasted no time and already, before the treaty was signed, had started to establish its posts, mainly along the south coast of North Island with its main settlement at Wellington. Land was being purchased by the Company's thrusting agents and settlers were on their way. It soon transpired that its activities were in contravention of the undertakings given to the Maoris by the Treaty of Waitangi, pledges which the Company did not consider as legally binding on its own land purchases. The Company was quickly disabused of this notion by the Colonial Secretary in London, but the whole question of land purchase and ownership was to prove one of the most complex problems to be resolved by Hobson and his successors. There were so many conflicting factors: the validity of land purchases made before the treaty; the Maoris' claim to own all the land, whether it was lived on and cultivated or not; the ownership of all tribal territories being invested in the whole tribe, not all of whom might be agreeable to the sale of any parts of it; the Company's desire to obtain the most fertile tracts for its settlers; and the Governor's wish to protect the rights of the Maoris while at the same time purchasing land which could be sold to settlers at a profit, thus raising revenues for the colony.

To attempt to resolve this vexed problem a Land Commission was set up to investigate all claims, and though it pursued its enquiries with complete impartiality, inevitably it left displeasure in its wake for Maoris and settlers alike, and it could only be a matter of time before the conflicting interests of both parties clashed violently. In June 1843 the New Zealand Company tangled with two of the most formidable chiefs in the south of North Island, Te Rauparaha and his nephew Te Rangihaeata, over a tract of land at Wairau across the Cook Strait in the South Island. The Company claimed it had bought the land in 1839; the chiefs declared the sale was invalid. A survey party in the area led by Captain Arthur Wakefield, a brother of Edward, was ordered to cease its activities by the chiefs. When Wakefield refused to do so, the Maoris began to harass his operations. He determined to arrest the two chiefs, shots were exchanged, one of which killed Te Rangihaeata's wife, and in the ensuing mêlée led by the enraged Te Rangihaeata, nineteen Englishmen and four Maoris were killed.

News of the Wairau massacre, as it came to be called, spread rapidly through the colony and on to England where the stock of the Company fell. At Auckland the Governmental view was that, while deprecating the slaughter of the survey party, the Maoris had been provoked by Wakefield's foolhardy action. The colonists, on the other hand, alarmed for their safety now that blood had been spilled, began to clamour for protection in the shape of military reinforcements.

Following the installation of the Lieutenant-Governor in 1840 about 150 men of the 80th (Staffordshire Volunteers) Regiment of Foot had been sent from New South Wales and were deployed chiefly at Auckland, with detachments at Wellington and the Bay of Islands. They were kept busy with police duties and constructing barracks and defences, and in 1842 quelled a disturbance between two warring tribes at the Bay of Plenty by the simple expedient of occupying the ground between them. The Maoris found 'the men who wear red garments' of absorbing interest, perhaps because red was their favourite colour, and were particularly intrigued by the bugle calls which regulated the troops' movements; they were less impressed by the principle of minimum force displayed at the Bay of Plenty, where they would no doubt have preferred a bloody trial of strength with these new warriors. The missionaries were considerably less enchanted with the men of the

80th. In 1843, following the departure of a detachment from the Bay of Plenty, a missionary was constrained to write: 'The soldiers to our great joy have left but I fear the abominable example that they set to the natives of drunkenness and fornication will long continue its pestilential influence.' The conduct of the detachment commander, Captain Best, who elected to enrich his lonely existence by the attentions of two Maori girls, brought forth a pained complaint from Bishop Selwyn to the General commanding in New South Wales.

By the time of the Wairau massacre the garrison had been reinforced by a company of the 96th Regiment and the whole force was concentrated at Auckland with no troops in the south at all, much to the anxiety of the colonists. The authorities in New South Wales reacted promptly to the news of the incident by despatching a further fifty men of the 80th and a company of the 99th (Lanarkshire) Regiment, but, with the situation in the south quietening down, these reinforcements were returned to Australia.

Meanwhile, far in the north around the Bay of Islands, news of the massacre had reached Hone Heke Pokai. Since he had signed the Treaty of Waitangi, he had become increasingly disillusioned with the British administration. The old raffish character of Kororareka had gone and a sober respectability now reigned at the settlement. Its population was greatly reduced, many of the inhabitants having departed for Auckland, taking with them the bulk of the trade on which the local Maoris had come to depend. Not only had the prosperity formerly engendered by the whaling fleets declined, but the Government had imposed customs duties on incoming ships and their cargoes. The Maoris could no longer exact their own tolls on the ships, and the storekeepers increased their prices to pay for the duty levied on the goods. Heke began to see his people's standard of living deteriorating, and when the British set up their flagstaff on Maiki Hill, he conceived this as a warning that in time the white men would start taking over his tribe's lands.

Heke at this time was in his thirties. A great warrior in the inter-tribal wars, he had nevertheless been drawn to Christianity, and, though distrusted by the missionaries, he always showed respect and concern for their safety. Opinions as to his appearance varied. One officer described him as 'a fine-looking man, with a commanding countenance and a haughty manner which appears habitual to him', but another thought 'his person is very disgusting; an ugly wide mouth; drunken eye; a broad stout fellow of upwards of six feet high'. Though intelligent, he was totally unpredictable and, probably as a result of his close kinsmanship with the great Hongi Hika, 'rash, impetuous and imperious, he was intolerant of all authority save his own'. One missionary had doubts about his sanity.

Daily he brooded on the fate of his people, his mind inflamed by whispered warnings from French and American traders in the Bay that the Union Jack signified slavery for the Maoris. The Americans had a particular axe to grind since their profitable smuggling activities, particularly in the most modern firearms, had been discovered and for which they had been heavily fined. Even the American Consul at the Bay of Islands was not averse to filling the fuddled mind of an old chief named Pomare with dire threats that no good could come to the Maoris from British rule. Pomare of course passed on these remarks to Heke, who became increasingly obsessed by the sight of the flagstaff on Maiki Hill. What made it even more intolerable was that the tall tree from which it had been made had once stood on Heke's land, and he had presented it as a gift to the former Resident, Mr Busby. His truculence was steadily building up and when he heard of the Wairau massacre, he is said to have asked: 'Is Te Rauparaha to have the honour of killing all the *pakehas*?'

In July 1844 the dam of his frustration broke. On learning that a girl of his tribe was living with a European butcher in Kororareka, he sent men to order her to return to the tribe. She received the emissaries with contempt and, pointing to a pig's carcase hanging in the shop, she likened it to Heke. Such an insult required immediate *utu*. Heke sallied into the town with a band of warriors, looted the butcher's shop and carried off the girl. Then, for good measure, they cut down the flagstaff.

Heke's act of defiance spurred the Governor to action. Hobson had died in September 1842 and had been replaced by another naval officer, Captain Robert Fitzroy,[1] who now sent a detachment of the 96th, who had relieved the 80th, to

[1] The captain of H.M.S. *Beagle* during the voyage of Charles Darwin.

Kororareka, and sent messages to Sir George Gipps, Governor of New South Wales, for reinforcements. In the third week of August 170 men of the 99th with two six-pounders arrived at the Bay of Islands, escorting Fitzroy himself aboard a sloop, H.M.S. *Hazard*. With troops at his back, the Governor summoned the chiefs of the Ngapuhi and other neighbouring tribes to a conference.

This lowered the tension, largely due to the intervention of Tamati Waaka Nene, who had spoken so strongly for the Treaty of Waitangi. Assuring the Governor of his friendship and loyalty, Waaka guaranteed that the older and wiser ones among his fellow-chiefs would keep the younger hotheads in order. The troops, he said, could return to Auckland. Pleased with this response, Fitzroy undertook to remove the unpopular customs duties. Somewhat ominously Heke did not attend the conference himself but sent as conciliatory a letter as he was capable of to Fitzroy, offering to replace the flagstaff:

> Friend Governor: This is my speech to you. My disobedience and rudeness is no new thing. I inherit it from my parents—from my ancestors. Do not imagine it is a new feature of my character; but I am thinking of leaving off my rude conduct to Europeans. Now I say I will prepare another pole inland at Waimate, and I will erect it at its proper place at Kororareka in order to put a stop to our present quarrel. Let your soldiers remain beyond the sea and at Auckland. Do not send them here. The pole that was cut down belonged to me. I made it for the native flag, and it was never paid for by the Europeans.
>
> > From your friend,
> > Hone Heke Pokai.[2]

All might now have been well but for two things. First, rumours reached the Maoris' ears, possibly through the missionaries, that their unoccupied land might, in future, no longer be regarded as their territory to dispose of as they pleased. This fear, though it proved to be groundless, was aggravated by the increasing number of Europeans arriving in New Zealand. Secondly, Kawiti, an old pagan chief of the

[2] Quoted T. Lindsay Buick, *New Zealand's First War* (Wellington, 1926).

...ert Hattaway, soldier of the 58th and
...or of *Reminiscences of the Northern War*. He
...ht at Ohaeawai and Ruapekapeka. A
...ograph taken later in life when he had
...me a prosperous member of the New
...and community.

William Isaac Speight, sergeant of the 58th. 'In
the field he is gallantry itself.' Recommended in
1856 for a retrospective award of the Victoria
Cross for bravery at Ruapekapeka. Photograph
taken in later life.

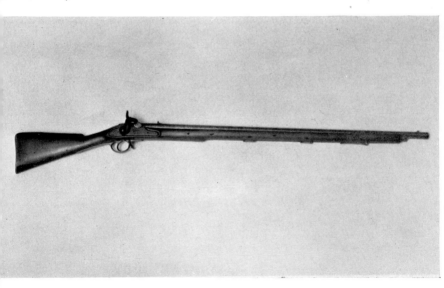

1839 pattern percussion musket used by the 58th in New Zealand.

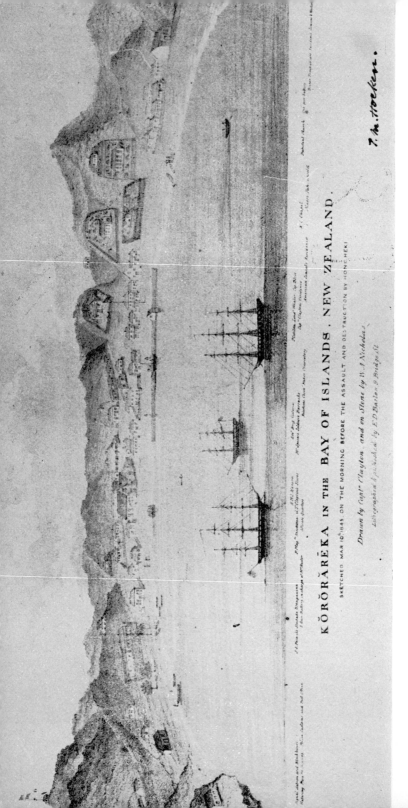

KŎRŎRĂRĔKA IN THE BAY OF ISLANDS. NEW ZEALAND.

SKETCHED MAR 10ᵀᴴ 1845 ON THE MORNING BEFORE THE ASSAULT AND DESTRUCTION BY HONE HEKI

Drawn by Capt Clayton and on Stone by W. J. Nicholas

Lithographed & published by E.D. Barlow 9 Bridge St

J. M. Hooker.

Kororareka on the Bay of Islands, 1845. (Lithograph after Captain Clayton)

Ngapuhi and leader of the *hapu*, or sub-division of the tribe, at Kawakawa, who had spent his life in slaughter and plunder against rival tribes, now felt tempted, perhaps encouraged by Heke's defiance, to test his strength against the white tribe. If there was going to be fighting, Heke had the sense to see that uncoordinated efforts by himself and Kawiti would get nowhere. It was time to assert his leadership, and on 9th January 1845 he cut down the flagstaff for the second time.

Once again a detachment of the 96th was sent up to the Bay of Islands with orders to replace it. To many of the settlers this seemed sheer provocation, a pointless exercise which could achieve nothing but goad Heke into ever more desperate measures. To the soldiers this fixation over a flagpole must have appeared incomprehensible. One of the 96th evolved the theory that Hone Heke was in reality an Irishman, Johnny Hickey, burning to avenge the wrongs done to his country. Nevertheless up it went, and no sooner up, than down it came for the third time.

Heke was clearly hell-bent on a trial of strength and measures had to be taken to meet it. A taller and stronger pole was put up and protected by iron around its base. A blockhouse was constructed at its foot and garrisoned by a permanent picquet of troops, while at the same time defences began to be built in the town itself. The tension was growing and, as reports of unrest among the tribes increased, building up as has been seen to the most destructive of all Heke's assaults on Kororareka, Fitzroy realised he must have more troops. He wrote hurriedly to New South Wales. In Government House at Sydney Sir George Gipps considered whom he could spare. Two of his four regiments were in Van Diemen's Land, the 51st King's Own Light Infantry at Hobart and the 96th, less those detachments already in New Zealand, at Launceston; the 99th were at Sydney. The 80th had left for Madras but the greater part of its relieving regiment had now arrived from England. The regiments in Van Diemen's Land were too far away and the 99th were well established in Sydney so it would be a pity to uproot them. The newcomers were only commanded by a major but he seemed alert enough, so them it should be. Orders went out to prepare for active service the 58th (Rutlandshire) Regiment.

4

We Mustered for the War

It was the tenth of April from Sydney we set sail
And fortune did us favour with a sweet and pleasant gale
We landed in New Zealand upon that very day
And at Auckland we got orders to sail straight for the Bay
Alexander Whisker.

THE FIRST INTIMATION THAT THE 58TH MIGHT HAVE TO CHANGE their comfortable quarters in New South Wales for what the Regimental record called, 'the disagreeables of New Zealand', came on 13th February 1845, when the Regiment was ordered to hold a detachment in readiness to sail for Auckland. The troops selected were from No. 9 Company, commanded by Captain Matson, an officer of over thirty years' service, and the Light Company under Captain Denny. Some delay ensued owing to a shortage of shipping but on 10th March, the very day Heke was planning his assault on Kororareka, they embarked on H.M.S. *North Star*, a twenty-eight-gun frigate commanded by Sir Everard Home, and the transport *Velocity* and sailed for Auckland.

After a voyage of fourteen days, the ships entered New Zealand waters, as Robert Hattaway, then a private in No. 9 Company, describes:

I can well recollect the event. It was a beautiful clear night, a full moon overhead, while serenity reigned around. We neared Point Britomart, and the ship cast anchor. On the same day the troops disembarked at Mechanic's Bay. This was the first detachment of the old 'Black Cuffs' to arrive in the colony. The company of Captain Matson marched up

Shortland Street to old St Paul's Church and halted, the rank and file extending their formation down to where the New Zealander printing office stood. There was a crowd of natives assembled, and they were in a great state of excitement, rushing up and down the lines, counting and recounting the numbers. After a considerable delay, the greater portion of the men were sent to Point Britomart, the residue, of about 60 men, to Hardington's old hotel; the officer retaining one room, and the men being distributed throughout the rest. After relieving ourselves of our accoutrements, and spreading our greatcoats on the floor for a mattress, and our knapsacks for a pillow, we lay down and enjoyed a short repose. After resting we looked round for refreshments, and found an old lady who supplied our wants. On tendering some silver coins, in change she handed me several small cards with IOU on them. We looked at the cards, and then at some nice refreshing drinks, and the drinks won the day. The issue of these small debentures was a great convenience for small tradesmen in these days. After the arrival of the troops money became more plentiful, and the IOUs disappeared from circulation.

As is the way with soldiers, the question of the next meal was of more pressing interest to the young Hattaway than any observations on the new country in which they had just arrived. He soon found that: 'The provisions issued to supply our daily wants consisted of 1 lb bread, and 1 lb pork and vegetables; coffee in the morning and tea in the evening. Boiled pork and fish continuously was not too appetising.' Fortunately this dull diet could be supplemented from the wares of Maori traders, who set up their provision stalls on the beach: 'Their supplies for disposal consisted of pigs, potatoes, pumpkins, kumaras, maize, fish, and, in the season, splendid peaches, the prices for which fruit were reasonable. The natives, especially the women, were keen hagglers in exacting the last farthing, and many amusing scenes ensued in the purchase of pigs by the knights of the cleaver.' The British soldier's well-known fondness for liquor met with a ready response from the local colonists who, grateful for the arrival of the reinforcements, 'presented to the men on outpost duty intoxicants, contrary to stringent orders. Some of the men partook too freely of intoxicants at a time when sobriety was so necessary for the very safety of the people whom they had come to protect.'

As soon as the troops were settled in their quarters, outlying picquets were posted around the town to guard against surprise and to give time, in the event of an attack, for the women and children to be concentrated in two places of safety: one at St Paul's Church, where the windows were boarded up and the walls loopholed, and the other at Point Britomart, where a fort was under construction, work which required the provision of a daily fatigue party by the troops. Auckland had grown in four years from a collection of huts and tents to a sizeable town with a Government House, a Supreme Court, a Mechanic's Library and Institute, newspaper offices, even its own racecourse, boasting the name of Epsom. With this expansion, the local community had become settled and domesticated, so that the news of the rising in the north, with its reality made manifest by the arrival of refugees from Kororareka, had caused considerable alarm and fear, which the arrival of the troops and the measures taken for the safety of the town did much to allay.

The military experience of the men of the 58th had hitherto been confined to garrison life in England and Ireland, and a few months in the peaceful surroundings of New South Wales, with no more urgent duties to perform than the finding of guards for the convict settlements. Now that they were on active service, with the prospect of an attack by a dangerous and ferocious enemy of whom none of them had any knowledge, inevitably a certain nervousness permeated the ranks, as is shown by an incident shortly after their arrival, described by Hattaway:

On April 1, about two a.m., a dark and cloudy morning, we received a great scare by a musket being discharged in the vicinity of Government House, then occupied by Governor Fitzroy. The alarm was sounded by the bugler of the guard. The troops assembled at the appointed place, and the volunteers[1] arrived at short intervals, some rushing up Shortland-street with their bayonets fixed at the trail—a

[1] The local militia raised in Auckland.

dangerous practice of a dark night. After the men had been formed up and told off, ready to be moved to any point required, Lieut. Balneavis was despatched to visit the different outposts, to ascertain the cause of alarm. The rear of the Governor's residence was covered with a low scrub and dense fern, which at this time surrounded Auckland. A non-commissioned-officer commanded a picket whose sentries were placed extending from Government House grounds to where the Choral Hall now stands. One of the sentries stated that he heard something stealthily approaching the post, and after listening some time he heard the crackling of the scrub. Seeing some object approaching he challenged three times, received no answer, and fired according to orders. The report which circulated after our dismissal at daylight was that the object was one of the Governor's cows, which had not answered the sentries challenge, and thus caused all the commotion that ensued. That sentry had a bad time of it afterwards. Even at the Antipodes All Fools' Day was not forgotten.

Meanwhile, although the arrival of two companies of infantry had restored confidence in Auckland, the shock of Heke's attack on Kororareka had convinced the Governor that more troops would be needed if the rebellion was to be crushed. Accordingly a further request for aid went off to the authorities in New South Wales and, on 4th April, Major Cyprian Bridge, commanding the 58th at Parramatta in the absence of Lieutenant-Colonel Wynyard, opened his Journal with the words:

Received orders to hold the Head Quarters of the 58th Regt stationed at Parramatta in readiness to embark on the shortest notice for New Zealand on special service, alarming accounts having just been received from thence of another outbreak among the natives, and the total destruction of one of the principal settlements in the Bay of Islands and the loss of 13 Europeans killed and 19 wounded.

John Mitchell, then in the Grenadier Company which was under orders to go, had only landed in Australia on 6th March and, throughout the voyage out, had been looking forward to

being reunited with his fiancée, Julia Maher, daughter of a
sergeant who had come out on an earlier boat. On landing at
Sydney he had been disappointed to find that Sergeant Maher,
with his family, had left on detachment a few days before for
Port Macquarie, some 200 miles up the coast. Mitchell had
been ordered to help out in the Paymaster's office, but finding
there was little for him to do there, he had applied for leave,
hoping to get away to see his Julia:

> I approached the Adjutant about it, he smiled & said 'your
> leave will be granted, I know your object in due course'. My
> leave was signed by Major Bridge & I intended starting by
> the first boat. Just as I was leaving for Sydney a despatch
> from the General to Major Bridge was received, ordering
> the headquarters and all available men to proceed to Sydney
> with the greatest despatch & there embark for New Zealand
> where serious trouble had broken out with the Maoris. My
> leave was immediately cancelled. I was naturally disap-
> pointed but consoled myself with the prospect of taking
> part in war.

The first troops to leave were from Captain Russell's Company, who, embarking on 8th April, sailed for Wellington
where trouble was anticipated from rebellious tribes in the
Hutt Valley. Two days later Bridge himself sailed with the
reinforcements for Auckland: the Grenadier Company, with
the sorrowing Mitchell in its ranks, under Captain Grant,
Captain Thompson's No. 3 Company, and the Band, a total
strength of eight officers and 204 men. The rest of the Regiment was to follow as shipping became available. Whatever
the future held in store, they could enjoy a pleasant voyage
since the ship on which they sailed was the barque *Slain's
Castle*, a comfortable and spacious vessel commanded by Captain Dawson which, prior to being chartered at Sydney as a
troop transport, had been used by the New Zealand Company
for ferrying emigrants out from home.

The crossing was made in six days but off the New Zealand
coast the ship was becalmed and it was not until the 22nd that it
could get into Auckland. Bridge records their arrival:

Reached the harbour about half an hour before daylight.

Beat the 'Reveille' on board, after which were cheered by our soldiers from the shore. Went on shore after having been boarded by one of H.M. Ship *North Star*'s boats. I returned on board having heard we were anxiously expected as the town of Auckland was threatened to be attacked by a chief of the name of Kawiti. Waited on the Commandant Lieut-Col Hulme 96th Regt, and reported my arrival. Afterwards the Governor (Capt Fitzroy R.N.) who told me in confidence that an expedition was to proceed immediately to the Bay of Islands to put down Hone Heki and the rebellious tribes there assembled. Was requested by His Excellency to meet him again at two o'clock and join a conference between him and Sir Evered Home and the Commandant as to further steps. Did so, and it was all arranged that the *Slain's Castle* should take on board 80 more of the 58th from the shore, and the *North Star* all the 96th under Colonel Hulme, and proceed at once to the Bay of Islands.

While their commanders conferred, the soldiers were getting their first sight of the Maoris. To Alexander Whisker and his comrades of No. 3 Company, many of them simple Irish country boys who can scarcely even have seen any human beings other than white men, the natives of New Zealand must have seemed astonishing:

There was great numbers of the Blackes came along side of our ship and they seemed very civil. They had a Blanket lapt round them from the waist Down and the officers Brought some of the Chiefs on Board. The moment they got onto the Poop they sat down and they would not rise to they were going away again. They are men of great looking strength and from about 5 feet 8 to 6 feet high. They have large canoes and they sit in the bottom of it with there feet turned Back under them and sits fair on their heels. There faces is frightful to look at and they have all kinds of things in there ears: some pieces of Bone and ivery, others with piece of sticks, others a great lot of worsted drawn through there ear and I seen one with a Brass Padlock in his ear. They brought fish, cabbage, potatoes, onions and different other things along side and we had great fun makeing bargains with them for we could not understand each other. All they could say was shilling and 6 pence.

After several days of heavy rain and squalls, which resulted in a number of the contradictory orders so often associated with military operations of this kind, the force for the Bay of Islands eventually embarked on 27th March under the command of Lieutenant-Colonel William Hulme of the 96th Regiment. Receiving an ensign's commission in 1803, he had served with distinction in the Pindari campaigns in India in 1817–18, for which he was granted a brevet-majority. It has been written of him that he was 'an alert and intelligent man, endowed with a good measure of common sense and a strongly marked characteristic of always appearing smartly dressed.'[2] Though his sartorial precision was unlikely to prove a decisive factor in the forests of the North Island, his sensible approach to military problems might have avoided much of the hardship and loss of life that was to ensue, when he was superseded by a more senior officer later in the campaign, as will be seen in due course.

Hulme and his detachment of the 96th boarded the *Velocity,* some of the Auckland volunteers were carried on the schooner *Albert,* and the 58th contingent under Bridge, of the Grenadiers and No. 3 Company, were joined on the *Slain's Castle* by eighty men of Denny's Light Company; Matson's company was left to protect Auckland. At six in the evening the little convoy sailed out of Auckland harbour for the north.

The ships reached the Bay at half-past two in the afternoon of the following day and as they drew alongside H.M.S. *North Star,* which had preceded them, Whisker recalled that 'the sailors gave 3 harty cheers which we returned'. Then, as the *Slain's Castle* cast anchor, the Band of the 58th rose to the occasion by breaking into 'Rule, Britannia!', followed, perhaps as an oblique tribute to the men they had come to fight, by 'The King of the Cannibal Islands'.

Gathered to welcome the troops was the force of friendly Maoris, some 400 strong, under the loyal and devoted chief, Tamati Waaka Nene, whose support throughout the campaign was to prove invaluable and unwavering. Tamati

[2] T. Lindsay Buick, *New Zealand's First War* (1926), page 21.

Waaka, always referred to by Whisker as 'Timothy Walker', had been infuriated by Heke's last attack on Kororareka, which he regarded as a betrayal of the assurances of good behaviour given by himself and other older chiefs to the Governor. He had determined on hunting Heke down and the arrival of the British force at the Bay was largely due to the request he had sent to the Governor for assistance. Now that the troops had come, Waaka's people did them honour with a war dance, which, in Mitchell's words, 'with Tomati's wife in the front rank amazed us very much indeed'.

Since, to the rank and file, one Maori must have seemed much like another, great care was taken by Colonel Hulme to differentiate between the loyal and rebellious natives, writing in Garrison Orders that:

> He considers it necessary to explain to the Troops, that there are about the Bay of Islands, several loyal Native Tribes who are at this time harrassing the Rebels, and to caution them to shew forbearance in their intercourse with the Natives who are not in a state of resistance, for they must be sensible that none but friendly aborigines will come near them unarmed, for he is determined to punish with the greatest severity any Soldier who shall offer violence to any Native who is entitled to our protection.

Cyprian Bridge, keen to get on with the task in hand, reported to his superiors:

> Went on board [the *North Star*] and saw Sir E. Home and Colonel Hulme and heard what were his orders: first to proclaim martial law, and hoist Her Majesty's flag at Kororareka, and then go up the river KawaKawa about 4 or 5 miles, and attack and destroy the *pa* and tribe of Pomare,[3] that being accomplished to proceed to cut off Kawiti and his tribe, and afterwards to land the whole force at Victoria and march into Heki's territories and endeavour to capture him.

The re-establishment of British authority at the Bay of Islands took place with due ceremony that very afternoon:

[3] Pomare was suspected of sending subversive letters to another chief, Te Wherowhero, south of Auckland.

At ½ past 4 sent the Grenadier Company ashore with Colonel Hulme to plant Her Majesty's flag and proclaim martial law. A salute from the *North Star* and three cheers from all the ships, after which they returned on board the *North Star*. Dined with Sir Evd Home, met Colonel Hulme, when it was arranged we should sail at break of day up to Pomare's *Pa* and knock it about his ears and raze it to the ground.

A lack of wind the next day delayed the departure and it was not until around midnight that the ships anchored at the junction of the KawaKawa and Waikare rivers, opposite the *pa* which stood on a high promontory with its rear covered by tea-tree scrub. At dawn a white flag was seen flying in the *pa* and the troops were disembarked. Bridge continues:

On reaching the shore myself I found that Pomare himself had come down to speak to Colonel Hulme and had been taken prisoner, and a loaded pistol was taken from him. While I was carrying out Colonel Hulme's orders in placing a line of skirmishers along the brow of the hill between the landing place and the *Pa*, many natives were seen lying in the grass within twelve or fifteen paces of the advanced skirmishers with arms in their hands, evidently determined to oppose our entrance to the *Pa*, until they were ordered by their Chief to disperse themselves, and then our men were called in.

Colonel Hulme took Pomare on board the *North Star* and persuaded him to order his tribe to hand over their arms within two hours, failing which the *pa* would be destroyed. Directions to enforce this were conveyed to Bridge on shore, but the latter, ever careful, felt rather more was required:

I got no orders to take precaution that the natives should not make their escape into the bush with their arms. I however sent a party of observation on a hill to watch their movements and [sent] my interpreter along with Awarre,[4] who shortly returned with three stand of arms which was all he

---

[4] Probably a Maori guide.

said [were] in the *Pa*, and he told me he had seen at least 21 men stealing along into the bush with their arms. I therefore desired him to go with Awarre after these men and tell them that unless they returned we would proceed against them as rebels and destroy their *Pa*. To this they turned a deaf ear, and made off with themselves into the bush. I was then sent for by Col Hulme, and I reported to him what I heard and done about the arms, and it was finally decided that the *Pa* should be burned as soon as the two hours were out.

It had been Hulme's intention that, after Pomare had been dealt with, the force should immediately advance to attack Kawiti, Heke's ally, but it was now decided that such a venture would be too risky without trustworthy guides, and that the force should re-embark once the *pa* was destroyed. Bridge goes on:

About 5 o'clock I was sent into the *pa* with my pioneers and some small armed men from the ship to search for gunpowder. A little boy accompanied us; he said he knew where the natives kept it, but we found it had all been taken away. The men were then allowed to take whatever they found of use, and kill pigs and poultry. A most laughable scene took place. Officers and men running after pigs, turkeys, ducks, and goats, shooting and cutting off their heads with their swords. Some few old arms were found and a good deal of the plunder from Kororareka, some of which we managed to bring off. All I managed to get was a small rifle with the lock out of repair, and a Native war club before the place was in flames all round.

John Mitchell was among the party ordered into the *pa*:

Some amusing incidents occurred in the looting. A few of the soldiers on this duty were married men, their object was to get domestic utensils such as frying pans, kettles, clothing for both men and women. A large number of joints, sheep & pigs were sent on board. I was very busy in this department, hunting from hut to hut I came across a small keg, about 9 gallon. Ah, thought I, I'm in luck, smashed in the head with my musket when lo, it was treacle (not spirits). My musket was in a terrible mess. My next act was chasing a pig about 40 lbs weight. The Adjutant assisted me in the capture by cutting it across the back with his sword. I sent it off to the ship with a lot of other things.

Permission to loot the *pa* had only been given after the measures to destroy it had started, but the conduct of part of the force brought forth some censorious remarks from Bridge, although he was plainly satisfied, even a little smug, about the behaviour of his own men:

I never saw men behave better in my life than the 58th. The 96th on the contrary commenced plundering before the fire began, or before any instructions were received on shore relative to the *Pa* being destroyed; so did many of the Volunteers from Auckland. The 58th had to place sentries to prevent these depredations.

Mitchell, too, ended the day somewhat disgruntled with the indiscipline of others, for when he finally reached the ship after the *pa*'s destruction, he found 'those on board had a fine time of it feasting on the spoil we had sent off, giving no thought to those away on duty'.

It was after nine at night before all were embarked and the following day the force sailed down to Pahia, where a conference was held to decide the next step of the campaign. The first task had been accomplished without loss of life, but the men of the 58th had yet to test their fighting prowess against the Maori warriors.

5

Baptism of Fire

At 6 oclock the 3rd of May we mustered for the war
the 58th and 96th Likewise some gallant tars
To face Bold Honi Heke—that Dareing Maorie Chiefe
And Likewise Bold Kowitta that came to his Reliefe
We fought on the 8th of May. although we were not Beat
At 5 oclock that evening we were forced for to Retreat

Alexander Whisker.

HULME NOW DECIDED THAT HIS NEXT MOVE SHOULD BE AGAINST
Heke's *pa* at Puketutu on Lake Omapere,[1] some fifteen miles
inland up the Kerikeri river and very close to Waaka's stronghold at Okaihau. He planned to convey his force by sea to the
mouth of the river, where it would land and advance on the
objective up the left bank. His infantry strength was
unchanged but British forces in the north had now been
increased by the arrival of H.M.S. *Hazard* (Acting Commander Johnson R.N.), an eighteen-gun sloop, which brought a
three-pounder rocket battery under Lieutenant Egerton,
R.N., to provide Hulme's only form of artillery. Shore parties
of seamen and Royal Marines were also landed from both
Hazard and *North Star*.

As the Royal Navy was to have an important role ashore
and afloat in this and the ensuing operations, something
should be said of its officers, men and ships at this period.
Though much reduced in ships and men since its days of fame
in the Napoleonic Wars—240 ships and 40,000 men compared
with over a thousand ships and another 100,000 more men—it
had not greatly changed in the intervening thirty years. As the
naval historian, Christopher Lloyd, has written, 'it was a

---

[1] Bridge called the lake Mawe, the old Maori name for it.

season of old man's glory reflected from battles long ago', when 'never was professional conservatism more rigid, nor opposition to new-fangled ideas more unyielding'. Changes there were however: the Board of Admiralty was reformed and modernised in 1832; steamships were slowly and against considerable opposition coming into service; the sailor's life was increasingly more humane; and the reduction of the size of the Navy no longer necessitated the use of the press-gang to man its ships.

Like the Army, the strength of the Navy in the Napoleonic Wars had brought into the ranks of its officers men from varying social backgrounds, but after the peace the officer class became much narrower. Since promotion in the Navy was entirely by seniority, and since there were not separate active and retired lists of officers, the upper ranks were extremely congested, with captains and admirals in their sixties and seventies, and promotion was laboriously slow. In short there were too many officers in the Navy and too few sea-going posts for them to fill.

Potential naval officers joined the service early at between twelve and thirteen years old, being selected for cadetships after passing a somewhat farcical examination, a process only instituted in 1838. The cadet learned his trade aboard ship. After four years at sea he could qualify as a midshipman and, with that achieved, he had his foot on the lowest rung of the promotion ladder, up which he climbed according to his seniority, subject to acquiring certain qualifications and passing various examinations. For appointment to the more desirable posts he had to rely on 'interest', derived either from the influence he could command from relations or senior officers, or by making his mark as a good officer.

By the 1840s all seamen were volunteers, drawn mainly from seafaring men of the southern counties, such men from the north tending to favour the merchant service. Unlike soldiers, and except for those who joined as boys, they were only taken on for limited, as opposed to continuous, service, being discharged when their ship was paid off, a wasteful system which was not remedied until 1853 when continuous service was introduced. The only long service men aboard a man-o'-war were the Royal Marines, enlisted, organised, uniformed and equipped similarly to soldiers. Their task was to provide the ship's police, to form the nucleus of landing-parties, to man some of the ship's guns or to act as sharp-shooters aboard ship in action.

Although Naval officers had, in the 1840s, a dark blue dress uniform cut on similar lines to that of Army officers but worn with a cocked hat, there was as yet no official uniform for the lower deck. Sailors were served out with garments from the ship's 'slop chest' or made up their own clothes, but, in the mid-nineteenth century, when great emphasis was laid on 'spit and polish' aboard ship, most captains liked to have their crews uniformly dressed and the traditional garb of round, tarred hat or straw hat with ribbon bearing the ship's name, short blue jacket, black neckerchief, shirt or blouse, and wide white trousers was more or less uniform, if not official. For their daily working dress sailors wore what they pleased, while officers had an undress uniform with a peaked forage cap.

The first steamship to enter the Royal Navy, a paddle tug named *The Comet*, had been launched in the 1820s. While this may have been useful enough for its purpose, the Lords of the Admiralty bilked at the idea of applying such a principle to ships-of-the-line. For a start, where would the guns go? The huge paddle casings would scarcely permit the serried rows of cannon which had produced the broadsides of Nelson's day. This particular problem was solved by the introduction of the screw-propeller and the celebrated tug-of-war in 1845 between H.M.S. *Alecto,* fitted with paddles, and H.M.S. *Rattler,* fitted with a screw, which resulted in a convincing win for the latter, marked the beginning of the end for the 'wooden walls of Old England'. However, at the time of this story, due largely to the innate conservatism of the Navy, the bulk of the fleet was still composed of full-rigged sailing ships.

Since the end of the Napoleonic Wars the chief function of the Navy had been to protect British commerce and link the world-wide possessions of the British Crown. This involved charting the oceans, policing the sea lanes against pirates and slavers and generally showing the flag. In 1839 the Mediterranean Fleet had been in action off Syria to restore British influence in the Near East and at the same time the Far East Fleet had given valuable support to land forces in the First China War. As British influence and power spread throughout the world, the task of policing the far-flung colonies and possessions with only a small Regular Army became ever more difficult, and the practice of landing sailors and marines to assist the troops ashore became a common occurrence as the Victorian age progressed. It was in this role that men of the Royal Navy, with guns landed from the ships, would be chiefly employed in the Maori War.

Shortly after dawn on 3rd May Hulme's force landed at Onewhero Bay, a place-name doubtless unpronounceable to the 58th, for they re-christened it Rutland Bay, after their regimental title. As the sun came up, with the promise of a warm day's marching, the troops fell in along the shore, with Thompson's No. 3 Company in front as the advance guard, followed by the Grenadiers and the Light Company, then the 96th detachment, the landing parties of seamen and Royal Marines from *North Star* and *Hazard* with the rockets, the Auckland volunteers, and lastly, in rather looser order, the friendly Maoris. The 58th were in their forage caps, red shell jackets and dark grey trousers. They were spared the burden of their knapsacks but were nevertheless hung about with muskets, bayonets, heavy leather ammunition pouches containing sixty rounds, water bottles and haversacks filled with five days' biscuits and an additional thirty rounds, while a greatcoat and blanket were strapped to their backs. The Maoris were constantly amazed at the sight of British soldiers on the march, 'straight as a flight of curlew in the sky' and, seeing them so heavily accoutred, observed, 'if we Maoris were loaded up in that way we would neither be able to fight or run away'.[2]

Before the march began a small ceremony took place, observed by Mitchell:

Before leaving Tomati Waka received gifts of naval uniform consisting of a cocked hat, blue coat with epaulettes, a military one on one shoulder & naval one on the other, a pair of military trousers & boots. Mrs Waka accompanied carrying their guns. He was a most amusing figure but did not seem very comfortable in the costume. We had proceeded about two miles when he began to disrobe. First off went

Auckland, *c.* 1843. (Artist unknown)

Interior of a Maori village. (Lithograph after J. A. Gilfillan)

Hone Heke Pokai, *c.* 1846, leader of the rising in the north against the Crown. 'A broad stout fellow of upwards of six feet high.' (Water colour by J. J. Merrett)

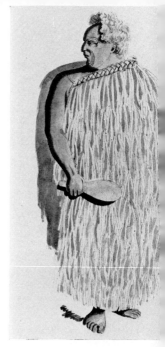

Kawiti, *c.* 1846, a chief who fought the prowess of the British soldier. H chief ally throughout the war. (Wa colour by J. J. Merrett)

The redoubtable chief, Tamati Waaka Nene, loyal friend and ally to the British throughout the First Maori War. (Etching attributed to Robert F. Way)

'The Old Serpent', Te Rauparaha, c the Ngatitoa tribe, which committee Wairau Massacre. (Drawing by J. A Gilfillan)

the hat, then the boots, next the frock-coat & finally the trousers, donning once more the beloved blanket. The cast off uniform was all carried by Mrs Waka. We all really enjoyed the fun.

Although the day was hot and the track narrow, the first day's march went well and ended in cheerful mood, as Bridge records:

Halted about 5 in the evening in a pretty valley with a running stream through it. Here we had to pass the night in the open field on the fern, no tents having been provided for us, there being no trees or wood near to erect huts. The night was fine [and] before we retired to rest we witnessed a most amusing scene, and one I dare say never seen before in an encampment, of British Soldiers and Natives sitting in perfect amity around the fires and singing songs alternately. A man of ours, John Smith of the Light Company, astonished and delighted them much with a song called the Irish Policeman in which the irish howl and shilelagh is introduced as well as the irish dancings. It was a truly wild and picturesque scene. Another thing was also worthy of remark and had a beautiful effect amongst all this noise and joviality, which was old Tamati Waka and the more sedate of his tribe singing (and very correctly too) the evening hymn.

However, this euphoria was not to last:

Before 10 o'clock it came on to rain heavilly and continued all night. Never passed so miserable a night, had to get up and stand round the fire. We were in a pretty plight in the morning, Officers and men wet through, Arms, Ammunition and everything.

Mitchell, with the unerring instinct of the private soldier for the correct priorities, also noted sourly, 'the food in our haversacks was unfit for use, the want of transport left us without the usual allowance of ration rum too, the loss of which was sorely felt & comments [made] which I need not write.'

The downpour continued unrelenting, so it was planned to make a detour to the Kerikeri Mission Station, where shelter could be found, the troops dried out, and the weapons rendered serviceable. By the time it was reached, between nine and ten o'clock, the force was more sodden than ever, for, 'by some blunder', they got on the wrong track which not only took them four miles out of their way but, as Whisker ruefully remarked, 'we had to march through 3 rivers to above our kneese'. Fortunately Mr Kemp, the missionary, met them with 'great civility and attention' and by the evening of the 5th all were fit and ready to advance once more.

On the 6th, Bridge led off again:

Marched at daybreak for Waka's *Pa*. The first part of it very rough and open country but towards evening came to a dense wood through which we had to cut our way, the pioneers going on in front with some natives soon made us a good broad path through it. This would have been a fine position for Heki to have attacked. He might have done us much mischief if he had, but we were not molested, although we heard he had sent men down to watch our movements. Reached Waka's *Pa* safely before dusk and found the people [had] errected two large huts for the Soldiers and two small ones for the Officers. Had to set to work to build another for a magazine.

Waaka's *pa* was only some three miles from Puketutu, so the next day Bridge set out with Hulme to get their first sight of their objective:

Went out with Colonel Hulme to reconoitre the enemies' position. Could distinctly see the men carrying in loads of flax leaves with which Heki was fortifying the different faces of his *Pa*, putting it up so thick between the pallisades as to be musket proof. Found the front and left faces of the *Pa* were very strong and were flanked by angles so as to bring a cross fire on assailants. The other faces we could not see, but were told they were not so strong, although there were two or three lines of pallisades on each face, with a ditch between them, and a stone wall inside the height of a man, and loophold below from which the defendent fired from a trench. Lieut Egerton went to look for a position for his rockets.

Despite the obvious strength of the *pa* and notwithstanding his lack of heavy weapons, Hulme decided to attack next day so, on the morning of the 8th, the whole force advanced and halted some 200 yards short of the *pa*. His plan was to bombard the position with the rockets and then, while holding the Grenadier and No. 3 Companies as a reserve behind the brow of a low hill opposite the front face, to assault from the right with three storming parties: the first formed by the 58th Light Company under Denny; the second, under Lieutenant and Adjutant M'Lerie of the 58th, consisting of the 96th and Royal Marines; and the third composed entirely of sailors, led by Johnson of the *Hazard*. Waaka's men were to guard the left flank and the right was protected by the waters of Lake Omapere, at the edge of which was a belt of swampy ground.

Great interest centred on the rockets for the Maoris appeared to believe they were a form of guided missile, which could pursue an enemy until it killed him. Egerton's first discharge thus came as something of an anti-climax, since the rocket sailed wildy and ineffectively over the *pa*, much to the sardonic amusement of Heke, who stood watching the proceedings from his main gate. With the third shot, Egerton struck the palisade, causing a great deal of noise and excitement within, but otherwise little damage. As the remaining nine projectiles were fired off, Bridge watched the advance of the storming parties:

They had to cross a narrow ravine between the lake and the left face of the *pa* under a heavy fire. When half way over they found themselves opposed by a party occupying the heights near the opposite sides, so that previous to taking up their seperate positions for Storming the *Pa*, it became requisite to dislodge this party, who would otherwise have harrassed them in their rear. This they did in most gallant style with the loss of only three men, and took possession of a breastwork from which they kept up a fire on the *Pa* as well as the wood in rear of it, into which they had driven the enemy.

As the Light Company hugged the breastwork, firing whenever they could see a target and regaining their breath for the assault on the palisades, a friendly Maori, Honi Ropiha,[3] suddenly spotted about 300 of the enemy, led by Kawiti himself, rising from the scrub behind to attack the stormers in rear. These had been the defenders of the breastwork who, on being thrown off it, had worked their way round through the tea-tree scrub. Hearing Ropiha yell the alarm, Denny leaped to his feet, bellowing at his men, '58th, about face! Present! Fire!', followed, after the volley crashed out, by 'Charge!'. Levelling their bayonets, the Light Company 'came with a rush, yelling horribly, grinding their teeth and cursing.'[4] The sudden on-slaught shattered Kawiti's men but, as the Light Company pursued them into the ravine, the other stormers, still on the hillock, were charged by a party from the *pa*. While the 96th and bluejackets opened fire, Denny reformed his company and led them up to support their comrades. A savage fight ensued around the breastwork but eventually the discipline of the troops began to get the upper hand and the Maoris were driven back behind their palisades. Both sides were now exhausted, the rockets were all expended, and it was clear that the mus-ketry fire which was kept up from the breastwork was quite ineffective against the defences of the *pa*. A stalemate had been reached, so Sergeant James Mathews of the Light Company volunteered to inform the main body of the situation and, under a heavy fire, made a dash across the intervening ground to the position held by the reserve.

Hulme now realised that further action was hopeless and that, without artillery to breach the enemy defences, he had no choice but to withdraw. At this point, Mitchell, in reserve with the Grenadiers, entered the battle:

About 3 p.m. I was selected to carry a despatch to the officer commanding where the force were engaged most of the day. I had to cross a swamp about a quarter of a mile under fire from the *pa*. My brother William[5] heard the order given

[3] Called Johnny Hobbs by the troops, or Jack Robinson.
[4] Maori account, quoted Gibson, page 41. The account ends with the words: 'It was wrong of the red tribe (the soldiers) to curse us. We were doing no harm; we were merely fighting them!'
[5] His younger brother, regimental number 1906.

& said I should not go alone. I tried to persuade him not to but he would [not] be gainsaid. It was a dangerous undertaking but we accomplished the task [and] delivered the despatch which was directing the force to retire, not in a body, but at intervals of three or four men at a time. Everyone seemed very much exhausted. My brother and I returned with them. On our way by the side of Lake Omapere, heard moaning. It proved to be a wounded man, one of our Regt named Yates.[6] My brother procured water from the lake in his cup for him to drink, but alas! the poor fellow died in a few seconds.

While with the stormers, Mitchell observed some quick thinking by one of the sailors:

One of the bluejackets discovered a maori behind a clump of titree in the act of firing at him. His carbine being unloaded with bayonet fixed, called out, 'I can't shoot you but I will harpoon you'. [He] cast his weapon piercing the native through the body killing him at once, thus saving himself.

Meanwhile steps had been taken to cover the retreat of the storming parties. No. 3 Company was extended on the hill opposite the *pa* to cover by fire the advance of the Grenadiers, as Bridge describes:

The Grenadier Company was sent across the swamp at the edge of the lake to support and protect the retreat of the parties that had been so long engaged and so greatly cut up. This Company lost one man killed whilst in the reserve and had four men wounded crossing the swamp and another on its return to the reserve. After waiting in some suspense, we had the satisfaction to see the storming parties making their retreat in order across the swamp about 4 in the evening, having been hotly engaged for upwards of 5 hours. We continued another hour forward under cover of the hill with [No. 3] company extended and firing from the end of it, lest the enemy should attempt to make a sortie from the *Pa*. But they did not attempt it, and about 5 o'clock Lieut-Col

[6] This was, in fact, 1352 Private Robert Yetts, Light Company.

Hulme gave orders to commence our retreat and left me to conduct it with two companies. This I effected in regular order without loss of a man, the friendly natives, as we retired, taking up the firing and protecting our rear and flanks. This was the first time I had ever heard a shot fired in earnest; it has a sharp discordant sort of sound when whistling close to your ear, but after a little one gets accustomed to it and does not heed it. Reached our camp after dark and found nothing to eat but potatoes—poor fare after fighting all day.

After the action, perhaps even that very night to take their minds off the 'poor fare', sketches were made of the battle, one by Bridge, the other by John Williams. Both show, from slightly different angles, the essential features of the fight: No. 3 Company extended along the hill, giving covering fire for the Grenadiers to form up behind, prior to moving round to support the storming parties, who can be seen across the swamp. Bridge shows a group of sailors manning a rocket tube, directed by a top-hatted boatswain, and within the *pa*, in both paintings, can be seen what Whisker described as 'the English flag and the bloody flag beside it'. The former may have been that taken by Heke at Kororareka and flown over his *pa* as an act of defiance.

It was believed that Heke and Kawiti had lost about forty-seven killed and eighty wounded, including Kawiti's two sons and Heke's 'fire-eater'. The British suffered fourteen killed and thirty-eight wounded, of which the 58th's share was eight killed and seventeen wounded. The bodies of the seven dead men of the Light Company had to be left where they had fallen, but that of the eighth was brought back to çamp for burial. He was an old soldier of the Grenadiers, Samuel Wandrum, No. 645, known to his comrades as 'Gunner'; once a labourer from County Tyrone, he had been soldiering since he first enlisted on 7th December 1829, and his death in action would leave a sorrowing widow in Parramatta. Mitchell knew him well:

Poor Wandrum's body was carried to our camp & laid for the night in a breakwind neither rain nor windproof. By the time we all got back it was dark & heavy rain set in. All very tired and hungry, having had no food that day or the day before. Rolled ourselves in our blankets & lay down in the shelter, soaking rain pouring in. It being very dark, I laid myself down with the rest, with my head resting on the body of a sleeping comrade. When daylight appeared, to my horror, it was poor Wandrum's body which had been my pillow.

The following day was spent in camp, under heavy rain, with the force dispirited. Mitchell wrote that it was 'no good, all in a most deplorable wet & dirty state, the wounded especially so. I chanced to get a cob of corn from a native to whom I gave a black silk handkerchief in exchange & shared the corn with my brother.' Even Bridge, who seldom complained, even to his Journal, had to confess that, after visiting the wounded, he 'passed a miserable day and had wretched food'. Only Whisker who, being with No. 3 Company, had had a relatively easy day of the fight, managed to keep his spirits up by visiting Waaka's men:

The Blacks or Mowreys acted very well. They found us hutts and Plenty of sweet yames and Pork and Beef which they cooked it under the ground for us. The way they cook, they make a hole in the ground and fill it up with wood, and lays a heap of stones on top of the wood, and when the stones is red hot, they take all the wood away and strew green leaves over the stones. They pour some watter to raise a steam, they then kill a Pig or Bullock and cuts it up and lays the meat on top of the green leaves, then about a Bushel of Potatoes on top of the meat. They then cover the Potatoes over with mats and throws clay over all same, as we would cover new dug Potatoes in the field, and in about one hour they are as nicely cooked as they could be Done in a Pot.
The Natives ware no clothes at all but some old shirt tied arround there weastes. They are great people for trafficking. They wil give anything for old clothes or hankerchiefs, and if one Buys aney article, they are not sattisfied to they all get the same.

Whisker was clearly one of those cheerful scroungers to be found in the ranks of any army at any time, who, when others are down to their last crust, are never without their creature comforts.

Hulme now learned from informers that some of Pomare's men had joined Kawiti, ('so much for our letting them go when we burnt their *Pa*', Bridge could not resist noting), but that the latter, infuriated by his casualties being greater than Heke's, left him in disgust and returned to his own *pa*. It was believed that Heke, for his part, would remove from Puketutu and take to the bush. Hulme appreciated that nothing would be gained by a further attack, so he ordered a return to the shipping.

In his entry for 11th May, Bridge wrote:

We were very long in getting stretchers enough and men to carry the wounded and had to employ our men chiefly. Commenced our return march about half past nine or ten A.M. and had more trouble in getting along with the wounded, did not reach Kiri Kiri until after dark. We fully expected to have been attacked but were not molested. Got a bed at Mr Kemp's, the missionary at Kiri Kiri, and a good tub of hot water to wash before retiring to rest; a great luxury after having slept in our clothes for eight days and nights. Did not however sleep so well as when I had no bed, owing perhaps to having taken a strong cup of coffee, or possibly being too comfortable in a bed, after having slept in my clothes so many nights on the ground and frequently wet.

The following day, a Sunday, Sir Everard Home pulled in to Kerikeri with ships' boats full of supplies, 'delighted to see us all safe, having heard a report that we had been defeated and all cut to pieces'. The thought of this rumour reaching his wife's ears caused Bridge some anxiety but, after another day's march, all was to end happily:

It was decided that the soldiers should march down the left side of the river Kiri Kiri at once, the day being fine and moreover to avoid the possibility of Heki and his tribe attacking us; he having deserted his *Pa* and, it was said, was looking out for us on the other road. Sir E. Home took down all the wounded in his boats as well as the seamen and

Marines, and about 12 o'clock we started. Had to ford the
river, many men fell into the water, the stones being slippery and wet, their ammunition much of it was thus lost.
The road ran up hill and across deep ravines and streams,
and was a very fatiguing march of at least 15 miles. Reached
a small bay at sunset, off which the *Hazard* was at anchor.
She immediately sent off her boat and Captain Johnson
most kindly insisted on the whole of the officers and men
going on board his ship for the night; the *North Star* and
Slain's Castle not being arrived from Pahia, which Col
Hulme consented to, otherwise the poor fellows would
have had to pass the night on the beach. Got a comfortable
dinner and about 9 o'clock Sir Evd came along side in his gig
for me and kindly took me on board the *Slain's Castle* to see
my dear Louisa. Found her asleep in her cabin, but my
entering awoke her and she received me with open arms and
her usual affection. This was indeed a happiness after 8 or 9
days separation and having encountered so much discom-
fort and danger.

Refreshed by his wife's embraces, Bridge was up early on the
12th to supervise the transfer of his men from the *Hazard* to the
Slain's Castle. After breakfast Hulme sailed off in the *North Star*
to report to the Governor at Auckland and, as the *Slain's Castle*
weighed anchor and headed across the Bay for Kororareka,
Bridge sat down in his cabin to compose an Order to mark his
Regiment's first action since the Peninsular War. After prais-
ing 'the ready obedience to orders, cheerfulness under severe
privations and steadiness and gallantry displayed during the
engagement, particularly of the Light Company', he singled
out for special mention, 'the Individual Bravery of Lieutenant
and Adjutant M'Lerie, Sergeant-Major Moir and Sergeant
Brown, Orderly Room Clerk, who volunteered their services
with the storming parties', and also the afore-mentioned
Sergeant Mathews. The dash by Mitchell and his brother
across the swamp to recall the stormers, he appears to have
overlooked. Perhaps his mind wandered, musing on his dear
Louisa and her 'usual affection'.

Note on the 58th Light Company killed at Puketutu-Okaihau
A note made many years later by W. I. Speight, a Sergeant in

the Light Company on 8th May 1845, lists the names of the men killed, besides Samuel Wandrum, as: William Moore (1674), James Fleming (2053), Edward Summers (318), Charles Stevens (1190), Robert Yates (Yetts 1352), Andrew Larrett and John McMillan. These names, with the exception of Moore, are also listed in Whisker's Memorandum Book, though he calls Yetts, Yeats and Larrett, Tarriot. However, the 58th Muster Rolls (P.R.O., WO 12–6745), while confirming the six names given above with regimental numbers, have no reference to Larrett or McMillan but list also as killed on 8th May, Thomas Morton (1366) and John Punched (1449). This must have been a clerical error in the Rolls, since Morton and Punched are also shown as killed on 1st July, which is confirmed in Whisker's book.

The other men killed at Puketutu, according to Speight, were: Private Mills, Royal Marines, a seaman who died of wounds on 9th May, and of the 96th: Corporal William Kelly, Privates William Fowler, Christopher North, John Norman, and Richard Turton (died of wounds at Auckland).

The action against Heke's *pa* at Puketutu was commonly referred to as Okaihau by the troops.

6

Bridge in Command

We marched to Keri Keri for hopes to get away
And we Burned the Waicaro *Pah* on the 16th of May
Alexander Whisker.

BEFORE LEAVING FOR AUCKLAND, HULME HAD TOLD BRIDGE HE
could use his discretion about attacking a *pa* up the Waikare
river, where the Kapotai tribe were rumoured to have stored
much of the plunder taken from Kororareka. The chance of an
independent command was not to be missed so, on the very
next day, while the troops rested aboard the shipping after
their efforts at Puketutu, Bridge set about making careful
plans for this undertaking:

May 13th. Went to Pahia with Captain Johnson to see Mr
Clendon, the Pahia Magistrate and the Rev^d Mr Williams,[1]
and got all the information we could with regard to the
feasibility of attacking the Waikari's; Mr Clendon described
the river and creek up which we had to proceed, and situation of the *Pa*, promised to procure small boats enough to
convey troops—large ones could not get up the creek—and
sent one of his men who knew the country up to the
Waikari's *Pa* that night, to recconnoitre and report what he
saw. The man has a son who is living up close to the *Pa* in the
house of a Mr Baker, a missionary—the son of a native
woman, and he went to see him and learn from him what
the natives were about, and how we could best surprise
them.

Two days later the man returned and, after hearing his

[1] Henry Williams, later Archdeacon of Waimate. See Chapter 3.

report and the views of Ripa, one of Waaka's chiefs, Bridge, Clendon and Johnson drew up a detailed plan:

> Arranged to embark the troops about 11 at night so as to go up the river with the tide, reach the *Pa* before daylight, surround it and prevent the escape of the natives. Captain Johnson gave me twelve pounder carronade and men to work it under a midshipman, and put one armed seaman into each boat to steer it; after the disembarking of the troops, these with a small party of soldiers in addition were to guard the boats. Lieut Philpot[2] was sent in command of the seamen and floatilla.

Apart from the sailors, eight marines, and four of the Auckland volunteers as guides, Bridge decided to take only the three companies of his own regiment, leaving the men of the 96th at Kororareka; accompanying the force would be one hundred Maoris in their own canoes under Ripa and another chief, Mohi, or Moses, Tawhai, a body of men described by Whisker as 'the 40 thieves'.

At eleven o'clock on the night of 15th May, the troops began to clamber down from the *Slain's Castle* into the boats arranged by Clendon and, when all were assembled, the long haul up river began under the rising moon. The soldiers, according to Whisker, did not take too kindly to this:'We had to go up the River 12 miles and we had to Pull the Boats ourselves with Rough made Paddles, same as the Mowreys uses for there canoes, which tired us greatly not being used to it'; to make matters worse, 'it Rained on us very hard for half the night', although what appeared as a deluge to the private toiling at the oars could be shrugged off by Bridge, his mind on the responsibilities of command, as 'some sharp showers'. The latter continues:

> Got up the river very well but when we approached the creeks, there was the greatest confusion among the boats, some sticking in the mud flats, others going up the wrong creek, in fact it was most infamously managed; there required to be a guide in each boat. The consequence was

[2] Lieutenant George Philpotts, R.N., H.M.S. *Hazard,* the defender of Kororareka. See Chapter 3.

that, when I reached the shore where the main body was to land, I had only about 20 men there. 30 more shortly came up in another boat, and with these few men I found myself close under the enemy's stronghold, and could hear them talking and directing each other to be firm and stick to their *Pa* and fight to the last. I had directed a party under Captain Grant of 50 and Subaltern to go up a creek to the left of my position and proceed towards the right of the *Pa*, my intentions being to go round by the left of it and so meet on the inland side, and cut off the enemy's retreat, but I could not tell whether the boats containing this party had reached their proper destination or not. I had therefore to send the friendly natives under Ripa round to the left of the *Pa* to flank it, whilst I drew up my small band in its front under cover of a low bank and some scrub. This was just at the dawn of the day. I sent Pine[3] and another person down to the creek to endeavour to get up other boats or bring up men out of those that were aground on the mud flats. Some men landed lower down and marched through the swamp and mangroves, and joined me shortly after daylight; at this time the inmates of the *Pa* were at prayers or had about finished.

The men Bridge had with him were from No. 3 Company, Whisker among them:

We concealed ourselves behind some ferin [fern] and heard there horns and bells going every minute. The[y] rung there Bell just after us lieing down and they went to Prayers. We got an order to not fire without our Majors order. We had not being lieing many minuets when the[y] fired about 5 or 6 guns to try what side we were in but we did not move. They then fired again and we still lay quiet. But During the time we were lieing, walkers tribe Slipped arround to they got in sight of them at Prayers when they fired on them. They soon started from Prayers and took to there heels. We then give a Cheers and Walkers tribe pursued them up the hill.

[3] Chilley Pine, Surgeon, 58th Regiment, 5th December 1843. A veteran of the China War of 1841, where he served with the 26th Regiment.

A running fight ensued between Ripa's men and the Kapotai, while the troops entered the *pa* to search for the plunder. Little was found other than 'pigs, potatoes and onions' and Bridge ordered the place to be burned. As the huts and palisades went up in flames, messengers came from Ripa saying he was running short of ammunition and was being beaten back. Bridge responded with alacrity:

I gave them ammunition and sent the Grenadier Company back with them at the same time. I disposed the rest of my men so as to prevent our being surprised and attacked in our flanks. Went down to the boats to see that all was right there and ascertain when the tide would serve to embark the men again and return to our ships. Found it would be an hour or two before it would be high enough. Found the gun mounted on the bank, and Pine attending to the wounded Maoris; saw him cut a ball out of the breast of poor Jack Robinson[Hobbs], the fellow who behaved so well at Heki's, *Pa* and saved all our chaps from being cut off by Kawiti; he bore it most manfully. On returning to the *Pa* found Captain Grant had brought his Company back as he could not act in the fern so high and his men were exposed for nothing. The fight seemed to continue pretty hotly between the natives. I therefore went forward and directed Captain Thompson who was in advance to send a line of skirmishers up on the ridge of the hill where the Maoris were to keep up a fire with them on the enemy. This soon had the desired effect of reducing their fire and driving them off.

Bridge's words suggest a modest satisfaction with his handling of the tactical situation, which indeed he had well under control, but his sudden deployment of Thompson's company was not entirely to Whisker's liking:

I was down in the *Parr* getting some plunder which I lost after when our compy marched off but when I returned [to the ranks] I soon found an opportunity of following my master [Thompson]. We lay behind some pailing for a short time, then we marched up the hill into the Bush, us and 10 files of the Light Compy. We extended on the hill and fired down on them But the[y] either ran or hid themselves from

us. We fired for about one hour to try to raise them but it
was all in vain.

With the *pa* destroyed, the Kapotai held in check, and the
tide now high enough to float the boats off the mud, Bridge
decided to withdraw:

I began to conduct the retreat and was fortunate enough to
bring all my men off into the boats and get them safely
down the river and on board the ships by half past 3 o'clock.
We had no men killed or wounded, our Maoris had 2 killed
and 6 or 7 wounded, and they say the enemy had 9 or 10
wounded but none killed. We were all in a pretty dirty state
having had to wade through a muddy swamp to and from
the boats and heartily glad to get on board ship again.

The measures taken by Bridge to prepare for this raid had all
the ingredients for a well-organised operation: the gathering
of intelligence beforehand, the combined planning with the
naval commander, the local experts and his native allies, the
night approach to obtain surprise, and the planned cordon
around the *pa* at dawn, all this should have achieved complete
success. That it did not do so was due to the failure of the
guides and the navigational difficulties imposed by the mud
flats. However, Bridge did not allow this setback to ruin his
plan; like the Duke of Wellington, he 'tied a knot and went on'.
The over-eagerness of the friendly Maoris turned the operation into a mêlée, rather than the neat cordon and search
envisaged by Bridge, but his calm handling of his force
enabled him to search the *pa*, deny its further use to the enemy,
and withdraw his troops to safety, all with the minimum
casualties. On the debit side, he had failed to round up the
Kapotai, and, in one quarter, pro-British sentiment had
changed to hostility: the death of one of the friendly Maoris
moved the man's sister to such grief and rage that in her
funeral dirge she claimed her brother's death could only be
avenged when she had eaten the Governor, Captain Fitzroy,
R.N.!
Johnson had brought the ships down to meet the returning
boats off the promontory where Pomare's *pa* had stood. Here
the force remained at anchor throughout the next day,

strongly buffeted by high winds but sheltered from the driving rain which, had they remained at Waikare as Ripa, who feared an ambush on their return, had advised, would have reduced the troops to sodden misery. Once again Bridge could congratulate himself on his prescience. The storm blew itself out overnight and the next day, a Sunday, was bright and sunny, enabling Bridge and his wife to enjoy an almost domestic routine, with Divine Service in the morning aboard the *Slain's Castle*, and a stroll around the ruins of Pomare's *pa* in the afternoon, finding a few souvenirs and cutting some grass for their goat.

Sterner matters intruded in the evening:

Received a letter from Tamati Waka telling me that Heki deserted his *Pa* the very day we left him and that he had gone and burnt it down, and said that Heki had gone away about 7 miles to Tianui and was fortifying his *Pa* there, and that he wished I would return with the soldiers and go and attack him. Had his own men been all with him his chiefs Ripa and Moses he would have gone by himself and attacked him.

This letter arrived on the evening of 18th May and its contents must have caused Bridge some hard thinking. He had no knowledge of what Hulme and Fitzroy might be planning in Auckland and he had no authority, even if he had the means, to undertake any operations other than that just completed. On the other hand, Hulme was probably unaware of Heke's latest movements and the longer action was deferred, the stronger would the new enemy position become. Furthermore, failure to make some response to Waaka's summons might diminish his faith in British support, but to inform Hulme and obtain further orders could only be done by sending a ship to Auckland, which could take between one and five days to get there and the same to return. Yet despite these problems, Bridge curiously makes no comment in his journal besides recording the contents of Waaka's letter. The terse entry for the 19th, 'Went ashore at Pahia', suggests he may have gone to discuss the situation with Clendon, the Magistrate, but if so, nothing came of it for, on the 20th, he simply records, 'An American whaler came in. Bad day.' Whether

The attack on Heke's *pa* at Puketutu, 8th May 1845. In the water colour by Cyprian Bridge, above, skirmishers of No. 3 Company, 58th, and a rocket manned by sailors support the attack, while the Grenadier Company and friendly Maoris wait in reserve. Below, another view of the same incident in water colour by John Williams. The Light Company, 58th, are on the right above Lake Omapere charging the Maoris. Wounded men are being brought back by friendly Maoris to a collecting point in the foregound behind the Grenadiers.

Men of the 58th and friendly Maoris advancing to attack the Kapotai tribe's *pa* on the Waikare river during Bridge's raid, 16th May 1845. Note the forage caps worn in the field instead of the full dress shako. (Water colour by Cyprian Bridge)

these last two words refer to some trouble with the whaler's crew, the state of the weather, or his inability to decide what to do for the best, can only be guesswork but the lack of any record of action taken, or even his deliberations, suggests that he was playing for time. On the morning of the 21st, he diverted himself by boarding the American ship and bought 'some whale's teeth and other curiosities', and then his dilemma resolved itself: the *North Star* entered harbour that afternoon with orders for him to return immediately with his troops to Auckland.

The next day, as they were beating out of harbour, a new development occurred:

> The Revd H Williams came on board and gave intelligence of Heki having been down to see him, who, he said, was likely to come to terms, and requesting me to wait for his final answer to certain conditions proposed by him [Williams] in order to convey it to Auckland to His Excellency the Governor. Consented and sent off *Velocity* and troops on board and O'Connell[4] with dispatches to Col Hulme and Capt Fitzroy.

Neither the troops nor the despatches were destined to get far for, on the 23rd, bad weather forced the *Velocity* to return to harbour. The following day was the Queen's birthday which, since Heke's letter had not yet arrived, could be celebrated with due ceremonial:

> All the ships in harbour decked out with their flags had a very pretty effect, the day very fine. Had a visit from the native chief Hobson to know if it was right for them to hoist the English flag on shore. I told him it was, it being the Queen's birthday, but he had better take it up to the Hill on which stood the flagstaff that Heki cut down and hoist it there, and after the ships had saluted they might fire a salute with small arms. This pleased him much and he went ashore immediately to carry out my suggestion. They did it very well, put up the English Ensign where it formerly stood and

[4] C. P. O'Connell, Lieutenant, 51st Regiment. Detached to New Zealand as an extra staff officer from his normal duties as A.D.C. to his father, Lieutenant-General Sir Maurice O'Connell, commanding in New South Wales.

after the salute from the shipping, they fired a sort of *Fue de joie* and danced a war dance.

For some time Bridge had wanted to examine the site of Heke's attack on the flagstaff but had not hitherto had the opportunity. Now he could do so, and what he saw moved him to a brisk aspersion on the conduct of the 96th, who had guarded it: 'Went on shore and walked to the flagstaff Hill, splendid view from it. Cannot conceive how any man with a blockhouse and guard in so commanding a situation could have allowed himself to be surprised and let it be taken.' In the evening Heke's letter for the Governor arrived and it was decided to sail for Auckland the next day. Before departure Bridge, ever-mindful of how much was owed to their native allies, took steps to ensure their continued support:

> Saw the friendly chiefs and wrote to Tamati Waka to tell him of my departure and that I hoped soon to return with all the requisites for resuming the war against Heki. Gave Ripa, who had been so particularly active and useful to us on the march and on the field, a musket and some ammunition which delighted him much, also some clothes which some of the officers presented him with, and a sword.

On the 28th the *North Star, Slain's Castle* and *Velocity* sailed into Auckland to be greeted with three cheers from Matson's No. 9 Company drawn up to receive them. The following day Bridge reported to the Governor and handed over his despatches and the communication from Heke. The latter opened with a tirade against British policy and conduct in New Zealand which, while doubtless justified where the behaviour of the more unruly settlers was concerned, was couched in words so arrogant that they were hardly likely to endear the writer to the recipient. Heke went on to claim that he alone could prevent a wholesale massacre of Europeans, that Waaka had only allied himself to the British for gain, and that he, Heke, was ready for peace or war, whichever Fitzroy preferred. Incensed by the tone of the letter, Fitzroy decided on war.

Bridge was then invited to confer with the Governor and Hulme as to the next steps:

Col Hulme and myself were then consulted as to the practicability and expediency of immediately resuming hostilities against Heki, by sending back 300 men and artillery and proceeding to Waimate and taking up our quarters there where we should be near enough to Heki's *Pa* to take advantage of every favourable day. We gave it as our opinion there was nothing to prevent our going back and proceeding to Waimate, but we thought it advisable to allow a short time for the men to recover from their late fatigues, and to be put into an efficient state before they went back. It was then suggested that we sent a small force of 100 men and officers there at once to take up a position at Kororika till the main body arrived and then proceed into the interior. The remainder to be landed and put in order, and to follow in about 10 days.

Formal thanks to the troops for their recent efforts were sent by the Governor on behalf of the colonists in a letter, which also made public his appreciation of Waaka's support:

The complete unanimity between the English and the loyal natives have caused sensations not likely to be forgotten. I have no hesitation in asserting that mutual good feeling between the two races has been much increased by these proceedings; that each holds the other in greater respect, and that a more kindly intercourse will be the consequence.

Sadly this unanimity did not prevail in other quarters, which enabled Bridge to notch up another point against the 96th:

Whilst dining at mess an order came from Col Hulme to send as many 58th as could be spared to quiet a riot between the 96th men and townspeople. Matson and Balneavis had to go out. This was a disgraceful business and 40 or 50 96th men were taken up with their side arms rioting and breaking windows etc.

Unfortunately it was not only the 96th whom the return to civilisation had provoked to licence. Whisker and some of his cronies also felt that two months' active service deserved some celebration:

I went on shore with my Masters washing along with the rest of the servants and Married Men When we all got drunk. Hooks Duffey and me got Drunk and Remained ashore from Friday to Sunday evening. We then come aboard we remained Prisoners to Tuesday evening when we were told off By the Major. Me 7 & 10 and go to my Duty for not having the old fustin [clothing] Better. Captn Thompson took Painter servant on the morning of the 2nd. Hooks got 7 & 7 and sent to his Duty. On the morning of the 4th we washed the ship from top to Bottom.

Bridge was not standing for drunkenness in the 58th. Whisker's spree had not only cost him the loss of his valued position as an officer's servant, a task which spared him many of the fatigues and drills performed by other soldiers, but he now faced seven days' extra drills and, even worse, ten days' loss of ration grog. Still, it was better than a flogging and, in addition, he now found himself on garrison duty in Auckland, thus missing the rigours in store for his less drunken comrades.

7

Downright Madness

At 3 oclock that evening 2 hundred of our men
the 58th the 99th the sailors and marines
the[y] all like men did muster upon that fatal Day
to fight for Queen and country and show them British Play
But men been few the *Pah* was strong we could not Rightly stand
For in 7 minutes and a half we lost one hundred men

Alexander Whisker.

WHILST WHISKER AND DUFFEY WERE ROLLICKING THROUGH THE grog-shops of Auckland, a ship, *The Lady Lee*, arrived in harbour from Sydney bringing letters and despatches. Few things mean more to a soldier than his mail, particularly when its arrival is infrequent and he is far from home, so it was with surprise and disappointment that Bridge found there was none for him. His official correspondence, however, disclosed:

The news that Colonel Despard and the two flank Companies of the 99th Regt were on their voyage from Sydney to Auckland, and that he would take command here. This will alter all the arrangements, made by Col Hulme who had decided on remaining in Auckland and sending me in command of the troops to the Bay, and will completely put his nose out of joint.

It was not only Hulme who was to feel put out. The reinforcements arrived in the *British Sovereign* on 2nd June, and when Bridge, who by now was something of an old hand, reported to the new commander, he doubtless expected to be asked for his views on the current situation. The ensuing conversation, however, was both one-sided and unpromising:

Met Col D. who told me he was only going to remain in

New Zealand till the war with Heki was at an end; and then
he and his men would return to Sydney. Much disappointed
at hearing this. Hoped the 58th had a chance of going back,
but fear we are destined to remain here till relieved from
Home. He says he thinks Col Wynyard [58th] and the men
he is bringing out will be sent here as soon as they arrive at
Sydney and that Col Hulme and the 96th will be recalled to
V.D.'s land.[1] He told me that tomorrow he would be better
able to tell me his plans about proceeding to the Bay, that he
thinks of leaving a detachment of the 58th here but not the
head quarters.

Despard apparently decided against taking Bridge into his
confidence, since the next day the latter could only record,
'Dined with the Governor'.

Henry Despard, the man who was now to assume command of all forces on operations in New Zealand, had grown
up during the French Revolutionary Wars and had received his
first commission in 1799. As a young officer he had seen
considerable active service in India in the early nineteenth
century with the 17th Regiment, which he had eventually
commanded. In 1842 at the age of fifty-seven, when enjoying
the peaceful duties of Inspecting Officer of the Bristol Recruiting District, he had exchanged to the command of the 99th
(Lanarkshire) Regiment, then recently arrived in Australia.
When he joined his new regiment in New South Wales, he
found that a ball had been arranged by the officers of the 99th,
both to welcome him and his family and to repay hospitality
by the local community. This he refused to attend and the ball
had to be cancelled. He then proceeded to endear himself
further to the civilian population by closing what had been
hitherto a public road through the barracks and by having his
buglers practise in close proximity to their homes. The 99th
was a regiment well drilled in the current manuals but Despard
had learned his drill in an earlier age and saw no reason to
change the habits of a lifetime; the result was confusion in the
ranks and apoplectic fury from the new colonel. His rages in
barracks were ascribed by his officers to the nagging they
suspected he received at home from the formidable Mrs

[1] Van Diemen's Land, where the major part of the 96th were stationed.

Despard, and the nearest he came to geniality was a ponderous solicitude towards the welfare of his subalterns. On inspecting their wines accounts in the Officers' mess, he was heard to enquire who John Collins might be as he was clearly no friend to young officers.[2] Now, at the age of sixty, having experienced no active service for nearly thirty years, he was about to undertake a campaign against an enemy of whom he was ignorant, in a land he had never seen, with a force which included not only regular troops, but sailors, colonial volunteers and native allies. Bridge's rather bleak account of their first meeting does not suggest that Despard had any misgivings about his own capacity for such a task.

In the second week of June the force moved up to the Bay of Islands for the next stage of the campaign. It was the largest yet assembled in New Zealand: the 58th under Bridge provided the strongest element, consisting of the Grenadier and Light Companies and a composite company under Captain Thompson of men from Nos. 2, 3 and 9 Companies, totalling 270 men; 180 men of the flank companies of the 99th led by Major Macpherson; seventy men of Hulme's 96th; Captain Johnson's naval contingent of seamen and marines with Lieutenant Philpotts;[3] and eighty of the Auckland Volunteers to act as pioneers led by Lieutenant Figg. For the first time the force was accompanied by some artillery—of a sort. Lieutenant Wilmot, Royal Artillery, the son of and A.D.C. to the Governor of Van Diemen's Land, had been sent by his father with Despard to lend his professional expertise. He was accompanied by two retired artillerymen,[4] who had volunteered their services, and on arrival took charge of two ancient sixpounders and two twelve-pounder carronades, dug out of some store in Auckland and manned by a handful of hastily-trained militia gunners.

Bridge set off with some reluctance: 'My birthday, 37, not a very happy one having to embark and leave my wife in a strange place and go into the field. God only knows if I shall

<hr>

[2] N. C. E. Kenrick, *The Story of The Wiltshire Regiment* (1963), page 255.

[3] Buick gives the naval strength as thirty, a figure also quoted by John Mitchell. Despard's subsequent despatch dated 2nd July 1845 states thirteen only. Another officer and twenty-five sailors joined the force during the operations.

[4] Messrs Boyd and Kerr. The 58th Digest of Service says they were retired officers, but Hattaway thought they were 'two antiquated artillery sergeants, who had served under Wellington in the Peninsula War'.

ever return. Embarked after breakfast leaving poor Louisa very unhappy.' He and the 58th arrived at Kororareka on 10th June and while he waited for the rest of the force to assemble, he cheered himself up by shooting wild fowl and collecting oysters among the rocks. On the 13th came news of Heke:

> Our old friends Jack Hobbs, William Hobson and Ripa's brother and one or two other chiefs arrived from the interior and reported their having had a fight with Heki the day before. Also a letter from Waka himself: he said that Heki had come and attacked him in his *Pa* with 600 men, and he was obliged to fight in his own defence, otherwise he had not intended to have moved till the arrival of the troops. He had only 150 men with him but he gained a most complete victory over Heki, who was wounded severely through the upper part of the thigh. Mr. Williams the Missionary also came on board and corroborated the whole statement, having just returned from Waimate, and having seen Heki since he received the wound. He said he was in much pain and they all seemed much cast down by their defeat. He as well as Waka urged our hurrying up to Waimate, and follow up Heki who had gone to his *Pa*, without any delay.

Although it was now the middle of the New Zealand winter, with cold winds and heavy rainstorms which would turn the primitive communications into quagmires, Despard determined to start operations the following day at dawn. The plan was for the force to sail across the Bay to the mouth of the Kerikeri and then advance by land on Heke's *pa* at Ohaeawai, via the mission station at Waimate. The start was inauspicious:

> The *British Sovereign* [Despard's ship] contrived to get on shore on the reef between Kent's passage and Pahia. She fired signals of distress and all the boats of the other vessels soon went to her assistance and all the troops were immediately taken out of her. I went on board of her after breakfast with Captain Dawson and a pretty state of confusion they were in on board. Her rudder was gone and she was bumping heavily on the sand with the swell; the sea was pretty high out there, the wind blowing right into the

harbour. Every endeavour was made to get her off, and about 3 p.m. they succeeded and she was brought back to her anchorage, making about 2 inches of water per hour. Had to send a fatigue party on board to help in getting out Ordnance and Commissariat stores and in pumping the ship.

After a day spent in putting things to rights, a fresh start was made on the 16th and by the evening the whole force was concentrated around Kemp's mission station at Kerikeri. Here some bullock- or horse-drawn drays and carts were requisitioned to convey the guns, stores and ammunition and the next day, in heavy rain, the twelve-mile advance along the narrow, muddy track to Waimate began. Bridge led with the advance guard:

Marched from Kere Kere about noon. Had a most tedious and harrassing march owing to the heavy loads, ammunition, camp equipage, stores and Guns. 2 drays broke down and the barrels of small [arms] ammunition had to be carried by the men on their backs. A Capt, Sub, and 50 men remained all night to guard one of the drays, a similar party was left with the other and a Sub and twenty men remained with a gun which could not be brought as the bullocks and horses being quite done up. I came on with the advanced guard and brought in 20 casks of ammunition and reached Waimate about 12 at night.

John Mitchell was among those detailed off to carry the ammunition barrels:

The Kegs containing 500 rounds in each had to be carried a Keg to two men. It fell to my lot to have a very little fellow to share the burden. He tried but failed. I said, 'Well Hopkins it has to be carried somehow, you take my musket & [I] will try & manage the rest.' I knelt down and got him to roll the keg on my shoulders, it rested between my knapsack & the back of my head. By this time darkness had set in. The bush, stumps of trees, mud & slush was a caution, [but] at this time of my life I could stand any amount of endurance. Eventually I got through the bush & saw a light. Found it was the remains of a fire, eased myself of the load, laid down & was soon fast asleep.

The rearguard of the force did not reach Waimate until two thirty a.m., a delay which brought a rare grumble from Bridge who, as Field Officer of the day, had additional duties:

Before we got them all housed and I [had] posted the picquets, it was past 4, and I laid down quite exhausted with the hard day's work, having been on my legs from 7 a.m. on the 17th till 4 a.m. on the 18th and wet through without the means or opportunity of changing.

Robert Hattaway, now on campaign for the first time and escorting one of the guns, did not reach shelter until the following day:

Our gun and ammunition dray, to which were attached four miserable bullocks, became bogged in the track. Drenched, and without food, we had to remain for the night. The following day the ammunition was conveyed to its destination, and the gun was extricated with considerable labour. About ten o'clock in the evening we reached the Waimate, hungry and exhausted, but the arrangements made by our comrades afforded us a very pleasant surprise. They were located in a large kitchen, in one of the Mission buildings, whose inhabitants had fled. Large logs were burning brightly on the hearth, and on the floor were several large dampers,[5] a couple of large jars of jam, and plenty of strong hot tea. Our comrades relieved us or our arms, accoutrements, and our outer garments, which they kindly cleaned and dried. After doing justice to the good things put before us, we fell into a sound sleep on the floor.

By the morning of the 19th the force was more or less in one piece again, but the state of fury to which Despard had been reduced by this chaotic start to the expedition was obvious to all, as his 'somewhat vivid vocabulary' resounded about the huts of the Mission, no doubt bringing a blush to the cheeks of

---

[5] Flour made into a paste with water and baked in the wood ashes of a fire.

the missionary, Mr Burrows, and probably unnerving him from making any complaints about the depredations of the more expert foragers among the soldiers. 'Certainly,' as Hattaway observed, 'the station was minus of any food after our departure.' Had it not been for the tact of an interpreter, Despard's temper could have had a far more crucial result than offending Mr Burrows' sensibilities for, when Waaka arrived with some 250 of his braves to offer his services, Despard sourly remarked that when he wanted the assistance of savages he would ask for it.

The force remained at Waimate until the 22nd while fresh supplies were brought up from Kerikeri; Despard went off on a reconnaissance, and Bridge, determined to keep his men in trim, held 'a small field day, the natives were very much pleased at the movements to the bugle sounds'.

On the 23rd Bridge, again commanding the advance guard, paraded his men at three a.m. to move off although, as he complained, 'it was near 5 before all was ready to march'. Heke's *pa* at Ohaeawai was only six miles off but the state of the road and streams was such that it was not until nearly six p.m. that the force approached the *pa*. The value of Bridge's small field day was then proved, as Hattaway, among the leading company, describes:

We formed in skirmishing order under Lieutenant Balneavis. We were assisted by a few friendly natives. Very soon we were greeted with volleys of musketry. The surrounding scrub being eight to ten feet high their aim was ineffective, as I saw only one man injured by the fire. A friendly native on my left received a ball in the thigh, and his comrades speedily stopped the hemorrhage by plugging the wound with clay. We advanced in line, preserving our distance from the centre, taking every advantage of any cover or irregularities in the ground, the rebels falling back before us until they finally reached their stronghold. The advance skirmishers continued in their extended order, and halted on rising to undulating ground, until the whole force arrived.

It is evident from this and other passages that, in the 58th, the centre as well as the flank companies were trained, not only to

move in extended order, but also to make use of cover; such
skills required considerable mental and physical agility from
soldiers in an age when most of their drill was still designed to
train them to move, both in the field and on the barrack square,
in the close order required by line, column or square. To
intelligent officers like Bridge, the serried ranks of such forma-
tions would clearly be of little value in close country against a
savage enemy and he trained his men accordingly.

Some 400 yards short of the *pa* and to the north of it stood a
native village, situated on the crest of a low hill with, to the
west, a higher, conical hill, the top of which was about 600
yards from the *pa*. The force pitched its tents in dead ground
below the brow of the low hill, while Waaka took up his
position on the conical hill, thus gaining observation into the
pa and providing security for the camp; on the summit he
hoisted the British flag. A breastwork and battery for the four
guns was constructed by the pioneers about sixty yards in
advance of the camp. Hattaway and his comrades soon found
they were in for a hard time:

> Two single bell tents were allotted to a company, only
> sufficient for the accommodation of about 16 men. The first
> night in camp was miserable; the ground saturated from
> incessant rain, the flooring of the tents a soft pool of mud.
> The greater number of the men were allowed next day to
> construct means of shelter for themselves. My three com-
> rades and myself constructed a small tea-tree shed, with two
> blankets for roof protection, and procured fern for our beds.
> During the whole of that period, about a month in the
> middle of winter, an unusually wet one, the men had no
> change of clothing. Our accoutrements remained on us, and
> our arms by our sides, as our proximity to the rebel position
> necessitated every precaution against sudden surprise.
> There had not been stored provision for a winter campaign.
> Some of the bullocks were slaughtered for the use of the
> troops [but] biscuits and rum were the daily fare.

The enemy *pa* was built on rising ground with ravines
and the forest on all sides except the north, thus affording
cover for its inmates to come and go and a plentiful supply
of timber to repair any damage. To men like Mitchell, who

had been at Puketutu, the new position appeared twice as formidable:

> The *pa* was about 90 yards by 50 with projecting flanks at each angle. It was surrounded with three rows of palisades. Between each was a ditch 5 feet deep from which the enemy fired through loop holes on a level with the ground & this ditch communicated with passages under the palisades. Inside the *pa* there were huts underground. The timbers were trunks of trees, 15 feet high & from 9 to 20 inches in diameter. The enemy were estimated to be about 300, but I think there were a much greater number.[6]

These defences, which were supplemented by four ships' guns, had been constructed by Kawiti who commanded in the *pa*, Heke having gone into hiding to recover from his wound.

On the morning of the 24th Wilmot's makeshift artillery opened fire, observed by Bridge:

> The 4 gun battery opened its fire on the *Pa*, but did no execution. About 10 a.m. they [the enemy] commenced and musket shots were exchanged. A constant fire was kept up by the guns of shell, ball and grape till dark. Many hit and burst in the *Pa*, and I fancy they must have lost many men. All quiet during the night, and although our pioneers and working parties were throwing up a breastwork and battery for the guns in another position more to the right and nearer the *Pa*, they never molested them.
> 25 June. The guns being brought into the new battery within 200 yards of the *Pa*, great hopes were entertained that a breach would soon be made. The guns made some very good practice and many shells burst in the ditches and the *Pa*, but owing to the elasticity and tenacity of the flax [covering the palisades] which closes up as the ball goes through, it was impossible to see what extent of damage was done to the fence.

As the day went on it became obvious that no breach was

---

[6] Mitchell's estimate of the size was fairly accurate. A ground plan of the *pa* gives the dimensions as 'Length 300 ft, Mean Breadth 125 ft'. The height of the palisades is shown as 12 ft.

going to be made 'owing to the shot not being directed all to one point, and to the fire not being kept up, half an hour elapsing between each shot by Colonel Despard's directions'. Meanwhile some of Bridge's men were under heavy fire:

> Lost one of my grenadiers today. He was shot a little to the right of the battery where we had posted 15 good marksmen to fire at everyone who showed himself in the *Pa*. The shot came thick enough about us but the mantle of flax protected us. Some balls came in at the portholes through which the guns fire, and strange they hit no one; poor Doherty was the only man hit today.

After these two days' bombardment, Despard concluded that since shot and shell had failed to force an entry, the bodies of his men must effect one. Bridge was warned to lead one of the storming parties:

> The Colonel determined on storming the *Pa* by night, and ordered ladders etc to be ready at 2 in the morning. I laid down to sleep with no pleasurable sensations as to the occupation of the morning, doubting the successful issue of the night attack, although British valor generally carries everything before it. Still, there must be a frightful sacrifice of life.

A scheme to minimise the casualties had been devised, of which Despard thought highly, but the men in the ranks who had to operate it, like Hattaway, were less enthusiastic:

> All men off duty were employed in cutting tea-tree rods about 12 ft in length, and faced horizontally with flax. When finished they were six feet in height, and reported bullet-proof. Each company were provided with four, which were to be carried by each advancing party in front of them as a shield, thus protecting themselves from the enemy's fire as they approached the *pa*. Upon arrival they were [to be] placed in front of each porthole of the palisade. From whom this idea emanated I cannot say, but to think that orders had been absolutely issued to that effect by the officer in command is more astonishing. Did he think that this phantom

army advancing at midnight would act upon their superstitious fears?

As the men of the 58th huddled round their fires that night,
their Sergeant-Major, William Moir, who had proved his
courage at Puketutu, remarked to Mitchell: 'The chances are
against us coming out of this alive. I look upon it as down right
madness.' Fortunately 'merciful providence intervened to
prevent such a desparate and foolish order being carried out';
at midnight it began to rain and by one o'clock, as the storming parties endeavoured to form up in the pitch darkness, the
downpour was so heavy that the attack was countermanded.
'Hope some less hazardous mode of attacking the *Pa* may be
fixed on', wrote Bridge. The following day saw the justifica-
tion of the soldiers' scepticism when Mitchell witnessed the
testing of one of the 'bullet-proof' shields: 'A musket shot was
fired at it. It was then made clear how the old Col had been
gulled. The affair was commented upon in no measured term
by the whole force.'

Though this device was proved a failure, another scheme
was soon forthcoming from what Hattaway called 'our
ingenious artillerymen'. Perhaps the empty shell cases:

Could be converted into stench balls and fired in a vertical
direction by short time fuses. Great expectations were entertained by our artillery officers of the success of this scheme.
The shells contained some poisonous substance, the effect of
which was expected to deprive the rebels of all animation,
and leave them an easy prey to the European victors.

As might be guessed, the stench balls had no physical effect
on the enemy, whereas, as Hattaway knew from personal
experience, the troops' physique was daily weakened through
other causes:

The hardships that the men had to endure from incessant
rain and insufficient food, produced exhaustion and weak-
ness. They had no change of garments, were ragged, tattered and torn, many without boots or tied on their feet with
flax, their pants of many colours; blankets and greatcoats
reduced in size to repair their continuations. To add to their

troubles there were no needles or thread, and the soldiers supplied their wants by means of a piece of wood hardened at the point, and a hole pierced at the other end to carry the flax split to the necessary size. About this time the supply had been exhausted, and half a pound of flour per day was the only food supplied to the troops for several days, which the men had converted into skilley, by boiling in their mess tins. A gill of rum was supplied after break of day and in the evening. This never failed to be supplied. The effect of the stimulant with an inadequate supply of food was clearly noticeable, producing a buoyancy of spirits for some time, but when its effect had died out there came a reaction, and a craving for more took place. Personally, I disliked the very smell of rum, and seldom tasted it, but I craved for more food which was not to be obtained.

The soldiers' only succour came from their native allies:

> The women of Tamati Waka Nene, at the time when the men were half starved in camp, regularly visited the sentries on outpost duty in the early morning, carrying small kits of cooked potatoes, and deposited one before each sentry on night duty before they returned to their camp. The few old soldiers still alive remember with gratitude these acts of kindnesses, as well as the ingenious contrivance of the old chieftainess, Tamati Waka's wife.

Precisely what she contrived Hattaway does not disclose, but an allusion to other women of the tribe accompanying the potato carriers perhaps suggests that additional comforts were arranged to cheer the men at their lonely vigil.

During the night of 26th–27th, a new battery was constructed close to the right flank of the *pa* to support another assault, but by the end of the day, Bridge could only record further losses:

> The battery was completed about 8 a.m. [on the 27th] and opened its fire. So did the other batteries, for they had divided the guns. Very bad plan I think. This brought on a very hot fire on the new battery, which was so close that many of our men were wounded and one sailor shot dead at

the gun. The storming parties were all brought down and formed in rear of this battery under cover of a wall on the crest of the hill to await a favourable opportunity for making a rush on the *Pa* as it was believed the guns would soon make a breach. The bullets were flying over us all the time and we could not move without a shot being fired at us. We lay there for 2 or 3 hours and at length about 3 p.m. we received orders to return to the Camp. No breach was made and the storming was again given up. About 5 or 6 p.m. the enemy made a sortie from the *Pa* to endeavour to cut off the guns and party in this battery, whilst the guns were being withdrawn, but were repulsed; two more of our men wounded and one Voltr.

Infuriated by this set-back, Despard now sent a message back to Kerikeri for a thirty-two-pounder from H.M.S. *Hazard* to be dragged up to the camp. By the afternoon of Sunday 29th there was no news or sign of its arrival and Bridge was sent for by an increasingly impatient Despard who said 'it was his intention to take the *Pa* by storm before daylight the following morning. God grant we may be succesful but it is a very hazardous step, and must be attended with great loss of life'. Then, in the evening:

Mr Turner returned from the Keri Keri with the good news that the 32 pdr was at the Waimate, and would be up before morning. Thought it a pity as it was so near at hand that the attack should be made before it arrived, as it might open a breach for us and be the means of saving many lives. Finding this was the general opinion and that I was requested to suggest the same to Col Despard, I consulted the Commanding Officers of the other corps, Lt Col Hulme and Major McPherson who agreed with me, and the proposal was made. After some objections Col Despard entered into our views, and the assault on the *Pa* in the morning was countermanded.

The following day the big gun arrived, escorted by Lieutenant Morgan and twenty-five sailors of the *Hazard*. As the bullocks dragged it up through the camp, a hail of fire was opened from the *pa*, which intensified as the gun was hauled

up the conical hill where, throughout the night, a battery was
constructed for it, some little way below the top.

During the night a foraging party went out to raid a potato
dump only about thirty yards from the *pa*. The party was
surprised but got away, only to find on its return that one man,
a private of the 99th's Light Company, was missing, though
whether he had been shot or taken prisoner was, at this stage,
uncertain. According to Hattaway, this caused some unrest
among the soldiers, but when the next day dawned, all attention was fixed on the thirty-two-pounder, soon to open fire
from the conical hill.

The day, Tuesday 1st July, was bright and sunny. Just
before eleven o'clock, Bridge was standing near the foot of the
conical hill, watching the first few rounds of the naval gun,
when:

A sudden attack was made on Waka's position on the hill
from the thick bush in rear. So bad a lookout had his people
kept, that they were completely surprised, the sentry of the
58th at the gun was shot, and young Mr Clark the interpreter was wounded before they knew whence the shots came.
Then a general retreat commenced, Waka's men and
women running down in the greatest consternation and
carrying our people with them. Colonel Despard happened
to be with the lower battery [the 32-pounder] at the time
and he ran down towards the encampment, where the
troops had already fallen in, hearing the alarm, calling out
for me and the 58th to charge up the hill immediately and
retake it.

Among the first to answer the strident blare of the bugle's
urgent summons was Hattaway who had just been borrowing
a camp kettle in which to cook a small pig he and his comrades
had acquired from a Maori woman for ten shillings. He now
stood ready, bayonet fixed, waiting for the word of command:

'Right face; double march!' The track from the camp was a
circuitous one, leading around the base of the hill, and
continuing up the ascent until the top was reached. We
commenced independent firing when within easy range of
our guns by turning to the left, making a temporary halt,

delivering our fire, and moving up to the right of our companions in arms.

Bridge continues:

We did this in double quick time, cheering all the way, and carrying the hill in a few minutes under a hot cross fire from the *Pa*, as well as from those that had possession of it. We had 2 men wounded going up. Found one of Heki's slaves dead on the top and a poor woman was shot through the body. Her husband was absent at the time the hill was taken, and finding his wife wounded on his return he was nearly frantic and was nigh putting an end to himself, he had to be held. It was a most affecting sight. The object of this attack was evidently to get or kill Waka, for three men rushed immediately to his hut and pointed their muskets at the very corner he always occupied. So intent were they on shooting him, that they let his wife and a european escape from the hut, whilst they satisfied themselves that he was not laying under the blankets. It was fortunate for Waka and for us too, that he had gone out with about 20 of his men to try and cut off some of the enemies foragers.

Once the position was restored:

Colonel Despard desired me to leave Captain Thompson and 60 men on the hill and to march the rest of my men back to camp. After this he informed me it was his intention to storm the *Pa* at 3 o'clock. The men were ordered to get their dinners and we also sat down to ours, and made a hearty meal notwithstanding a feeling it might be our last.

After the brief action Hattaway looked forward to doing justice to the piglet but, on returning to his hut, found that the object of his 'promised treat' had been stolen.

Despard's patience had run out. He personally had had a narrow escape on the hill and now nothing would satisfy him but an all-out assault on the *pa*. He stormed back to his headquarters, summoned his Brigade Major[7] and dictated his orders for the attack:

[7] Lieutenant R. B. Deering, 99th Regiment.

The principal attack will be made on or near the right angle on the front face (the north-west corner) and the whole column for this attack will be formed as follows:

2 Serjeants and 20 Volunteers from the three Corps will form the advance, and will proceed with the most perfect silence till they reach the Stockade.

This party will be followed closely by the assaulting body under Major Macpherson, composed of 40 Grenadiers of the 58th and 40 Grenadiers of the 99th, and will be accompanied by a small party of Seamen, and by 30 pioneers from the Volunteer Militia: the Seamen, and as many pioneers as there are sufficient tools for will be supplied with Axes or hatchets for the purpose of cutting down the Stockade; those pioneers that cannot be supplied with Axes or hatchets are to carry the ladders as well as strong ropes, which will be supplied by the Artillery Department, for pulling down the Stockade. Major Macpherson's party will be closely followed by Major Bridge of the 58th Regiment, having under him the remainder of the Grenadiers of the 58th to be made up to 60 Rank & File from the Battalion [company] of the same Regiment, and 40 Rank and File of the Light Company of the 99th Regiment in all mounting to 100 Rank & File.

A strong supporting party will be formed under Lieutenant Colonel Hulme 96th Regiment, consisting of the whole of the Detachment of the 96th completed to 100 Rank & File by the Battalion men of the 58th.

The moment an entrance is made into the *Pah*, this party will instantly follow the preceeding parties: the remainder of the Force will be under the personal command of Colonel Despard, for the purpose of directing assistance wherever necessary.

Apart from confirming the time of attack as three p.m. and the need for Thompson to maintain his picquet on the conical hill, that concluded the orders; no reference was made to the part to be played by the artillery.

Command of the advance party, traditionally known as the 'forlorn hope' from the hazardous nature of its task, was given, at his request, to Lieutenant Jack Beatty of the 99th Grenadiers. When volunteers were asked for, Hattaway said:

The whole of the men of the 58th took a pace to the front, indicating that they were all willing to join with that party. Being more than was required, the right hand man, front and rear rank, of each section of the company, was ordered to the front; a similar number of the 99th constituted the forlorn hope.

Among the 58th men thus selected were Corporal William Free and his fellow Irishman, Charles Stapp, both of the Light Company. They had enlisted at the same time and together they would face the coming ordeal.

At three o'clock the storming parties fell in along the muddy tracks between the tents. They would have made a shabby sight: battered forage caps pulled down over cadaverous faces, threadbare red jackets faded to a dirty brick-dust colour, patched trousers and broken boots; their cross-belts, once white with pipeclay now soiled; only the musket barrels, topped with bayonets, reflecting any brightness. With them stood the seamen from the *Hazard* in their black tarred hats, and the blue-smocked Volunteers, grasping their axes and scaling ladders. Leading his sailors was the irrepressible George Philpotts, who throughout the siege had openly derided every action of Despard's and had vehemently protested against this new assault; now, as he joined his men, he drew off the pair of soldier's trousers he usually wore, threw aside his forage cap and scabbard, and stood, ready for the onset, clad in a blue sailor's shirt and flannel drawers, monocle in his eye and bared cutlass in his hand. Viewing the scene with choleric eye as the troops moved to their assault positions was Despard, clutching the walking stick he habitually carried, his field bugler behind him, ready to sound the advance.

The point of attack selected by Despard was the north-west angle of the *pa*, the nearest to the conical hill. The assault parties formed for the attack in dead ground, some one hundred yards short of the palisades; Beatty's forlorn hope took up a position north-west of the objective, with Bridge's party behind them, while Macpherson's men were poised due north of the angle. Here they waited for the bugle. Within the *pa* a chief called, 'Stand every man firm and you will see the soldiers walk into the ovens.'[8]

[8] Quoted Buick.

Bridge felt the suspense of the moment:

I was posted under cover of a thick clump of trees in front of the point of attack and whilst here there was an awful pause. The defendants ceased firing, and not a sound was heard except the occasional report of a cannon from the hill, the Colonel having ordered a few shot and shell to be thrown in before he sounded the advance, when we were all to rush rapidly on the *Pa* and endeavour to force an entrance. What were then the thoughts of many a brave fellow whose spirit might soon be wafted into eternity? As for myself I thought only of my darling wife, and poor old mother, and how deeply they would feel my loss if I fell in this engagement, and I offered up a prayer to Almighty God to grant me his protection for their sakes, unworthy as I am, and a full reliance of my fate being in his hands, I calmly await the signal to advance. After waiting about a quarter of an hour, I was asked by the Brigade Major if I was ready, and answered yes. Shortly after the bugle sounded the advance, and with a hearty British hurrah on we rushed.

With the forlorn hope went Free:

We formed up in close order, elbows touching when we crooked them; four ranks, only the regulation 23 inches between each rank. There we waited in the little hollow before the *pa*, sheltered by the fall of the ground and some tree cover. We got the orders, 'Prepare to charge'; then, 'Charge'. Up the rise we went at a steady double, the first two ranks at the charge with the bayonet; the second rank had room to put their bayonets between the front rank men; the third and fourth ranks with muskets and fixed bayonets at the slope. We were within 100 yards of the *pa* when the advance began; when we were within about 50 paces of the stockade front we cheered and went at it with a rush, our best speed and 'divil take the hindmost'. The whole front of the *pa* flashed fire and in a moment we were in the one-sided fight—gun flashes from the foot of the stockade and from loopholes higher up, smoke half hiding the *pa* from us, yells and cheers and men falling all round. A man was shot in front of me and another was hit behind me. Not a single

Maori could we see. They were all safely hidden in their trenches and pits, poking the muzzles of their guns under the foot of the outer palisade. What could we do? We tore at the fence, firing through it, thrusting our bayonets in, or trying to pull a part of it down, but it was a hopeless business.

Mitchell was with Macpherson's party:

I was in the leading section of our Grenadiers. The enemy reserved their fire until the leading sections got to within 5 paces of their out work. We were then met with such a fusillade, I can only describe it as the opening of the doors of a monster furnace. We expected scaling ladders, axes & etc to have been brought up, but alas there was but one ladder & that was brought up by a darky named Brown (a volunteer). It was placed against the outer fence by Lieut Philpott R.N., he was killed in the attempt to get over the fence & fell over. In the meantime we could only pull off the flax which was hung on the outside as a sort of screen. The party was literally mown down. My nearest comrades in the affray were Capt Grant & Sergt Major Moir. We could see inside the *pa*, but could not reach the maories lying in the ditches. One of them a big fellow I could just reach with the bayonet, but could not use it with effect. He was intent on shooting me. I called Capt Grant's attention to the fix I was in, he shot the fellow with his pistol in the forehead. He, Grant was killed almost immediately. At the same time Sergt Major Moir called to me he was wounded. I was also wounded above the left knee. We both retired, the whole area was strewn with wounded & dead, a very frightful sight.

Bridge's men had followed Macpherson's party with such speed that they reached the palisades together:

When I got up close to the fence and saw the strength of it and the way it resisted the united efforts of our brave fellows to pull it down, and saw them falling thickly all round, my heart sank within me lest we should be defeated. Militia and Volunteers who carried the hatchets and ladders would not advance, but laid down on their faces in the fern. Only one ladder was placed against the fence and this by an old man of the Militia. Several officers were cutting at the ties with their swords and pulling at the portion of the fence they had partially loosened, when a bugle in rear sounded the retreat. This at first was thought to be a mistake and was not attended to, for all went to work supposing the *Pa* must be taken or die in the attempt. After a little it was repeated and then all that were left prepared to obey its summons carrying off the wounded with us. We had suffered very severely and many were killed or wounded whilst retiring as the enemy increased their fire upon us as they saw us in retreat. It was a heartrending sight to see the number of gallant fellows left dead on the field and to hear the groans and cries of the wounded for us not to leave them behind. Several fine fellows behaved very well, in returning two or three times to bring off a wounded comrade through a hot fire, and one man in particular (Private Whitethread of the 58th[9]) carried off 5 or 6, not only of his own regiment but the 99th as well.

According to Hattaway, one of the 99th rescued by White-thread was Major Macpherson; the latter was 'said to be 18 stone in weight', but aided by a comrade, Jonathan Pallett,[10] Whitethread succeeded in bringing him to safety. Lieutenant Beatty had been one of the first to be hit but Charles Stapp saw him fall and, despite the point-blank fire, rushed to rescue him from the mêlée round the stockade. Another man of Hattaway's company, Private McKinnon, lifted the wounded Corporal Stewart on to his back but was himself killed as he tried to reach safety. Free recalled: 'I picked up a wounded man and was carrying him off on my back when he was shot dead. Then I picked up a second wounded comrade, a soldier named Smith, and carried him out safely.' Ten years later many of these acts of rescue under fire would have earned men the Victoria Cross, but in 1845 there were no medals for gallantry and no incentives to risk their lives for others, save for the bonds of comradeship and regimental pride.

[9] His regimental number was 2180, which would indicate his being one of the youngest soldiers of the regiment. Mitchell's brother, No. 1906, had volunteered for the assault but had been told by the Adjutant that he was too young.
[10] No. 1086, the son of a sergeant-major killed at Waterloo.

Had it not been for prompt action by Hulme with his supporting party in covering the retreat, casualties would have been even higher. As it was, in an action which only lasted between five and seven minutes, a third of the storming parties were killed or wounded. Grant of the 58th and George Philpotts were dead, and Jack Beatty's wound was to prove mortal; Macpherson was seriously wounded, Ensign O'Reilly of the 99th had his right arm shattered and Lieutenant Johnston of the same regiment was also wounded. Of the N.C.O.s and men, thirty-three had been killed and sixty-six wounded, of whom four later died from their wounds.[11]

Bridge had emerged from this disastrous day physically unhurt but obviously shaken by all he had seen and heard. The night was to afford no respite:

Mr Williams the missionary who was in the camp came and asked the Colonel's permission to carry a flag of truce towards the *Pa* to get our dead. Having got it, he went towards it, but the savages would not allow him to approach, and told him to go back and come next morning. After this they assembled and danced one of the most savage and frightful dances I ever heard in exultation of their victory and defiance of the Pakehas (the white people). It was nearly dark before we returned to the camp, tired and dispirited and disgusted beyond expression at having been defeated by a mob of savages, and with such fearful cost too. The two Surgeons[12] were employed more than half the night attending to the wounded; many were very severe and several amputations were performed. I went round the tents in all of which there were two or more wounded men to see if I could be of any use, whilst the Drs were engaged with the most serious cases. We passed a wretched night, during the whole of which the savage enemy were yelling and shouting and threatening to attack us in the morning and make *Kai Kai* (food) of us all, whilst now and again the most frightful screams were heard to issue from the *Pa*, as if from

[11] Figures from Despard's despatch, dated 2nd July 1845, see Appendix 2.
Bridge writing on the night of 1st July, gives thirty-six killed or missing and seventy-four wounded, exclusive of officers.
Whisker lists twenty names of 58th men killed and forty wounded but these include casualties for the whole of the Ohaeawai operations.
[12] Pine of the 58th and Galbraith of the 99th.

some poor wretch being tortured. These horrid sounds positively struck terror and dismay into the hearts of the men on picquet, some of whom left their posts and came into the camp, they were so horrified by these dreadful cries.

The following day Mr Williams again sought permission to remove the dead but it was not until the morning of the 3rd that the Maoris agreed. Bridge was appalled at the condition of the pathetic corpses and one in particular sent a shudder of horror through the British camp:

It was most disgusting to see the manner in which some of the bodies were mutilated and the want of respect shewn to them, even by our own natives. Poor Philpot was scalped. One had his head severed from his body, another the skull battered in. A third had the flesh all burnt and torn off his thighs and a hole in his body, with his clothes and flesh singed, proving that a red hot iron had been thrust into him. His arms extended stiff over his head, and his wrists and ancles bore the marks of having been tied together with flax. This was the poor fellow of the 99th who was missing on the morning of the 1st of July, and who had evidently been taken prisoner, and had been put to death and tortured in this inhuman and savage manner and whose screams were heard the whole night of the 1st.

Eventually, after the 'mournful task' of collecting the bodies had been completed, all the dead were accounted for except Captain Grant. When asked, the Maoris said they had buried the body and would not give it up. Bridge was furious:

Went to Colonel Despard to report this, and request he would ask Tamati Waka to write to Kawiti or some chief in the *Pa* and endeavour to get poor Grant's body given up to us. Met with a most ungracious and unfeeling reception, and was told I was too fond of interfering—as everyone who is rash enough to offer an opinion generally is by him.

Tempers were growing short all round and, to make matters worse, difficulties began to arise with the friendly Maoris. Most of the wounded soldiers had been sent down to Waimate in the drays but, by the 4th, these had not returned and there were still nineteen men to get away. The friendlies were asked to help by carrying these men down but they would only do it on payment of four blankets each. 'This exhorbitant demand was of course refused', wrote Bridge. Later in the day he attended a meeting at which Despard informed the chiefs that, since nothing further could be gained by remaining at Ohaeawai, that his men were growing sick from exposure to the cold and wet, and since the wounded at Waimate were unprotected, he had decided to break up the camp and return the whole force to Waimate. The chiefs' response was hostile in the extreme and even Bridge, who hitherto had been entirely well-disposed towards the allies, began to question their loyalty:

> Several of them made some very violent speeches, using most insulting gestures and language. As to the number of our wounded and the prospect of our men getting sick, they said what matter, are we not all alike, and when we talked of our unfortunate wounded being cut off at Waimate, 'Oh never mind your wounded, let them die and rot', and such brutal remarks. They evidently care nothing about us or what became of us, so that they get what they want, the land and plunder of their enemies. We are to stop and keep guard over them and force the enemy to leave the *Pa*, that they may take possession and derive all the benefit, a more selfish, covetous, ungrateful race I believe never existed. We certainly are in no enviable position, and have a very difficult card to play, surrounded by savages and cannibals, those professing to be our friends scarcely to be depended on, who at the slightest cause of offence might turn against us.

For once, Despard allowed tact to overcome temper and, realising that no good could come from antagonising his allies, he agreed to wait for two or three days to see what the enemy would do, though he still planned to leave on the 8th. The following day, the 6th, Waaka appeared, having completely changed his tune and agreeing it would be best to withdraw. 'He has some motive for this, I have no doubt,' wrote Bridge darkly.

On the 7th, the remaining four rounds of the thirty-two-pounder were fired into the *pa* and, apparently encouraged by the wailing heard from within, Despard changed his plans again. 'The Chief', wrote Bridge, 'intends standing his ground, and has at last done what he ought to have done a week ago, sent down for more shot and shell for the 32 pdr and more provisions for the men. It is thought the defendants will not hold out much longer.'

When the ammunition arrived two days later, another gun, a twelve-pounder, was taken up the conical hill; the bombardment re-opened and continued all day. That night, all the dogs in the *pa* started howling, a sign, the friendlies said, that the enemy were leaving. Despard forbade any movement by the troops before dawn, with the result that, when they marched in next morning, Bridge found much of his suspicion about his allies to be justified:

> We found the natives in possession of everything and even made a favour of letting the soldiers have some potatoes, although there were tons of them in the *Pa*. The enemy must have made a most precipitate retreat for they left behind them all the arms, accoutrements etc taken off our killed on the 1st instant, and some of their own ammunition and guns, firelocks and tomahawks, boxes full of plunder from Kororareka, and potatoes and indian corn enough for six months.

In addition:

> Poor Grant's body was found buried a few inches below the surface of the earth, outside the *Pa*. The flesh had been all cut off the buttocks and thick part of the thighs, and roasted and eaten I suppose by these brutal cannibals.

Utterly sick and disillusioned, everyone was now in haste to leave this ill-fated place but, before the *pa* was destroyed, the officers still had enough professional interest to examine carefully the extremely sophisticated defences, which had so effectively resisted their efforts. Despard wrote: 'The strength of this place has struck me with astonishment and I feel convinced that some European has had the direction of it.'[13] More realistically, Bridge thought: 'This will be a lesson to us not to make too light of our enemies, and show us the folly of attempting to carry such a fortification by assault, without first making a practicable breach.'

It seems strange that this lesson had had to be learned at such cost and that Despard, once the thirty-two-pounder had arrived, did not mass all his artillery against one point of the *pa* to see whether a breach could not be made, before ordering the assault. Despard's despatch of 2nd July claims that he had planned at least to weaken the defences:

This attack [by the enemy on the conical hill] shewed me the necessity of coming to an immediate decision and I accordingly determined on attacking the *Pah*, by assault, in the afternoon, as soon as the few shot brought up from the *Hazard* (26 in number) were expended: which I expected would so loosen the stockades, so as to enable the men attacking them to cut and pull them down.

Later in the same despatch he attributed the main cause of the failure to the axes, ropes and ladders not being brought forward. He appears to have issued a verbal order for 'a few shot and shell' to be fired into the *pa* before the attack but it is not certain that all the twenty-six rounds of the big gun were expended before he ordered the charge.[14] Moreover, the point selected by Despard for the assault, the north-west angle, was not the most vulnerable, even if the pioneers' tools had been available. Bridge wrote:

In my opinion we should not have succeeded if they had been brought up, but possibly lost more men. The fact is, the attack (which with the small force he had ought not to have been made at all) was directed on the strongest part of the Stockade where the guns had done no damage, when 50 or 60 yards to the right, the fence was very much battered by the cannon balls and shells.

[13] His despatch dated 12th July 1845, see Appendix 2. There was no evidence for the presence of any European, but presumably he had to restore his self-esteem somehow.
[14] Bridge only mentions the 'occasional' shot being fired before the advance, and as late as 7th July there were still four thirty-two-pounder rounds left, unless more had been brought up; Bridge's account suggests that none had.

Admittedly Despard's written orders had specified the point of attack as being 'on or near' the angle, a somewhat imprecise definition in itself, but in his despatch he made no criticism of the stormers on this score. Therefore his claim that he planned the attack to follow up, if not a breach, then a weakening of the stockade by the artillery, seems weak, and the laying of blame on the pioneers, however justified, appears an abdication of his own responsibility. The question remains: why did he persist with this sudden attack before the effect of the new addition to his artillery could be gauged?

Hattaway had a theory that the unrest caused by the disappearance of the 99th man on the night of the 30th[15] was so exacerbated by the surprise attack on the conical hill that Despard, fearing a breakdown of discipline and morale, ordered the attack simply to quench the men's 'desire for retribution'. However, Hattaway was writing from hindsight and, if there was such unrest, Bridge would almost certainly have been aware of it; yet there is no mention of it in his journal. In any case, the theory does not seem to accord with what is known of Despard's character; if he was unwilling to heed his officers' advice, he most certainly would not have bowed to the wishes of the men. On balance, his decision to attack seems to have been born out of anger and frustration, following the enemy sortie when he had had to run for his life, and determination that his desire for a physical assault should not again be thwarted. With the shrewd instinct of the man in the ranks, Free seemed to sum it up, when he said: 'We just went at the strong stockade front under orders from a Colonel who did not know his business and had a contempt for the Maori.'

On the 14th, leaving the smouldering pa and the demolished siege works behind them, Bridge led the rearguard away from Ohaeawai and marched down to Waimate. He was delighted 'to get back again, even to such indifferent quarters, having been three weeks under canvas and crowded with 9 officers in one small subaltern's tent. Enjoyed a thorough good wash, a luxury I had not had for 3 weeks during which time I never had my clothes off.'

[15] 'The men assembled in small parties and approached the sergeant-major, who conveyed their demand to be led to the attack of the pa to Adjutant M'Lerie, who reported to his superiors the state of the men's feelings.'

So ended Despard's first attempt against the Maoris. Kawiti and his warriors had escaped, Heke had recovered from his wound and was fortifying a new *pa*, and many good men had been lost. The campaign was no further forward. The best that old campaigners like Bridge and Hulme could hope for was that their commander might echo the sentiment expressed ninety years before by an officer of similar temperament, General Braddock, who, after his defeat by American Indians, said: 'Another time we shall know better how to deal with them'.[16]

[16] On 9th July 1755 General Edward Braddock, with a force of 1300 British regulars and provincials, was routed near Fort Duquesne by a force of 650 Indians under French command.

8

Ruapekapeka *Pa*

It was on the 10th of January to fight we next did go
We had large guns and mortars and Rocket tubes also
the[y] being in there strongest *Pah* and well secured all Round
We fired on all sides of them in hopes to Break it Down
We made 3 Breaches in the *Pah* and scattered it about
We kept the fire up all night but could not get them out

Alexander Whisker.

THE BODIES OF THOSE KILLED AT OHAEAWAI WERE BROUGHT
back and buried in Waimate churchyard with, according to
Whisker, 'a willow tree and a Red Rose at there heads'. He
went on:

the officers greaves are all neatly Raild Round and a very
Well finished head stone at the head of there greaves. They
lie in a Beautifull spot and the Grenidears and No 9 Company has Raised a Railing and head Board Round there
greaves as a token of Respect to there late Comrades [who]
now lie as comfortable as those who often commanded
them and if aney thing they have nicer greaves than they
officers.

Whisker had arrived at Waimate with the detachment of the
58th which had been left in Auckland under Captain Matson,
who had been ordered to relieve the 99th in the north. The
latter regiment, the 96th and Colonel Despard had all returned
to Auckland, leaving Bridge in command at Waimate, 'much
to my disappointment and that of my dear wife, who had been
fondly expecting my return to Auckland'. However disappointment was not his for long, as on 2nd August Louisa
arrived with Matson and his men and was installed in Mr
Burrows' house.

She must have enjoyed a robust constitution for she was at this time some four months pregnant, and the journey from Auckland had not been easy, beginning with a violent storm just after they embarked, then a journey down the Kerikeri river in boats (it was now the New Zealand winter) and finally a rough march to Waimate, as Whisker found:

> We had to march through a very bad piece of Road and some of the Boys Stuck in the mud so the Maories had to take horses for them. When we come in sight of the Barracks the whole of our men came running to meet us. When we came in we were very tired But Sargt Sullivan had a Rum and grog for us.

Life at Waimate was neither restful nor secure as there were frequent reports of Heke and Kawiti massing to attack the settlement and hardly a night passed without some alarm. Bridge found the strain of these alarms, most of which proved false, 'very annoying and harrassing—my dear wife bears them most heroically—still I cannot but feel uneasy and have serious thought of sending her down the Keri Keri'. But the next day: 'Changed my mind about sending my wife away, she fretted so at the idea. Besides I do not believe any attempt will be made to attack us.' Nevertheless he was determined not to be caught napping and therefore began the construction of defences around the mission station, keeping his garrison at instant readiness. Hattaway, who had received his first step to non-commissioned rank after Ohaeawai, noted the routine:

> Our duties at this time were conducted as if we were in the presence of an enemy, namely, parading an hour before dawn, and remaining in formation till daybreak. After dismissal of the parade rum was issued, diluted with water. Breakfast at eight a.m.; morning guard took place at halfpast ten a.m.; then came garrison or camp parades, when all officers and men off duty had to appear.

Money now arrived at Waimate to pay the men who had been without any for some time, but this, welcome though it was, brought disciplinary troubles, as the keen young N.C.O. Hattaway observed: 'The money paid to the men caused a good deal of gambling, and some drinking. From whence the old topers got the drink it is difficult to say.' He soon discovered one source:

I was placed in a very unpleasant position at this time, being non-commissioned officer in charge of some commissariat stores, over which, together with a barrel of rum, a sentry was placed. The guard occupied a small wooden building, and the hogshed was on a dray in our front. I knew the necessity of being watchful myself, owing to the presence of two men of intemperate habits. My suspicions were soon aroused by whisperings between the two men. They thought me asleep, but I was never more awake in my life. One of the men was married with a large family, and the sentry in charge. Through a small opening in the wall I observed one man tampering with the barrel. I surprised him in the act, and made him a prisoner, taking his arms and accoutrements from him, and keeping him as such till early morning. Fortunately, I detected him in time, or otherwise my duty would have been enforced. This was one of the most important duties of a sentry, a breach of which would have caused a heavy punishment, if reported. He begged very hard for a chance, and the rest of the guard interceded for him. If tried by court-martial and found guilty, a flogging would probably have ensued. I thought of his family, then in Parramatta, and decided to exercise leniency.

He also recalled that it was not only 'the old topers' of the 58th who caused trouble:

Among the Volunteers sent from Auckland was an American, who was a source of great trouble to the officers of that force by his acts of insubordination. It eventuated in his cursing the flag that he was serving under. He was confined at eight a.m., tried by a drumhead court-martial at half-past ten a.m., and sentenced to 50 lashes before the parade was dismissed. He begged for mercy but the answer was, 'Drummer, do your duty!' He gave no more trouble during his term of servitude.

With the constant night alarms and the need for men on

duty to carry loaded firearms, it was inevitable that accidents would occur. One such happened to a friend of Whisker's:

On the 10th of September Prt Ingate of the Lt Compy was Shot on guard and died at ½ one a.m. the 11th and was Buiried at 11 a.m. the 12th in Waimatta church yard. The whole of the 58 and 96th and 99th Regts all went to his funeral, the whole Band and Drummers Playing at it. Poor Ingates greave looked the best of aney of the greaves, his head Board Being a great deal Better done than the Rest, haveing a Rock Drawn on top with a weeping soldier reclineing on it with his right hand covering his face, while in his left hand he holds his firelock with trees growing on both sides of him. He is deeply Regretted by the whole who knew him. He was wounded on the head at Heki's *Pah* on 8th May and after getting Better he volentiered to Rejoin his compy at Waimate. He allways told us he would never Be shot by a Maorie. It was true for him, he was accidentely shot by the Corple of the guard when going on sentry. He died in the 22nd year of his age.

Born in the tiny village of Kirby Cane in Norfolk, Ingate had been a farm labourer before he took the shilling. His only living relative was his sister Debra, living at Rumburgh in Suffolk and it would be many months before she heard of his death, so many miles away from the East Anglian fields in which they had grown up.

What with all these difficulties and his concern for his wife and the safety of his post, Bridge had more than enough to contend with, but September brought him yet another cross to bear—the return from Auckland of Colonel Despard. If Bridge was expecting any commendation for the measures he had take to ensure the security of the garrison, he was sadly disillusioned. The irascible Despard took one look at Bridge's neat earthworks and exploded: 'I could never admit that a European force of between 300 and 400 men well supplied with arms and ammunition and four pieces of cannon, required any rampart to defend them in open country against a barbarian enemy'.[1] He ordered the hard work of Bridge's men

[1] Buick, page 197.

to be immediately flattened, making it abundantly clear that his invincible pig-headedness had not been dented by his failure at Ohaeawai.

Luckily for Bridge help was at hand in the shape of a buffer between him and Despard's temper for, on 6th October, Whisker was able to record the arrival of Lieutenant-Colonel Wynyard with seven officers and 214 rank and file of the 58th, who had not hitherto left New South Wales:

> It being a wet day we turned out in loose coats [greatcoats] to welcome our gallant colonel home to his Regt. As soon as he seen what we were up to he took the front. He was Joyfully received with 3 cheers. He saluted us and then called out, 'How are you my Brave fellows?', when we gave him 3 cheers again and he got 3 cheers more Before going into his Quarters, so he could not but say he was received by his Regt with 3 times 3.

Apart from the two companies still at the convict settlement on Norfolk Island, the 58th was now complete in New Zealand under its own colonel, although Hattaway thought that the sight of the veterans of Okaihau and Ohaeawai must have been something of a shock to Wynyard:

> A more motley body of Her Majesty's troops could hardly be conceived. Their original regimental uniform could hardly be recognised, owing to large patches of various colours, and some with boots and others without. What a contrast his men must have presented to the eyes of the old Colonel to what they were some ten weeks previously when entering upon the New Zealand campaign.

While Despard had been at Auckland, Governor Fitzroy deferred any further action against the rebels in case there was any possibility of getting Heke to come to terms. This had found no favour with Despard whose view was that 'the New Zealander is not a man who can be treated with any sort of hesitation. He must be talked to with the bayonet.'[2] However Heke's continued intransigence gave Despard the opportunity

---

[2] Quoted Gibson, page 55.

to return to the north with more troops and supplies, ready to continue the campaign. Before he did so, further communications from both Heke and Kawiti reached Fitzroy which, while holding out little hope of Heke's accepting Fitzroy's terms, did contain certain assurances that Waimate and the surrounding missions would not be attacked. Resting his hopes for a peaceful settlement on the activities of the missionaries, Fitzroy ordered Despard to withdraw the troops to Kororareka, and by the end of October the whole force was encamped among the ruins of the settlement, with the warships and transports lying in the bay.

At this juncture events took a surprising turn. Fitzroy received notice of his recall and the appointment of a new Governor, Captain George Grey, who recently had been Governor of South Australia. Grey, who at this time was in his thirty-fourth year, had been an officer in the 83rd Regiment and had first attracted the attention of his superiors by his exploration of the Australian deserts. Competent and energetic, he had a quick understanding and sympathy for his subjects, and was to have a long and distinguished career both in New Zealand and other parts of the Empire. Accompanied by his wife Elizabeth, a dark beauty of great charm, he landed at Auckland on 14th November and lost no time in bringing himself up to date on the state of affairs in the colony. Realising that the main problem lay in the north, he quickly disposed of the most pressing matters that awaited him in Auckland, and embarked on the Honourable East India Company's eighteen-gun sloop *Elphinstone*[3] for the Bay of Islands.

On 24th November he disembarked at Kororareka. Bridge recorded his reception by the troops and friendly Maoris:

His Excellency landed and was received by the whole camp under arms and guard of honor, and the usual salute from the men of war, as well as the guns on shore. Held a Levee and then received all the native chiefs, who assembled their people and danced a war dance in honor of his arrival and made several speeches. His Excellency fixed on a day when

---

[3] Up until 1860 the Honourable East India Company employed its own naval and land forces, which were part European, part Indian.

he would see all the chiefs who were loyally disposed, and when he would address them.

Whisker was a little more precise about the honours accorded:

At 12 oclock he landed at Kororarika, the *Elphinston* fireing 15 guns, the soldier artillery fireing 13 guns, then the *North Star, Race horse* and the Brig *Ospray*[4] fired 15 guns each. The 58th and 99th flank Compys they all formed a guard of honour for him, the 58th Colours flying and Band playing. At one oclock the Maories danced the War Dance.

On the 28th Bridge continued:

His Excellency landed again under the usual salutes to receive the friendly chiefs. Many spoke and all were warlike. His Excellency told them he was sent here by Her Majesty the Queen to endeavour to settle their differences and he hoped to make peace, but as the rebellious chiefs Heke and Kawiti did not give a favourable answer to the terms that had been already proposed to them by his predecessor Captain Fitzroy, and that by Tuesday night next he would have nothing more to say to them, and as he had heard many chiefs professing to be neutral had allowed their followers to fight for the rebels, and had indirectly assisted them, he would if this continued treat these deceitful chiefs as enemies. All the friendly chiefs seemed much pleased with this speech, and expressed their earnest wish that he would remain amongst them and not return to Auckland. The Governor and suite and heads of departments dined with the officers at the camp, at a garrison dinner.

After a few days reconnoitring and a fruitless journey to Pomare's *pa* in the hope of meeting Kawiti, Grey decided to make one more effort to see the rebel chiefs and then return to Auckland. If, as he was beginning to suspect, Heke and Kawiti had no intention of coming to terms and were merely making peace overtures to gain time, there were arrangements to be

[4] H.M.S. *Racehorse*, eighteen-gun sloop, had arrived with Grey, H.M. Brig *Osprey*, twelve guns, a little earlier. H.M.S. *Hazard* had sailed for China on 8th November.

made in Auckland for the furtherance of the military campaign: the raising of more volunteers, the collection of supplies and the cutting off of arms sales to the Maoris. Before leaving he sent Bridge a message:

His Excellency sent a message to me that he was going to Auckland and would take my dear wife with him, and place her in Govt House in Mrs Grey's charge. He was going up again to the Kawa Kawa to see if Kawiti, Heki and Pomare would come down and meet him as they had promised, and, if not, he intended to return immediately and sail for Auckland in the *Elphinstone,* and leave orders for the troops under Col Despard to proceed up the river and take up a position at Puketutu *Pa,* so that it would be impossible [for Mrs Bridge] to remain at Kororareka. I therefore decided on accepting His Excellency's very kind offer, and took her on board about 9 p.m. (the Governor having given up his own cabin to her servant) as His Excellency had failed again in seeing the rebel chiefs; the ship sailed at daylight the next morning.

Between 7th–11th December the whole force moved up the Kawakawa river to set up a new base at its head near the *pa* at Pukututu,[5] beyond which ten miles of difficult country stretched to Kawiti's *pa* at Ruapekapeka, the 'Bat's Nest', lying, according to Whisker, 'in the middle of a Bush on the side of a hill'.

Now that the force was again in fairly close proximity to the enemy, a certain jumpiness infected the night guards and picquets, whose task was not made easier by the high winds and drenching rain. Frequent alarms brought the troops staggering from their sodden bivouacs to stand peering into the darkness in anticipation of a surprise raid by the rebels. Whisker was on guard during one of these alerts:

On the 15th I went on guard and at 8 p.m. we heard 4 shots fired beyond the outlieing Picquet. The alarm was sounded and the men turned out. The inlieing Picquet was marched up and it was one of the Sentrys, J Stuart of No 9 Company.

[5] Not to be confused with Puketutu *pa* on Lake Omapere which was attacked on 8th May. See endpaper map.

He was Drunk and had his ammunition laid on a stone and was fireing away for his own amusement.

Hattaway, too, remembered this incident:

The whole force was speedily under arms, and the field officer of the day with a strong patrol proceeded to go his rounds of the picquet. The cause was soon discovered, as the patrol were dragging into camp a drunken man, who was resisting with all his might and shouting, 'Mighty men! There are thousands of them!' It transpired that he had a bottle of rum hidden on his person when he paraded, and was passed as fit for outpost duty. At sundown, when placed on sentry, he satisfied his craving for intoxicants at the expense of being on the following morning tried by drumhead court-martial, sentenced, and received 100 lashes with the cat-o'-nine-tails. He was a very intelligent man, but his drunken habits were a source of much trouble to his superior officers.

On the 19th one of the naval picquets alerted the camp, 'firing at cows, pigs or dogs in the bush,' Bridge thought, 'as no shots were returned'.

That day the Governor had returned from Auckland bringing supplies and reinforcements. All was now ready for the advance and a sizeable force had been collected: a naval brigade under Commander Hay, R.N., totalling thirty-three officers and 280 men from the H.M. Ships *Castor* (a thirty-six-gun frigate), *North Star, Racehorse* and H.E.I.C.S. *Elphinstone*; a Royal Marine detachment of four officers and eighty men under Captain Langford; twenty officers and 543 of the 58th under Lieutenant-Colonel Wynyard, the largest unit in the field; the flank companies of the 99th commanded by Captain Reed, seven officers and 150 men; Captain Atkyns and forty-two Auckland Volunteers; and 450 friendly Maories led by Waaka, his brother Patuone, Mohi Tawhai, Nopera Panakereo and Ripa. The artillery was manned by the sailors and fifteen men of the Honourable East India Company's Bengal Artillery under Lieutenant Leeds, and consisted of two naval thirty-two-pounders, two twelve-pounders, one eighteen-pounder, one six-pounder brass gun, four five-

and-a-half-inch mortars and two rocket tubes. In all the force mustered just over 1600 men.

At six o'clock on the morning of 22nd December the advance guard under Wynyard set off for the next staging post at Waiomio, followed next day by the remainder of the force. Although the distance was only five miles, the heavy rain had so churned up the single track that it took all morning to cover the distance, with soldiers and sailors pulling on drag ropes to supplement the efforts of the bullocks harnessed to the drays on which the guns were placed. Whisker complained that 'we were wet to the skin before we got our tents up' and, so miserable were the conditions, the soldiers had only their grim sense of humour to keep their spirits up. When a sailor accidentally shot off Private James Connor's finger, 'some of the men Burryed it in front of the camp', with due ceremonial.

From the camp at Waiomio, Kawiti's *pa* at Ruapekapeka was visible and the sight of his objective fired Despard into activity. Accompanied by the Governor, he set out on Christmas Eve with an escort and some rockets for a reconnaissance. Bridge watched their movements from camp:

Could see the party winding along over the hills nearly the whole way, and when they got as near to the *Pa* as the wood would permit, could see the rockets fired. One of the rockets fell in the wood and accidentally amongst a party of the enemy and sent them flying, and firing off their guns at random. It is said to have killed a chief.

On Despard's return:

Orders issued for the march of the troops to the new position tomorrow morning—700 men and 2 twelve-pounder howitzers. The remainder to be left under my command. The two 32 pdrs not to be taken up—more folly. I hoped the chief had got a lesson at Ohaeawai but it will be the same thing over again if he goes to work in this hurried and unprepared manner.

Christmas Day 1845 dawned after another night of teeming rain and was celebrated, as Whisker mordantly remarked, 'with a fine Breakfast of Dry Biscuit'. Unfestive though it was, Bridge found some advantage in the miserable conditions for:

> The advance is countermanded much to everyone's satisfaction, as it had rained nearly all night and the roads would have been in a fearful state. It would have been madness to have attempted to move on without the 32 pdrs, with very few days provisions, heavy roads and insufficient number of drays and bullocks. Besides, Xmas-day should be a day of rest, and the natives themselves object to move today, shewing greater regard for it than their more enlightened allies.

Perhaps finding Grey in a receptive mood, he also managed to have 'a long conversation with the Governor and expressed my feeling (opinion) very plainly as to the expediency of getting up the heavy guns before we moved on to the *Pa*. He is quite of the same opinion and determined they shall be taken up with us'. This conversation seems to have borne fruit, for the next day the thirty-two-pounders were brought up to the camp.

On the 27th the main body with some of the heavier guns was sent forwards towards Ruapekapeka, while Bridge was left at Waiomio with a rearguard to protect the stores and reserve ammunition. The advance was again slow but by about midday Bridge observed fire being opened on Kawiti's position. During the day a friendly Maori came into Waiomio with the news that Heke had left his own *pa* and was on his way with 200 men to join Kawiti. That evening a further welcome reinforcement reached Waiomio when Captain Cockcraft, with four subalterns and 108 men of the 58th detachment from Norfolk Island, marched in to join the rest of the regiment. Hattaway observed:

> It was a pleasing sight to see this fine body of men in their bright scarlet uniforms and white accoutrements, a contrast to the men in the field. Many of those men who had joined the regiment in Chatham or Dublin had grown to be tall and stalwart men. These meetings amongst old companions in arms, after an absence of two years, afforded much enjoyment, as the nature of our occupation and the uncertainty of

our lives naturally created in us a strong humane feeling towards one another.

Bridge had to wait another two days for the drays to be returned from Ruapekapeka but, on the 30th, he received orders to join the main body, after he had sent back the tents and the six-pounder ('useless lumber') to the Kawakawa. He covered the five miles in around three hours, reaching the new position at about eleven a.m. Whisker evidently regarded this march as a full day's work, as he sourly remarked, 'we had to go on picquet after our March without a night in Bed'.

Bridge was unimpressed by what he saw on his arrival:

Found they had taken up a position and established a battery about 1200 yards from the *Pa*, on a knole in the centre of a wood with a deep ravine between it and the *Pa*. The 32 pdrs, 18 pdr and 12 pdr had opened fire on it, and the enemy had opened a hot fire of musketry on it, but from the distance had hit no one. Most of their shot fell short except some rifle balls which whizzed over our heads, whilst our guns and rockets were making good practice. Saw 3 rockets and 3 shells from the 12 pdrs thrown into the *Pa*, which set the fellows running out helter skelter but they always came in again as soon as the guns ceased fire, to put out any fire or to repair any damage done to their fences. This is not the way I hoped to see this *Pa* attacked. There is no use firing a shot till all the guns, ammunition etc come up, and everything prepared to carry on the attack with vigour. An incessant fire should be kept up by all the guns and rockets, till the *pa* is set on fire, or so battered that, by taking immediate advantage of their confusion, a part of the force might rush in before they could return to their defences, whilst the remainder should be posted to cut off their retreat into the woods. Alas, how deplorable it is to see such ignorance, indecision and obstinacy in a Commander who will consult no one or attend to any suggestion made to him, and also, in consequence, has neither the respect nor the confidence of the troops under his command. Every one looks disheartened at such a beginning and apprehensive for the result.

Bridge's disgust with Despard's arrangements and character

were echoed by the man in the ranks, like Whisker, who caustically remarked that, 'Colonel Dispart would not let aney more guns than one be fired at a time. He had to hold his head when they would fire like a piece of patch work, for fear of it tearing.'

Their first full day before Ruapekapeka *pa* was marked by a number of incidents which, though of minor importance, were all recorded by both Bridge and Whisker, and their entries for the last day of 1845 reveal an interesting comparison between the respective view of events taken by the major and the private. First, Bridge:

This day commenced with a thick fog which cleared off a little about 9 a.m. when the guns and rockets commenced again, firing a shot or two at a time at intervals. Whilst at breakfast a sharp fire was heard to the left of the rocket battery in the ravine, which on enquiry proved to be from a party of the enemy, who had crept up close to the pioneers who were at work, and finding one a short distance apart from the rest, who had gone unarmed to get some water at a stream, they most barbarously and dastardly shot him in 3 or 4 places and then made off. The friendly natives immediately sallied out to endeavour to intercept their retreat into the *Pa*. A party under Ripa came up with them and had a brush, and he, poor fellow, returned with the loss of 3 of the fingers of the left hand from a musket shot. Kawiti hoisted his flag today for the first time since we came up to this position, which signifies his readiness to fight, and that some of our shells and rockets must have killed some of his people and put his blood up. But our shot and shell are all being frittered away in this absurd manner instead of keeping up a constant fire. Whilst the enemy find out where they are safe and shelter themselves whilst the fire is kept up, and then return to their trenches to await our assault, which they expect is our mode of warfare, fully convinced they will serve us the same as they did at Ohaeawai. Some excellent shots were made by Lieut Bland of H.M.S. *Racehorse* with the 32 pdr, and one cut down the flagstaff with the enemy's colours and went through the rear fence of the *Pa*, behind which most of the natives were congregated at their dinner. The poor volunteer that was shot (a black man) died of his wounds 2 hours after he was brought in. He was completely riddled and the savages who committed this cold blooded murder must have been close to him, for some parts of his clothes were burned and blackened with the powder.

Whisker wrote:

At ten oclock a.m. one of the volentiers went down to wash some clothes and kowita's men come on him and shot him. There was 5 Balls in him. No 3 and the Light Company was marched up into the Bush and the friendly tribe being up in the Bush Before us. Ripper got wounded on the left hand haveing 3 fingers shot off at the midle joint. We could not do anything so we marched home at 3 oclock. Lieut Guner of the *Race horse* cut down Kowitas flag staff with a shell from the 32 Pr from our Camp. Our men give 3 harty cheers as soon as this was cut down, we put one up in our camp and hoisted the English Colour on it. In the evening Moses Waka made a speech which Kowita answered from the *Pah* when the gunners sent him over 4 shells and one Rocket for supper and all was quite for the night. We made Breast Works at the guns this Day.

On 1st January, after 'our New Years breakfast of Peppermint tea and Damper', a party of friendly Maoris sallied forth to exact *utu* for the loss of Ripa's fingers. Bridge said that 'William Waka killed a man with Ripa's gun and they returned in great glee and danced a war dance'. About noon the Maoris again showed excitement when:

A very curious and uncommon phenomenon appeared in the heavens, a young moon with a bright star near it was distinctly visible at the same time as the sun shone brightly. This, some of our Maoris who are very superstitious, interpret into a good omen for us, and say it is Kawiti's flag (which has a sun, moon and star upon it) that we knocked down gone up to the sky. Others say it was favourable to Kawiti, as the star was on his side of the moon and not on ours. This remains to be proved but I believe they all look on the fall of their flag as fatal to their cause. I hope it may dishearten the savages, and make them take themselves off, for I am heartily sick of this life on our side, and this the Governor wishes, as he wants to take possession of their *Pa* without any loss of life on our side, thinking that will be sufficient punishment for them, and prove to them that they cannot resist us.

The *pa* was now being bombarded daily but in such a desultory fashion that Kawiti's men were able to repair any damage, and put out any fires which had been started, without much hindrance. Furthermore, until batteries were constructed closer to the stockade, it was unlikely that a breach could be effected. To find suitable gun positions, patrols were sent out under Captain Thompson of the 58th, among which was Hattaway:

A party of 100 men and a contingent of natives was despatched from camp, the object being to ascertain the nature of the ground and the facilities for constructing a small redoubt in front of the left face of the *pa*. The forest here was open, free from supplejack,[6] the trees large, with little undergrowth, and very favourable for disciplined skirmishers. We were not long here until we were discovered, and a strong party of rebels from the *pa* were sent against us. We opposed them, taking advantage of the large trees and every cover that offered for protection. Our opponents retired before us, and at sunset returned to their former position. We had noticed in making this flank movement a small opening of a few yards in extent, in which was growing very strong fern, and from which a full view of the *pa* could clearly be seen. It was now dusk. Captain Thompson, after placing me in the position with three men, returned to camp. My instructions were to be vigilant, and, as advanced scouts, we were, if attacked, to fire and fall back upon the outlying picquet, about half a mile distant. After the captain left us we sank down in the midst of the tall fern and, by pulling that growing under our feet and placing it in a circle around us, we found a place of security. We rested our guns on the outer circle of the fern, facing outwards, keeping two of our number on the look-

[6] A tall climbing shrub.

out, where they could see and hear any hostile movement. We passed the night in safety, our position not being discovered by the enemy. The position was selected by Colonel Despard for the use of a two-gun battery, the distance being about 400 yards. The steep gorge or gully located in front of the left face of the enemy's position; the two other faces were adjoining an extensive forest. The rebel chiefs, therefore, had good reason to believe their position was unapproachable against heavy artillery. They were accordingly surprised to see batteries constructed on the opposite side of the *pa*.

On the 2nd work was begun constructing a battery on the site of Hattaway's listening post. This involved clearing the ground, erecting a stockade, and felling the trees in front so as to open up the field of fire. Bridge was sent out with a picquet of 200 men to protect the new position. As he went forward, the rebels made a sortie on some of Waaka's men who were lying up in the bush to the left of the *pa*. Bridge, who was becoming increasingly ill-tempered, found himself in a crossfire:

I was put out with a strong picquet of 200 men to occupy the stockade, which was about half completed and arrived there during the action. The balls were whistling over our heads in the stockade, the skirmish between the natives being in front and on the right of it. After sunset all Waka's people came in and went to their *Pa* on the right of our encampment, and we were left to pass the night on the bare ground, with a fence on one side of us, and only a small trench on the other. After placing my sentries, we all laid down and kept ourselves as quiet as possible, and although dark we heard the enemy searching for their dead, and those in the *Pa* talking over the fight. They acknowledged to having got the worst of it, lamenting that none of Waka's people had been killed, but the chiefs are trying to encourage them by telling them they would be succesful tomorrow or the next day they fought, exhorting them to be strong, firm and brave and they would serve us as they had at Ohaeawai. Yet, whilst those that were seeking for the killed were distinctly heard conversing, little thinking we were so close to them, they did not come near enough to us for us to see them, and we were not disturbed during the night, although some of the sentries fired at imaginary sounds in the bush. Passed a wretched night, was not relieved till 9 o'clock.

Over the next week work on the battery continued so that the guns could be dragged forward into position. Apart from musketry and a few shells from a gun the rebels had in the *pa*, the work surprisingly was not molested. The troops' conditions however were distressing. 'A miserable cold wet day,' wrote Bridge on the 6th; 'It come on and kept raining all day and night,' grumbled Whisker as he went on guard. They had no tents and had to construct small huts, called *whares* by the Maoris, about five feet high and six feet long, with beds of fern inside to lie on. 'We had not a place to put our heads in haveing anything but Ferrin warries to sleep in and all of them let in the rain.' Such billets afforded little comfort or warmth for men after a rainy night spent out on picquet. With the enemy so close at hand, constant readiness was called for, with little chance of cleaning and drying their filthy and sodden uniforms, or even taking them off. On 5th January Whisker wrote: 'At 5 oclock A.M. I went into the Bush to wash my shirt and socks and towel [taking] my arms and accoutraments. I then took off my clothes and washed my skin not haveing my jacket off nor even unbuttoned myself since the 29th of Decr.' He also observed how the rigours of active service levelled out the peacetime differences between officers and men, when he saw one with 'a gunk of mutton and Biscuit in his hand, eating it Ravenous as a Cat Would do a lark, and a stick of Cavendish Tobacco and his pipe stuck over his Breastplate. I often thought how proudly I have seen the same officer sit at his splendid mess table and now he was like aney of ourselves.'

To provide a base and form a link between the force at Ruapekapeka and the ships at the mouth of the Kawakawa, a post had been established at the *pa* at Pukututu under Lieutenant Johnson, R.N., and sailors of H.M.S. *North Star*. On 31st December H.M.S. *Calliope*, a twenty-eight-gun frigate, had arrived in the Bay of Islands and was given orders to disembark a detachment of sailors and marines. The sailors were to relieve the *North Star* men at Pukututu, who were

View from the British camp of the assault on Heke's *pa* at Ohaeawai, 1st July 1845, above. Below, soldiers and a friendly Maori sniping at the left angle of the *pa*. An officer observes from behind a screen of flax on the right. (Water colours by Cyprian Bridge)

The storming parties' assault at Ohaeawai, supported by a detachment behind a breastwork in the foreground. The figure in the long coat with a stick under the trees to the left is probably Despard. (Water colour by John Williams)

then, with *Calliope*'s marines, to join the force at
Ruapekapeka. Among the officers of *Calliope* was a midshipman, H. F. McKillop, who came from a long line of sailors and
had entered the Navy as an assistant clerk in 1839. He had been
recommended for appointment as midshipman, and, when
serving aboard H.M.S. *Belleisle* at the age of nineteen on the
China Station in 1841–2, had received the Royal Humane
Society's silver medal for saving a seaman who had fallen
overboard in a heavy sea. He later wrote an account of his
service in New Zealand,[7] which gives many entertaining
insights into the life of a sailor on land service.

> As soon as the men were told off, and the officers named
> who were to compose the army (which, by the bye,
> included nearly every officer in the ship), the muster of
> dangerous weapons was alarming, the costumes ludicrous.
> The costume adopted by all the officers was a serge frock
> and sword-belt outside, with the ammunition pouches
> attached to it; most of us having double-barrelled guns, and
> wearing the same havresack as the men, and a blue cap
> without a band; our object being to assimilate our appear-
> ance to that of the men, the natives usually selecting officers
> as a mark on which to try their skill. With a few exceptions,
> we made our wills and wrote home, leaving the letters with
> the ship-keepers. After we were pretty well prepared, we
> had a convivial meeting in the gun-room, which lasted
> nearly all night: few if any of the junior members indulged
> in sleep. Captain Stanley very nearly shot one of the officers
> in the gun-room, whilst showing him what safe things the
> patent six-barrelled revolving pistols were; one of the six
> barrels going off *mal-àpropos*, passed through the bulkhead
> on one of the cabins.

After landing, the *Calliope*'s men marched up to Pukututu,
where McKillop found:

> a clear space of ground, including about two acres of land on
> the top of a hill, enclosed by stakes of various dimensions,
> the largest being about the size of a man's thigh, and the

[7] H. F. McKillop, *Reminiscences of Twelve Months' Service in New Zealand* (London, 1849).

smallest mere sticks, rather neatly arranged, and tied together with flax: the shape was an indescribable one; it had probably been added to at various times to suit the number of inhabitants. The huts had undergone considerable improvement since the arrival of the English, both in appearance and comfort; the grass roofing having been made water-tight, and doors put up, as well as a window in the one appropriated to the officers. The fires were lighted in the open air, and all the cooking done outside the stockade, for a time; our houses being composed of such combustible matter that a spark would have set the whole of them in a blaze: and as we had a considerable quantity of ammunition of various descriptions in a magazine, made by the boatswain of the *North Star*, in the stockade, it would have been a catastrophe not to be desired. Here we lived as it were on a perpetual picnic. Our duties not being very arduous, enabled us to drill our awkward squad, which they very much wanted. We were frequently warned of an intended attack. The excitement kept the men on the alert, and, consequently, many a poor stray pig and dog lost his life for not answering the sentries' challenge. We were all in light marching order, having nothing but a havresack and blanket besides our arms, and were obliged to wash our own clothes in the river, whenever we got a good drying day; and many a laugh we had at the first attempts of some few among us in the laundry line.

McKillop was eager to see something of the fighting and therefore counted himself lucky when he was chosen to accompany his captain up to Ruapekapeka, carrying some despatches for the Governor. His description of this task illustrates not only the spirit and humour of a young naval officer of the period, but also how strenuous sailors found land service after months of shipboard life, until they became accustomed to it:

We left with our despatches carried by the gig's crew, and two days' provisions, as wel as a tin box containing ammunition for guns and pistols, belonging to the captain. We had not gone far before we met a midshipman returning from the camp on horseback; and Captain Stanley, being rather lame, relieved him of his steed and mounted, finding he could not march very well with a sprained leg.

We found the road along the ridge of hills very warm; and I and the captain's clerks, who accompanied me as amateurs, frequently relieved the men from carrying the boxes. Their feet beginning to get very sore, we took a rest, having proceeded about eight miles, and began our lunch, or dinner, the tin box quite repaying us for the trouble of carrying it. We then took to the road again: the captain pushing on as fast as his own lameness would allow him to ride, we soon lost sight of him; and in about an hour after the second start, two of our men were completely knocked up, and obliged to lie down on the road; they were, moreover, parched with thirst, having eaten raw salt pork; and not a drop of water could we get for miles. We made sad travelling of it; and, considering the weight of what we carried, I don't wonder at it; the distance being about fourteen miles, and the hills so fearfully steep. The boats' crews had pulled some eight or ten miles before we started on our march; and we had none of us been refreshed with a night's rest, which fully accounted for our bad condition. As we proceeded, every one of us showed a deadbeaten countenance; and we were obliged to leave one of the clerks a long way behind, with cramp, after having supported him for a mile or two, finding it impossible to give him any more assistance.

We at last came to a river in a valley, thickly wooded, and beautifully cool, where we threw ourselves down and eagerly drank the delicious water. Here we made up our minds to await our straggling companions, who would of course exert themselves to their utmost in getting on, as they were at the mercy of the natives in their present situation. We also held a council of war over the tin box, the key of which the captain had taken with him. It was unanimously voted we should break it open and satisfy our hunger, now become insupportable since we had relieved the more pressing want of thirst. My sword was accordingly applied to the hasp which held the padlock, and open it flew. We did not take long in carving the remaining cold fowl, and whatever else it contained. We were, in the meantime rejoined by our lame friend, who revived considerably after taking a glass of the captain's port wine. We soon reached the camp after this last halt, and finding out the Governor's tent, delivered our despatches; we then proceeded to the head-quarters of the naval brigade, where we were kindly received by the officers of the *North Star* and *Racehorse*, who had a rough shed for a mess-place, which we shared with them.

One of the mids of the *North Star* good-naturedly invited me to partake of his hut; there were a few burning fagots in the middle, and, with my blanket, I made myself comfortable, and was introduced to some distinguished guests in the shape of maories, who joined us in our pipes, and favoured us with several songs. I gave all the news I could to those who had not been fortunate in receiving letters from their friends by the mail we brought out.

At the eight o'clock muster we were shown the trenches; and the position we were to take in them was pointed out to us, should there be an attack in the night, which was thought very probable; consequently, we all turned in like troopers' horses, fully accoutred. I for one should have slept soundly enough, notwithstanding this, had I been allowed; but the first interruption we had was a musket-shot, fired by one of the sentries at some imaginary spy from the enemy's *pah*; which complaint being very catching, about a dozen more sentries fired because the first had done so. The bugles immediately sounded the alarm, and the boatswain's mate piped all hands to the trenches; and out we turned, helter-skelter, jumped into the muddy wet ditch, and placed ourselves in a stooping position, which soon brought on the cramp in my legs. There was, however, no enemy to be seen; the night was dark and pretty cool; and the bushes and stumps of trees, to my uninitiated eyes, took the forms and faces of the tatooed tribes whose acquaintance I had so lately made. After cooling our courage for about an hour and a half, we were quietly dismissed without having had a chance of satisfying the craving for fight, which comes to all beginners stronger than it ever returns after it has once been gratified. The next morning, although not much refreshed by our night's rest, having had a second interruption soon after the false alarm, by one of the sentries nearly shooting an officer of the *North Star* when going his rounds, we started for Puketutu's *pah*, where we were to join our own party.

Early on 8th January, six days after McKillop's visit to Ruapekapeka, about eighty Maoris were observed by a sergeant's picquet leaving the *pa*, and later in the morning a woman appeared, carrying a flag of truce. Bridge discovered that:

This was the wife of a young chief named George King, a halfcast woman whose mother was amongst Waka's people. The poor thing came to tell our natives that she wants to get out of the *Pa*, but that they would not let her. She said the party that went over the hills this morning will not come back again. A chief accompanied her of the name of Hara, and appeared very much disgusted, and asked what more we wanted. We had been a month here, roasting them with iron, and we are not satisfied. He was told we should not be satisfied till they left the *Pa* and we got possession of it. The Governor sent a message to Kawiti to request he would send away all his women and children, as he did not come here to hurt them, and to express his sorrow that the woman and the child had been killed in the *Pa* on the first of the month. I fancy they are leaving the *Pa* by parties, and that they will shortly bolt, but I hope not before our batteries open upon them, as it is better that we should drive them out than that they should go of their own accord, just to show them what we can do, and to take the conceit out of the rascals.

Even if some Maoris were leaving the *pa*, the determination of the remainder was stiffened by the arrival of Heke who, with sixty followers, not the 200 previously reported to Bridge, managed to slip in to join Kawiti on 9th January. His arrival coincided with the last convoy of shot and shell to reach the troops and now, with the batteries completed, Despard was about to deliver his assault. Three gun positions had been constructed. One, in the camp, housed a thirty-two-pounder, a twelve-pounder, a six-pounder and two rocket tubes; within the stockade built 400 yards from the *pa* were two thirty-two-pounders and four mortars; and in another stockade, further to the right and closer to the *pa*, one eighteen-pounder and a twelve-pounder.

At ten o'clock on 10th January, 'our great guns', wrote

Whisker, 'all commenced a Cross fire on the *Pah* all takeing up the signal from the 32 in our camp. They kept on at it to about 5 oclock in the evening when they had made 3 Breaches in it.' Despard, now in a fury of excitement at the destruction caused by the massed guns (a tactic urged all along by Bridge) sought the approval of Grey before ordering Wynyard forward with a storming party to charge the *pa*. But, said Whisker, 'the governor was not well pleased at him'. Grey was not alone in this, for when the friendly Maoris saw Despard's intention, Mohi Tawhai rushed to stand in front of Wynyard's party with arms outstretched, as if to bar their way, shouting at Despard, 'How many soldiers do you want to kill? You shall not pass by me!'[8] Bridge wrote:

> Waka and Moses told the chief, if he attempted to storm he would only lose his men as he did at Ohaeawai, but if he waited till tomorrow, he would get the *Pa* which [was] only a bundle of sticks after all, not worth the sacrifice of life for nothing, as the enemy they were sure would be gone. Their good advice was fortunately taken this time by our Sapient Leader, and the party ordered back to the camp, and the guns kept up a fire on the breaches all night to prevent any attempt at repairing them.

The two advanced batteries were protected through the night by a picquet of 100 men of the 58th under Captain Denny. Denny himself was in the forward (eighteen-pounder) position with fifty men, while the remainder guarded the thirty-two-pounder battery. Among the sergeants of this picquet was 1542 William Speight, who had been severely wounded on 8th May with the Light Company stormers at Okaihau. Although not fully recovered from his wound, he had volunteered to accompany the force to Ruapekapeka. Another N.C.O. in this picquet was Hattaway, whose position so close to the enemy gave him an excellent view of the events of Sunday, 11th January, of which he left a graphic account:

Early in the morning, Tamati Waka's brother, Patuone,

[8] Buick, pages 253–4.

accompanied by the European interpreter, held a consulta-
tion with Captain Denny. After this they proceeded along
the margin of the forest, crossing the bottom of the gorge,
sometimes crawling along to conceal their persons from the
view of the garrison of the *pa*. The ascent from this deep
gulley to the outer works of the enemy's position had been
protected by acres of fallen bush, in such a manner that the
trunks of the trees, many of them very large, were a splendid
protection against the advance of any attacking force on that
front of the *pa*. The clearing was planted out in potatoes,
which looked a promising crop in its early growth.

All the men, excepting the sentries, were ordered to take
off their greatcoats, and prepare for a dash. After waiting
and watching for some time, we saw the chief and interpreter emerging from the forest into the potato plantation,
stealthily moving from tree to tree, listening, and proceeding nearer and nearer to the breach. At last, satisfying themselves that all was safe, they raised a white signal behind one
of the large trees. Captain Denny, at the head of his men,
gave the word to advance to the breach. We crossed the
gorge and up through the steep plantation at our utmost
speed. The foremost men, with a strong heave, pushed over
the damaged palisades, and they fell inwards with a crash.

This evidently was a complete surprise. We saw no one
until we passed right through the *pa*, with the reverse [side]
towards us, when a bell rang which had the effect of causing
the rebels to try and re-enter the *pa*. They were met by a few
of our men just in time. Several of their men were shot there,
and afterwards dragged a short distance away. The balls
from the 32-pounder had gone right through the palisading,
even to the back palisading, and it was from the holes thus
made that the troops kept firing, when the rebels made a
very determined attempt to recapture the *pa*. A companion
on my left and I were firing through the same perforated
opening, when a bullet struck him on the head, and killed
him. A splinter from the same shot struck me on the for-
head, but inflicted no injury. At this time men were fast
arriving from the camp. We rushed through the back entrance and raised a hearty cheer, still keeping up our firing as
we advanced from cover to cover. The many large trees
which had been felled afforded splendid shelter and facilities

for practical and experienced sharpshooters. As we advanced, we noticed a number of trees fallen directly in our front, and which was a natural barricade to our further progress. They were on the margin of the standing forest, to which we thought the natives had retreated. Suddenly they appeared behind these large trees, and delivered a volley amongst us. We retired, taking advantage of any cover that offered. One of my comrades, T. Hales, was bleeding profusely from the mouth. I went to his assistance, and found that his front teeth had been knocked out, and his gums injured. This was up to the time I speak a soldiers' skirmish.[9]

The enemy kept up a heavy fire from this barricade which successfully held up any further advance for some time. A number of sailors from H.M.S. *Castor*, whose first action this was having only recently arrived from China, attempted to charge, either singly or in small groups, but were shot down before they could get to grips with the enemy marksmen. Then Sergeant Speight, with Sergeants Stevenson and Munro, followed by a mixed party of soldiers and sailors, burst through a door in the *pa*'s stockade, behind which they had been sheltering, and hurled themselves at the barricade. This sudden attack was made with such dash and determination that the Maoris fell back from their defences and started to melt away into the undergrowth. Though they kept up a desultory sniping from the forest, their resistance was broken and, with reinforcements brought up by Wynyard, the *pa* was securely in British hands.[10]

It was learned afterwards that the Maoris, thinking that no attack would be made on a Sunday, had withdrawn to the far side of the *pa*, where a number of the Christians among them, including Heke, were holding a prayer meeting. Only Kawiti and a handful of non-believers had been in the *pa* when it was entered, and they had had to fight their way out to avoid capture. It was ironic that the rebels had lost their *pa* through showing greater respect than their adversaries for the religion

[9] i.e. Soldiers working independently and on their own initiative without waiting for orders from their officers.

[10] All three sergeants were commended in orders for their gallant conduct. In 1856, when the Victoria Cross was instituted, Speight's name was put forward for a retrospective award for his action at Ruapekapeka by Wynyard, then still commanding the 58th. However, no awards were allowed for actions prior to the Crimean War.

brought to their land by fellow-countrymen of those adversaries. In view of the ferocity with which they fought to regain the *pa*, it seems doubtful whether the friendly Maoris had been right in their prediction the day before that the rebels were about to withdraw.

Despite this lucky chance the British had not got off lightly, twelve men being killed, and Midshipman Murray of H.M.S. *North Star* and twenty-nine wounded, two of whom later died of their wounds. Of these casualties, the sailors suffered most, losing seven killed, all from H.M.S. *Castor*, and fourteen wounded, while the 58th lost two killed and ten wounded. One of the latter was Private Monaghan of No. 5 Company, of whom Whisker dryly wrote: 'Monaghan had his arm cut off after comeing into the hospital. He seemed to think nothing of it.' Of such stuff was the mid-Victorian soldier made!

As the Maoris were in the habit of carrying off their casualties, it was difficult to establish their losses, but a few of their dead were found lying in the undergrowth. Whisker noted that a party of the 99th:

> found an old chiefe lieing at the foot of a tree about 2 mile from the Pah. They took two Pouches off him. Colonel Wynyard sent Hanson the interpreter[11] to see who he was. Some of us went out for him and we Brought him home. He had a 96th Jacket on him, he was shaved all over, he had not a hair on him from head to foot. 4 of us carried him home. We found him to be the old Chiefe that Burned the 99th man and eat some of Captn Grant at Oheawai. The Maories wanted to Burn him but we Burried him.[12]

During the attack Bridge had been left in charge of the camp in case of an attack from the rear. After Despard returned from the captured *pa*, doubtless flushed with the success that had eluded him for so long, Bridge received permission to go up and look at the enemy's stronghold.

[11] A Maori or possibly a half-caste.

[12] How these gory details were attributed to this particular Maori is not made clear. He may have been identified by the friendlies as a witch-doctor who had been at Ohaeawai. According to Buick, the screams heard at Ohaeawai, which the troops believed to have come from the 99th man under torture (see Chapter 7), were in fact the witch-doctor calling down the wrath of the native deities on the troops.

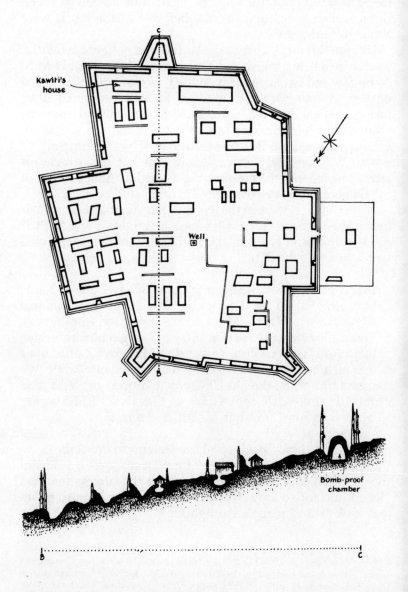

A near contemporary sketch of Kawiti's *pa* at Ruapekapeka. A—the palli-sades breached by the two 32-pounders. The cross section (below) of the *pa* from B to C shows the bomb-proof holes and chambers.

I found the *Pa* much stronger in its interior defences than the one at Ohaeawai, but the outer fences and ditches were very similiar, and all the faces well flanked. There were also deep holes under ground all over the *Pa*, which were so constructed as to be bombproof in which the men secured themselves from the shot and shell. Cross fences and breastworks inside, so that a fire could have been kept up upon us, even had we succeeded in forcing the outer fences by storm, as we advanced into the interior of the *Pa* which must have proved most destructive, had we not taken them so much by surprise.

Now that the operations were over, Bridge had other preoccupations for he was aware that his wife's confinement was imminent. Grey was keen to return to Auckland at once, so Bridge seized his opportunity, asked for and was granted a month's leave, and sailed with the Governor on 14th January. He reached Auckland on the 17th where, 'about an hour and a half after my arrival, she presented me with a fine son and heir'. The child was christened Cyprian Wynyard, in compliment to Bridge's commanding officer.

Meanwhile, at Ruapekapeka, the *pa* was destroyed and the force began the laborious business of moving the guns, ammunition and stores back to the Kawakawa for reloading on to the shipping. Whisker's account of the next few days suggests that, while the troops' morale when in face of the enemy had remained high, despite the wretched living conditions, the task in front of them caused some discontent; only the issue of the grog ration restored their spirits. First, all the ammunition from the batteries had to be manhandled to a central point. Then:

We were marched off from the Camp left in front[13] with one fife and small drum playing the British Grenidears. When we got to where we left the shot in the morning We were halted and the company had to go one at a time and as he marched past every man had to take up a shot. When they were all gone every 2 had to lift a box and carry it between us, and us in heavy marching order and our Blankets

[13] i.e., with the Light Company leading.

besides, We had very hard work. Some 4 men had to carry a 5 inch mortar on top of there knapsacks and one Divission had to pull the guns carrages after them. We only gott about 1 mile when we had to halt for the night. We got our grog and lay down not building aney huts that night but lay down on the top of a large hill with our Blankets over us and our knapsack formed our Pillow. But the night was Dry and the Moon shined Bright. We lay very contented for the night.

15th January 1864. The Bullocks not comeing to it was late we got up at 6 in the morning and carryed the shot shell and rockets down past the officers tents to give the Drays room to turn and as they were taking down the gun carriage it forced its Way too Quick and run over Spreckland, going over his arm and leg and takeing a piece out of his leg, left the bone Plain to be seen. About 7 oclock one of the officers went down and set fire to the ferrin below the amunition to make us carry it farther on so we carryed it on to another hill. At 2 minutes before 12 oclock we marched of from the Camp and we were halted at the amunition. We then got our first grog for the Day as an Inticement to carry the shot same as the Day before. I was confined by Captn Thompson for saying it was Bullocks Work. I then helped the Rear guard to Pull the gun carriage to the next camp where We arrived at $\frac{1}{4}$ to 4 oclock. The first of the Party arrived at $\frac{1}{2}$ past 3. I was then Released at that Place and got our grog. We then marched at $\frac{1}{2}$ past 4 oclock and arrived at Bugamators Pah Cowa Cowa[14] where we arrived at 20 minutes past 7 in the evening. Waka give 2 Baskets of Potatoes to each Compy free, all of us was glad of them.

On the 16th the troops went down the Kawakawa in boats, embarking on the ships that evening. The next day another soldier suffered the consequences of his actions during the march down: 'Prt Sutton of the 6 Compy was tried by District Court Martial for refusing to carry his accoutraments and disobeadince of orders to Captn Thompson and Colonel Despart. He got 150 lashes. He called out as he lay on board all night.'

[14] Puketutu *Pa*, Kawakawa.

It had been decided that a garrison of two companies of the
58th commanded by Bridge, when he returned from leave,
would be left at Victoria, across the bay from Kororareka,
while the rest of the force returned to Auckland. Whisker
found that his company, No. 3, and No. 8 were to remain but,
apart from grumbling that he was the first man selected for
guard at Victoria, his journal indicates no annoyance at being
left behind. Hattaway had badly sprained his ankle during the
move down from Ruapekapeka, having had to march without
boots while carrying a thirty-two-pounder shot. He was destined for Auckland and five weeks in hospital but, as he waited
on the dockside at Auckland, he witnessed the exhilarating
arrival from China of H.M.S. *Driver*, the first paddle steamer
to reach New Zealand. 'Those who saw the natives,' he wrote
in the closing paragraphs of his narrative, 'were much amused
at their antics and excitement, as the *Driver* slowly steamed up
the harbour, wreathed in smoke, against the ebb tide; meantime the Maoris were exclaiming, *"Taipo"* (the devil) and
"Haere Mai" (Come here).'

An even more exciting display to mark the end of the
campaign in the north was seen when the old hero Waaka and
his tribe returned from Ruapekapeka. McKillop witnessed the
extraordinary scene:

Waka being in his full uniform—epaulettes, cocked hat, and
all—a war-dance took place in honour of their return: this
was a series of the most extravagant distortions of features,
accompanied by the most discordant yells and shouts, as
well as dancing, which consists of jumping off their feet as
high as extreme excitement and great activity alone could
accomplish, flourishing their muskets and tomahawks over
their heads at each fresh scream; the chief giving the time for
these displays of diabolical manoeuvres, which, however,
they execute in the most excellent measure, keeping the
most correct time in these horrible choruses, as well as
jumping together with the greatest precision, the 200 muskets acting as one piece of machinery. At the first part of this
spectacle Waka stood with the officers who were looking
on, merely showing that his mind was with the dancers by a
slight movement of the leg, and every now and then slap-
ping his thigh with the palm of his hand, marking time; but

gradually becoming more and more excited, forgot the dignity due to his uniform and new station, and in a few minutes snatched a musket from the willing hand of one of the soldiers standing by who had been watching him, and joined in the noisy throng, soon taking the prominent part which his energy of character rendered him so well able to perform, losing all control of his gentlemanly self: this ended in a sad catastrophe happening to his blue dress pants, which could not stand the repeated tests of strength they were put to. We all laughed most heartily; but so excited had our tatooed officer become, that he did not discover the damage done to his limited wardrobe until the dance was over, when he felt rather ashamed of the figure he had cut'.

9

Drummer Allen sounds the Alarm

'A lad who was engaged in the last affray behaving
with great spirit and courage.'
Corporal John Mitchell, 19th March 1848.

BETWEEN 17TH AND 24TH JANUARY COLONEL DESPARD'S
despatches announcing the fall of Ruapekapeka were published in the Government Gazette in Auckland.[1] Despard described the operations at length, though somewhat distorting
the fortuitous circumstances by which the *pa* had been captured, and concluded by lavishing the most uncharacteristic
praises on all the naval, military and volunteer forces, mentioning by name all the officers commanding detachments,
the staff and medical officers, and even the interpreter Mr
Edward Shortland. Although he had expressed, in his Brigade
Orders of 11th January, 'His admiration at the brave and intrepid conduct displayed by our native allies', and somewhat
patronisingly commended their bravery at the assault on the
pa as 'fully equal to what might have been expected from Her
Majesty's bravest troops', he found no place for Waaka and his
followers among the list of distinguished officers in his last
despatch.

When the latter was republished in *The New Zealander* on
24th January, that paper sourly remarked: 'On this occasion
we fear that the drummers and fifers will feel themselves
deprived of their laurels in this assault, from the omission of a
paragraph complimentary of their services.' Furthermore, the
editor went out of his way to play down the achievements of

[1] See Appendix 3.

the force in general and of Despard in particular by saying: 'The manner in which possession was gained of Kawiti's *pah* did not, in our opinion, justify the lengthened, pompous, commendatory despatch of Colonel Despard, in which a mere casualty of the defenders—being at prayers without the *pah*, enabling our troops and allies to enter unperceived and unmolested—is termed "the capture of a fortress of extraordinary strength by assault, and nobly defended by a brave and determined enemy." '

Unpopular though Despard may have been, this belittling of their efforts by the colonial press was resented by the naval and military officers, particularly, as one naval officer pointed out, that of the large number of colonists capable of bearing arms in defence of their interests, a very small body had volunteered to take the field. As for Despard, the hostility of the press was of no consequence, for, when the article appeared, he was no longer in New Zealand. On 21st January Bridge observed thankfully: 'Lieut-Col Despard took his departure for Sydney, much to the satisfaction of the troops in New Zealand'.

Whatever *The New Zealander* may have thought, there was no doubt that the capture of Ruapekapeka had quelled the uprising in the north. After abandoning their *pa*, Heke and Kawiti first attempted to take refuge with Pomare, but that old chief had no wish to compromise himself by giving them aid. Both now realised that there was no alternative but to make peace, and appealed to their old enemy, Waaka, to act as intermediary between them and the Governor. On 29th January Kawiti wrote to Grey:

> This is my absolute consenting to make peace with the Europeans on this day. Exceedingly good, O Governor, is your love towards us, and I say, also, good is my love towards you. That is the joining (by peace) for ever, ever, ever!
>
> From me,
> Kawiti.[2]

Heke, stiff-necked to the last, wrote a less conciliatory letter, requiring Grey to come to him to discuss terms:

[2] Quoted Buick, page 272.

Sir George Grey, Governor of New Zealand. (Engraving by W. W. Alais after a photograph)

Pages from Private Alexander Whisker of the 58th Regiment's memorandum book.

The bombardment of Ruapekapeka *pa,* as seen from the British camp. Note the troops' huts, or wha and the sergeant supervising the issue of the grog ration in the foreground. (Water colour attributed John Williams)

The troops entering Ruapekapeka *pa* as seen from the lower stockade, 11th January 1846. Note the sailor to the left of the gun, right. (Water colour by Cyprian Bridge)

Friend Governor Fitzroy, Friend the New Governor. I say to you, will you come and let us converse together either at Paihia, or at Waitangi, or at the Waimate, that my thoughts may be right towards you concerning the stick [flagstaff] from which grew the evil to the world? Walker and Manu [Rewa] and others say they alone will erect the staff. That will be wrong; it will be better that we should all assemble—they, we and all the many chiefs of this place and of that place, and you too, and all the English also.

Now, this I say to you: come that we may set aright your misunderstandings and mine also, and Walker's too. Then it will be right; then we two (you and I) will erect our flagstaff; then shall New Zealand be made one with England; then shall our conversation respecting the land or country be right.

Mr Busby; the first Governor; the second Governor; the third Governor; the Queen: salutation to you all.

From

John William Heke Pokai.[3]

Once Waaka was convinced of their sincerity, he went to Grey to plead their cause, and to suggest that a policy of clemency would best ensure a lasting peace in the north. Grey agreed. Heke and Kawiti were granted free pardons, and the threat to seize their lands was abandoned. The war in the north was now over, and, a few weeks later, Kawiti, accompanied by Waaka, paid a visit to the garrison at Victoria. Whisker and his comrades thus had their first close sight of their old adversary:

Kowita accompanyed by his whole staff all carefully Rolled up in there Blankets Paid his first visit to us. He came in his War canoe with the Ensign of old England flying at Stern. He was allso accompanyed by Tomathy Waka. He landed and our men ran Down to the Beach to see him. He was greatly afraid of us But when we went forward and shook hands with him one by one, he began to feel ashured that we would not do him aney injury, so he come up to the camp his tribe walking after him with Waka at his side, and it was a struggle with a great maney of our men whitch of them would be nearest to him as he walked up to the officers quarters. There he was taken in and treated by them mutch Better than aney of us that fought long and hard and endangered our lives for what they Pleas to call the honour of old England. But ther he was coiled up like a Serpant in his Blanket. He got Plenty of Biscuit and Tobacco from the officers and they made him stupidly Drunk. He then got tired of being in the house so him and his tribe went out and lay down on the grass, there old favourite position for as soon as they come near the soldiers they throw them selves down eather sitting on there two heels or lieing there on one side, and they do the same no matter whoes Presence they are in. They stopped from ten oclock in the morning to 5 in the evening when they went away well satisfied.

In showing clemency Grey had not been solely inspired by humanitarian motives, for shortly after the return of the troops to Auckland from Ruapekapeka, news reached him of a fresh outbreak of trouble in the south of North Island around Wellington. Although another company of the 99th under Major Last had arrived from Australia, and the last 58th detachment from Norfolk Island under Major Arney had reached Auckland, Grey did not dispose of sufficient troops to cope with any further disturbances in the north, at the same time as quelling the new threat in the south. Thus the willingness of Heke and Kawiti to make peace came at the most opportune moment. The two-company garrison at Victoria under Bridge would suffice to contain the north, thus permitting Grey to deploy a sizeable force to the relief of the colonists around Wellington.

It will be recalled that the first bloodshed between whites and Maoris had occurred in the north of South Island in 1843, when Te Rauparaha of the Ngatitoa, and his nephew Te Rangihaeata, had massacred nineteen Englishmen at Wairau, following their foray across Cook Strait between the two islands. The Ngatitoa's lands lay to the north of Wellington around the Hutt Valley, which ran north-east from the town. Along the course of this fertile valley a number of farms had been established by settlers as a result of land deals made between the New Zealand Company and the local Maoris. Many of these deals were now being disputed by the Maoris, who claimed either that the land had been seized without compensation, or that they had not received a fair price. First intimidation, then raiding slowly began to force the outlying settlers off their farms to seek sanctuary in Wellington. At the back of this deteriorating situation lay the Ngatitoa and the formidable Te Rangihaeata, whose eyes were on not just the Hutt, but Wellington itself.

Te Rangihaeata was described by a European as 'a fine handsome man, very powerfully built, with piercing black eyes' but 'particularly dirty'.[4] He must have had a strong constitution for, on one occasion, he was believed to have swallowed a pint of rum which had been laced with arsenic, but this had only made him violently sick. He was implacably hostile to all Europeans and to Christianity, and saw in both nothing but a threat to the Maori way of life. Nevertheless he was more than ready to make use of their firearms, and was not averse to their tobacco and spirits. His part in the Wairau massacre had made him a much feared figure among the colonists, and his reputation as an uncompromising opponent spread alarm through the settlements of the Hutt Valley. Concern also began to be felt in Wellington, where there was only a small garrison of Captain Russell's company of the 58th and a company of the 96th, 180 men in all. Defences were built, the local Militia called out, and requests for help sent to Auckland.

With the departure of Despard the military command in New Zealand had reverted to Lieutenant-Colonel Hulme of the 96th, who embarked for Wellington with a force of 400: Major Arney and two companies of the 58th, Major Last and two of the 99th, and one of the 96th. Sailing in H.M. Ships *Castor, Calliope* and *Driver*, the transport *Slain's Castle*, and the Government brig *Victoria*, the reinforcements reached Wellington on 16th February.

Aboard the *Calliope* was the young midshipman, H. F. McKillop. On arriving at Wellington he, like many of his brother officers, was keen to see the town, particularly as they had been led to believe by the citizens of Auckland that 'the place was so inferior a settlement to the capital'. They were surprised to find that it boasted a theatre, where the perfor-

4 McKillop, page 46.

mance of a player dressed as Macbeth while performing a hornpipe 'brought forth such shouts of delight and uproarious peals of laughter, accompanied by such stamping and screams and other symptoms of excessive approbation, that in a few minutes down came the boxes, the supports having been knocked away from beneath'. Escaping from the ensuing shambles, McKillop next inspected the hotel—'far superior to anything we could have expected after what we had seen at Auckland'.

The situation of the town itself was, he thought,

more picturesque than convenient, the steep thickly wooded heights rising so abruptly from the beach as to make it necessary in many places to cut terraces in the side of the hill to build upon. There are some good substantial brick buildings, the bricks being made on the spot. The principal mercantile houses are all on the beach. There are also numerous roomy stores and commodious shops, many of them having wooden wharfs attached, running out into ten or twelve feet water, allowing small vessels to come alongside and take in or discharge cargo. The town also boasts of a steam and a wind flour-mill, a strong gaol, a bank, four chapels of various sizes, belonging to different sects of dissenters. The church is situated at the north end of the town, and is much smaller than many of the chapels. Near it are many of the principal residences, amongst which the one belonging to the New Zealand Company's principal agent, standing in a nice green lawn, with a pretty garden at the back, reminds one of an English villa. The Lieut-Governor's house has also been built here, as well as a new barrack. There are rather too many public-houses for the size of the place, which were generally well filled, owing partly to the unfortunate disturbances having thrown so many people out of work, and driven in numbers of the out-settlers from their farms, for the protection the town afforded.

The pleasures of this pleasant town were not to be enjoyed for long, as news came in of the murder of a settler and his son. Hulme therefore moved troops up the Hutt Valley and established posts to protect the more vulnerable farms. Stockades were constructed around the farm buildings and garrisoned by

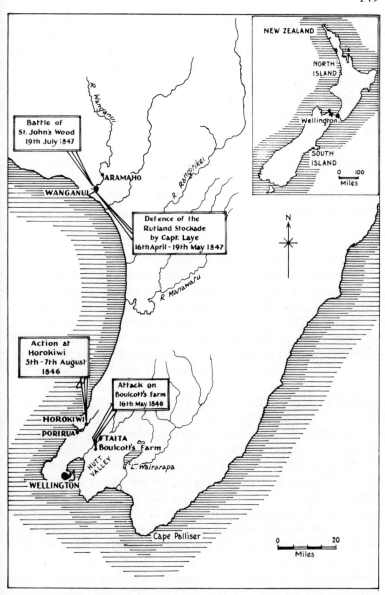

Action in the Hutt Valley and Wanganui, 1846–7.

troops or militia. One outpost, called Fort Richmond, was built by Captain George Compton, commanding the Hutt Militia, who had lived in America and modelled his fort on the same lines as those erected as a defence against the Red Indians. At one of these posts was the young soldier of the 58th, Joseph Hinton. He had missed the operations in the north, and in the account he left of his experiences, he says he sailed from Sydney direct to Wellington. Thus he must either have been a member of Russell's company, which had been permanently stationed in the south since its arrival in mid-1845, or come out as one of a reinforcing draft. He now found himself on active service for the first time, occupying a stockade on the banks of the Hutt River.

We were a happy and careless lot of young fellows and enjoyed the prospect very much. We lighted a large fire inside the stockade and, having posted sentinels, lay down to sleep. For three days we were engaged in completing the stockade, and when this was accomplished we filled mattresses with straw, and, having blankets to cover us, were more comfortable at night; and here we continued contented enough for about three months. While here, we were joined by the wife and children of our Colour-Sergeant, who had come from Paramatta with a draft of men who were to remain at Wellington.

On 27th February, after a dispute over compensation near the Maori village of Marae-nuku, about twelve miles from Wellington, some troops, who had not been informed of the peaceful solution to the dispute, burnt the village to the ground. When Te Rangihaeata heard of this, he embarked on a systematic campaign of retaliation against the farms in the valley. On 3rd March his men attacked Captain Eyeton's company of the 96th at Taita, who succeeded in driving off the dissidents. This attack gave Grey, who was now in overall command in the south, the opportunity to proclaim martial law and, at the same time, he strengthened the garrisons in the Hutt.

Te Rangihaeata was operating from bases to the west of the Hutt and receiving support from other dissident tribes in the Wanganui area, further up the west coast. Realising that Te

Rangihaeata's attention was fixed on the valley farms, Hulme decided to harass his rear and interrupt his communications with the Wanganui tribes, by landing a force at Porirua on the coast, under the command of Major Last of the 99th, consisting of two companies of that regiment, one of the 58th and a six-pounder gun detachment of the Royal Artillery. Unfortunately this strategem did not produce the results expected of it, as Last wasted so much time constructing a heavily defended base on the coast, thus allowing Te Rangihaeata as much time to build a *pa* close by, from which he could obstruct any moves made by Last. While this was going on Captain Russell's company began the construction of a road between Wellington and Porirua to open up the country. Friendly Maoris provided the labour, while the work had to be constantly guarded from sudden attacks by Russell's picquets. McKillop had the opportunity to observe the Maoris at work:

It was astonishing to see how anxiously the natives sought for engagements for this work. They were divided into parties, each under the superintendence of a chief of their own, who received two shillings a day, the labourers only getting one. They were paid regularly every Saturday, and it was amusing to see their delight when assembled for this purpose; it afforded them a never-ceasing topic of conversation and calculation as to how these earnings could be most advantageously laid out. This employment became very popular, and large parties came down the coast several hundred miles to offer their services: working and living together in their usual way, and the regular payment being the principal inducements, for they are naturally more mercenary than industrious: they delight in what horse-dealers in England call 'doing each other', and he who gets the worst of a bargain is sure to be laughed at by the others.

We found them very expert at felling trees, and were apt scholars in learning the use of the various tools necessary for such work, particularly carpenters'. I have seen them using the adze with great precision, steadying their work with the naked foot, which a false stroke would have cut to pieces. They also became clever at moving the huge trees, after they were felled, to the side of the road, as well as placing them across the streams to form bridges when necessary; using bars, levers, wedges, and other purchases necessary for such purposes.

Notwithstanding these diversions, the raids still continued in the Hutt, and in May Hinton found himself as one of a detachment of forty-eight under the command of Lieutenant George Page at Boulcott's Farm, the most advanced homestead up the valley. Most of Page's men were young soldiers, like Hinton, and his bugler, Drummer William Allen, was little more than a boy.[5] The farm was situated in a picturesque spot, with the river on one side, and its grasslands surrounded by forest on the other three. The buildings included Boulcott's cottage, where Page set up his headquarters, a few outhouses and a large barn, around which a stockade was built, loopholed for musketry. Most of the men were billeted in the barn, with a few in the outhouses, while near the river bank a guard tent was erected.

Just as dawn was breaking on 16th May, the sentry patrolling round the guard tent suddenly noticed that a group of bushes near the river bank seemed to have moved a little closer to him. Cocking his musket he watched the nearest bush closely, only to see a Maori face peering through the leaves. He took quick aim and fired but, before he could reload, the Maoris leaped from their cover and cut him down with tomahawks. The sound of his shot alerted the occupants of the guard tent. First out was Drummer Allen, raising his bugle to his lips to sound the alarm. As the first notes rang out across the clearing, a Maori almost severed his arm, causing him to drop the bugle. Despite being surrounded, he seized the bugle with his other hand and tried to continue the call, but the Maoris threw themselves on him, hacking at him until he was dead. Warned by the bugle, Page rushed out of the cottage with his soldier servant and another man straight into the midst of a group of the enemy. With sword and bayonet they tried to fight their way over to the stockade but were forced back to the cottage. He called out to another group of soldiers in one of the nearby outhouses, and together they made a concerted dash to the

[5] A proportion of a battalion's drummers were often boy soldiers, being usually soldiers' sons born and brought up in barracks.

stockade, where the rest of his command were already firing through the loopholes.

Hinton had had a narrow escape as he had just come off sentry duty before the Maoris attacked. He recalled:

I then went into the barn to sleep for a little while, but had not slept five minutes before I heard a shot. I called out to my companion, 'Look out, mate, there they are!' and out we rushed, and found about two hundred and fifty natives fording the river. Some had reached the picket tent and were firing through it.

We took up a position behind two trees that had been felled near the barn, and fired volleys into them as fast as we could. While we were firing, the wife of a volunteer, who was camping farther up the country, came out of the Colour-Sergeant's hut, and I called to her to go back or she would be killed. She answered, 'I'm all right; I suppose you want some more ammunition?' I replied, 'We shall very soon'. Whereupon she went into the barn, brought out a cask of cartridges, knocked the head off it, and handed the cartridges to the men, who kept up a steady fire until the Maories retreated across the river.

The fire-fight had continued for about an hour and a half, each section under its sergeant falling back into the barn to reload, while the remainder fired in turn from the loopholes, so that a continual volleying was kept up from all sides, holding the Maoris at bay. Eventually, with ammunition running low, Page decided to counter-attack. Leaving one section to hold the barn, he ordered the rest to fix bayonets, led them out of the stockade with a rush, and then, quickly forming a skirmishing line, advanced on the Maoris. As they went forward, they suddenly heard the sound of galloping horses and, in the best traditions of such frontier skirmishes, a party of Hutt Militia rode up to the rescue. The Maoris retreated across the river into the cover of the forest, from which they kept up a desultory fire for some time, but then made off.

When order had been restored, Hinton went to see if any of the guard had survived:

We found the guard tent riddled with shot; within it the men were all dead, and very much hacked about, except one who was unhurt, and who told us he had pretended to be dead, and that, although the natives had lifted up his eyelids and moved his arms, they had not discovered the fraud.

Poor Corporal Dockrill, in charge of the tent, had the top of his head cut off, and it was hanging down the back of his neck. Private Brett was also very much knocked about; and the bugler had three cuts on his right arm, four on his left, three gashes on his forehead, and his mouth cut from ear to ear, and, what's more, they stole his bugle, and we afterwards heard them sounding it in the wood.

In August, William Allen's bugle was recovered by another regiment in the Horokiwi valley, though whether it was ever returned to the 58th is uncertain. To commemorate his brave act, a record of his deed was inscribed on a silver bugle which was for ever after carried by a drummer of the 58th.

A month after the action at Boulcott's Farm another settler was murdered, and the next day a patrol under Captain Reed of the 99th was sent out to reconnoitre the area in which the incident had occurred. In the patrol was Lieutenant Herbert of the 58th. As the troops entered the forest, they were fired on by a party of Maoris lying in ambush. Herbert and four soldiers fell wounded. Reed ordered his men to take cover and return the fire, but the undergrowth was so dense, and the Maoris' positions so well concealed, that there was nothing for it but to retreat. As the troops fell back, Herbert, who had been hit in the shoulder, was inadvertantly left behind. Realising his dangerous predicament, he managed to clamber up a tree, where he remained until dark. Then, with the coast now clear, he painfully got himself down from his hiding place and made his lonely way across country to the nearest outpost.

After this incident Governor Grey decided to strike a major blow at the enemy's morale by arresting Te Rauparaha, Te Rangihaeata's uncle and chief. Hitherto the old man had not overtly assisted his nephew with his campaign, and indeed had even made approaches to Grey to assure him of his neutrality. However, Grey's suspicions had been aroused by rumours that Te Rauparaha had requested the Wanganui tribes to assist his nephew's operations, and, although he had no clear evidence against the old chief, he determined to forestall any mischief that might be afoot, by seizing him from his abode at Taupo, just north of Porirua harbour. Accordingly a plan was made, in which a major part was to be played by Midshipman McKillop.

McKillop had sailed with his ship to Porirua when Last's force had been transported there for the operations against Te Rangihaeata's rear. He had since been enjoying himself patrolling the coast line in order to prevent food supplies reaching Te Rangihaeata from the sea, and to forestall any attempts by the enemy to escape in their war canoes. He had been conducting his patrols in an eight-oared boat, but found this no match for the Maori canoes which held up to fifty men, most of them armed with double-barrelled shot guns. He therefore requested from his captain, Stanley of the *Calliope,* a more formidable vessel. 'A ship's long-boat was accordingly purchased, and converted into a gun-boat by the carpenters of the *Calliope* mounting a 12-pound carronade; which was brought round by the ship, and I was installed in my new command, Captain Stanley lending me a brass gun, which he had purchased for his own boat.' As crew he had eight sailors and two gunners from the Royal Artillery. To give his craft more protection, he lashed up his men's bedding in their hammocks and fastened them round the boat to make a bullet-proof breastwork.

He soon had an opportunity to test out his new command:

Having seen the natives through a glass in rather large numbers assembled on a point of land about a mile and a half from the camp, I thought it a good opportunity of trying if round shot and canister would compensate for the disparity in our numbers.

As we approached the point of land where I had observed the natives, it appeared to be quite deserted, not a living creature stirring; but knowing how well they lie in ambush, I pulled close in and raked the bushes with canister. The effect was like magic; upwards of a hundred tatooed faces were to be seen in a second in great confusion (for them), not having expected that our shot would have penetrated their cover. They, however, were not long recovering their usual coolness, and we soon found that they did not mean to allow us to have all the fighting on our side—every surrounding bush giving forth its fire; but they, finding the canister was too penetrating for the bush to afford them any shelter, showed boldly out, rushing into the water up to their waists, and keeping up an incessant and well-directed fire, nearly every shot striking the boat—many passing through although she was coppered nearly up to the gun-wale.

The water was very shallow, and we had approached so near the point that they made an attempt to board us, fancying we were aground. At this time, finding that I could not bring the carronade to bear so as to keep them all at bay, I directed the brass gun against a party who were making an attempt to board us on the quarter. Unfortunately the gun burst, knocking me down, blinding me for the minute, and also cutting my head with the lock, which, however, was all the harm it did. I soon washed the powder out of my eyes, and found that the artillerymen, under the direction of my coxswain, had checked the advance of the enemy with the other gun.

The maories had become so confident of their superiority, from their having formerly caused us to retreat, that they still persevered; but a few of the cautious ones took shelter behind the rocks. They must have sustained considerable loss by this time; and Rangihaeata was urging them to make another attempt to board us, he himself standing foremost and uttering yells of defiance. I now took my double-barrelled gun, and used it with some effect, keeping up a smart fire of canister at the same time, which caused them at length to retreat; which they did in very good order, taking their killed and wounded with them, and inviting us to follow them into the bush, using every provoking and insulting gesture and speech calculated to cause us to do so. I knew too well, however, the advantage of my position afloat, and contented myself with driving them into the bush, and then sending a few 12-pound shot after them, which brought down some young trees about their ears, but had not the desired effect of bringing them out to the attack again. We now took to our oars (which had been tossed up, one end resting in a socket at the bottom of the boat, to be out of the way of the working of the gun, and had been riddled with musket-balls), and pulled away, not having any of the crew wounded—which in New Zealand warfare gives a decided victory.

Adventures like this around Porirua had given McKillop an intimate knowledge of the coastline, its inhabitants, and of Te Rauparaha's own movements and circumstances, so that, when Grey determined on seizing the chief, it was McKillop who was entrusted with the task.

Accordingly it was arranged that we were to leave the ship before daylight the next morning, and land quietly on the rocks some little distance from the *pah* in which our treacherous allies [*sic*] lived; taking a mixed force of blue-jackets and soldiers, amounting to 200 men, to support us in the case of the natives rising before we had effected our object. It was the Governor's particular desire that we should not lay our hands on these men [three other chiefs of the Ngatitoa] until we had told them they were prisoners for treason, but on no account to let old Rauparaha escape.

I took Mr Dighton with me to act as interpreter, and four of our own men unarmed, giving them directions to seize upon the old chief as soon as he was made aware of the charge preferred against him, and to hurry him down to the boat before he could rouse his people—the principal object being to secure him. We landed at break of day; and while they were forming the troops on the beach, I with my small party ran on, as it was then light, fearing that conscious guilt might sharpen their ears and frustrate our plans. When we reached the *pah* not a soul was stirring, but our heavy steps soon brought some of the sleepers to the doors of their huts, knowing we were not of the bare-footed tribe. We could not wait to give any explanation, but pushed on to the hut which contained the object of our search, whose quick ears had detected strange footsteps; never having liked me, he did not look at all easy on perceiving who the intruder was, although his wife shewed no alarm, and received me with her usual salutation. Upon informing him that he was my prisoner, he immediately threw himself (being in a sitting posture) back into the hut, and seized a tomahɔwk, with which he made a blow at his wife's head, thinking she had betrayed him. I warded the blow with my pistol, and seized

him by the throat; my four men, immediately rushing in on
him, securing him by his arms and legs, started off as fast as
his violent struggles would allow of, which, for a man of his
age (upwards of 70), were almost superhuman. He roared
most lustily, 'Ngatitoa! Ngatitoa!' endeavouring to bring
them to the rescue; and in a few seconds every man was on
his legs, and came rushing to see what was the matter with
their chief; but the troops and the blue-jackets coming up at
the same time, and surrounding the *pah*, prevented any
attempt at a rescue, as he was already in the boat. His last
effort to free himself was fastening with his teeth on to my
coxswain's shoulder, who bore this piece of cannibalism
unflinchingly. I sent Mr Dighton off to the ship with him,
there not being much chance of his escaping from the boat,
particularly as he was informed that he would be shot if he
attempted to escape. I then returned to the *pah* to search for
arms and ammunition, and also to see if the other prisoners
had been secured. The interior of the *pah* presented a woeful
spectacle, the women all howling in chorus with the pigs
and children; the two latter being much knocked about in
the search for arms.

A quantity of arms and ammunition had been discovered,
evidence which, in view of Te Rauparaha's earlier assertions
that he had none, seemed to indicate that Grey's suspicions
were well founded. The old man was not, however, tried for
treason, but treated as a prisoner of war, later being sent to
Auckland, where he was allowed considerable liberty and,
like Waaka, developed a liking for British naval officers'
uniform in which he used to walk the streets of Auckland.
Te Rangihaeata was greatly disturbed by his uncle's arrest,
particularly as the old man had not heeded the warning his
nephew had given him, following a dream which prophesied
disaster. Rangihaeata therefore withdrew from his *pa* at
Porirua and moved with his warriors into the upper reaches of
the Horokiwi valley.
Last's force of 58th and 99th companies at Porirua was now
increased by the arrival of a company of a new regiment, the
65th (2nd Yorkshire North Riding), from Van Diemen's
Land. Together with detachments of seamen, the ubiquitous
McKillop among them, Hutt Militia and Wellington Armed

Police, he now mustered some 250 bayonets. To these were added 150 of Te Rauparaha's subjects, who decided to change sides and promised their assistance against their dissident fellow tribesmen. They were hastily served out with blue serge blouses, emblazoned with a large 'V.R.' in white on back and front, to ensure easy recognition by the British forces. On 5th August Last set out in pursuit of Te Rangihaeata.

The route up the Horokiwi was, according to McKillop,

very bad, even the natives slipping down in passing along the sides of some of the rivers, the wet weather making it worse than usual. Our path lay through the most dense wood it has ever been my fate to tread, being frequently crossed by small rivers, and fallen trees of such size as to make it necessary to change the direction of the road to avoid them. It was as much as the men could do to carry one day's provisions with their arms and ammunition.

At the end of the first day's march camp was made at the foot of a steep hill, on top of which some of the enemy were ensconced. McKillop wrote:

The ground was dreadfully wet, but by lighting fires and erecting huts, which we smoke-dried, we managed to pass the night more comfortably than could have been expected, considering that it was the depth of winter, miserably cold, and pouring with rain; our long walk also having made us quite equal to eat a good supper, had we been fortunate enough to have been provided with any. However, as it was, I marched out with a small party of sailors to take my post, an outlying picquet, having been previously refreshed with a small glass of spirits given me by one of the officers of the 65th, who was lucky enough to be provided with a bottle: and I must say I never felt more grateful for Dutch courage than on this occasion. We planted our sentries behind the trees right round our position, fearing that we might be surprised by the enemy before daylight, our post not being by any means a favourable one.

The following morning a patrol of the friendly Ngatitoa under Pauha, a relative of Te Rangihaeata, made contact at the top of the hill with Rangihaeata himself and a group of his warriors. Somewhat surprisingly the encounter went off quite amicably, Pauha pleading with his kinsman to give up those who had murdered settlers, and Rangihaeata refusing. The meeting ended, according to McKillop, 'by the two chiefs rubbing noses'.

Our two friendly tribes [he went on] now assembled for a war dance, previous to setting out to attack the enemy; for although it was the wish of the officer commanding to keep his movements as quiet as possible, he could not persuade our dark-skinned allies to dispense with this noisy and usual practice, although it gave good notice of our intentions to all within hearing. Several of us joined in this exhibition, much to the delight of our maori friends, who immediately advanced up the hill, dividing themselves into two parties, each under the command of their own chief, acting, however, under the orders of a European interpreter, who was, in fact, the captain of the party. After climbing the hill with great difficulty, but without molestation, although the men were necessarily much exposed, we began to think that they did not mean to dispute our further progress; we advanced a long way without seeing any sign of them. Our native allies, however, proceeded very cautiously after we reached the summit of the hill, crawling on their stomachs, and peering into every bush in the most searching manner, evidently expecting an ambuscade.

We advanced in this tedious mode for several hundred yards, until they discovered a breastwork thrown across the very top of the hill at the narrowest part, composed of several large trees which had been felled and thrown across; with a small clearing in front, which prevented our approaching unseen.

An exchange of musketry now ensued, chiefly between the friendly Maoris and their kinsmen behind the barricade. Pauha's men were unwilling to advance across the cleared field of fire immediately in front of the defences, and the narrowness of the track and thickness of the forest on either side did not permit the British regulars to deploy. It was clear that Te Rangihaeata held every advantage of the ground.

Boulcott's Farm and stockade in the Hutt Valley. (Water colour by G. H. Page)

Wanganui in 1847. (Artist unknown)

Major Last's column confronted by Te Rangihaeata's barricade across the track at the top of Horokiwi hill, 6th August 1846. The troops in the foreground are the 99th with two sailors (dark clothes) brandishing their cutlasses. (Water colour by G. H. Page)

Ensign Blackburn of the 99th, a very popular young officer who was acting as Last's brigade-major, was killed, and although the Grenadiers of the 99th pleaded to be allowed to charge to avenge their officer, Last was not prepared to accept the loss of life which would inevitably follow. Realising that he had no hope of dislodging the enemy from their strong position without artillery support, he ordered the naval detachment to return to Porirua, and escort Captain Henderson of the Royal Artillery with his troop of mortars up to the force.

Although the seamen had only five or six miles to cover on foot, with a further mile and a half in boats before Porirua was reached, this was no easy undertaking. Night was falling, the terrain had proved arduous enough in daylight, and the mortars and ammunition would have to be carried on the men's backs. McKillop's account captures vividly the difficulties of that night march:

> We started just before dark, and not with a very pleasant prospect before us, being both tired and disheartened with our day's work. We met the Governor coming up as we left the camp, and soon after Dr Ross, the assistant-surgeon of the *Calliope*, who had marched up alone, with his blanket and case of instruments on his back. From him we learnt that several soldiers, who had fallen lame on their way up, were lying about in the wood, and, unless some assistance was rendered them, would have to remain there all night. We heard the firing on the hill for an hour after we had left it, and feared that the rebels must have been driven from their temporary *pah*, and would probably retreat the same way that we were going. Darkness soon overtook us, which would have rendered it quite impossible to distinguish friends from foes, had we met any of the latter. We could not even see the blade of a sword held close to the face. We travelled in single file, having a maori in front to show us the path. The men were cautioned, when they found themselves off the track (which they would soon discover, as the mud was nowhere so bad out of it), to stop immediately, and call out 'Halt'; we should otherwise soon have separated, it being quite impossible to follow each other regularly over such ground. At length the repeated shouts of

'Halt', in all directions, made it most tedious, especially as we kept halting on our faces every now and then, through the assistance of some stump or bush, and not unfrequently in the river, which not being deep enough to break the fall, made it very dangerous. We travelled in this way for about an hour, until those in front getting tired at the continual halts, and fearing we should have to remain all night in this wood, pushed on, leaving every one to make the best of his own way; of which I for one was very glad, having had several tumbles over my leading file, or the man before me, whom I soon passed on learning the last order; and, with the exception of coming in contact with a tree or two, which made my nose bleed, I soon reached the clear space about a mile from the beach, where our optics were again called into requisition.

We mustered our party on reaching the boats and found there were many absentees; but leaving one boat for the stragglers, we pushed on and reached the camp, half famished and caked with mud, where I discovered I had had a musket-ball through my cap. The other boat soon followed us, having brought all the party except the drummer of marines, who had not turned up when they left the place of embarkation. Having refreshed ourselves with a good meal and four hours' sleep, we again started for the camp, taking with us the two small mortars, every man carrying three shells and a fifteen-pound bag of powder; our men taking it turn and turn about with the artillery-men to carry the heavy parts of the apparatus; the officers themselves each having a bag of powder to carry, and frequently a musket or two belonging to the men. We were obliged to make frequent halts, and had the greatest difficulty in ascending some of the steep and slippery hills, the men not unfrequently coming down with their loads, which rolling to the bottom of the hill, gave us the extra work of taking them up a second time. We had a few shot-boxes of shells, some of which went to pieces from the repeated tumbles; and we had to divide them amongst us, carrying them in the bosoms of our blue frocks. Thus loaded we reached the camp, where we were greeted with three hearty cheers from the combined forces, our little iron friends making us a very welcome reinforcement.

As soon as the two mortars had been set up, fire was opened on Te Rangihaeata's position. The dense foliage of the tall trees made it difficult to observe the fall of shot, but McKillop crawled forward through the bush until he could watch the *pa*, and from that position called back corrections to the mortar-men. Despite this harassing bombardment, the enemy continued to fire back, and any movement into the open ground in front of the barricades drew such a volume of musketry, that any attempt to launch an assault must have incurred heavy casualties. Moreover, Last guessed that, even if a succesful attack could be made, Te Rangihaeata would not await the ensuing hand-to-hand encounter but would simply retreat further into the forest. In addition, Last was running short of supplies and his line of communications to Porirua was threatened by flooding, so that, when the friendly Maoris offered to remain on the position and endeavour either to capture Te Rangihaeata or force him to fly further inland, he decided, after consulting the Governor, to withdraw.

It was with some relief that the troops, tired and wet through as they were, fell back to their camping ground at the foot of the hill where, McKillop wrote,

We were agreeably surprised to find that the day's rations had been issued, some of the force having been three days on very short allowance; the wet and the cold, as well as the fatigue we had undergone, making our gill of spirits most acceptable. There were many extraordinary modes of cooking invented this night—such as frying pork in a tin drinking-cup, grilling pigeons on ramrods, boiling water in a glass bottle, and such like. Hunger being the best sauce, enabled us to make a hearty meal; and we soon forgot our little privations, and should have been jolly enough, had not the loss of poor Blackburn, who had been the gayest amongst us on the last night of our being together in this place, cast a gloom over our little party. We stretched ourselves out, warning the long-legged ones to keep their feet out of the fire. We were disturbed, however, by the groans of an unfortunate one of that species, who in his sleep had stretched himself beyond the accomodation which our dwelling afforded; consequently, thrusting his feet into the fire, had burnt his boots, and partly roasted his pedal digits before he was awakened from his sound sleep. Early in the morning we retraced our steps over the vile roads, taking back with us the mortars which had cost us so much labour to bring up. When we reached our camp at Porirua I took off my clothes, for the first time for a week, on going to bed; and my hut here, rough as it was, appeared quite a palace after my late muddy couch.

When the whole force was back at Porirua, information was received that Te Rangihaeata had abandoned his position and moved away, far up the valley. Though he would never come to terms with the white man, he was no longer a threat. He found an inaccessible spot, surrounded by flax-swamps and lagoons, where, with some hundred devoted followers, he constructed a *pa* in which he was to remain until he died, in 1856, after taking a cold bath to cure an attack of the measles. Rather than compromise, he chose isolation. Though he had lost his lands, he had fought strenuously for his beliefs and his rights, and had never been defeated.

With Te Rangihaeata's removal from the scene of operations, peace returned to the Hutt Valley. As the south and the north were now pacified, it seemed as though the war was over, and that Grey could begin the task of reconstructing the country and persuading Maori and settler to live peaceably together. However, events were to prove that the soldiers' task was not yet completed.

10

Now the War is Over

So now the war is over and we have saved our lives
So let us join Drinking to our sweethearts and our wives
                                    Alexander Whisker.

WHILE ORDER WAS BEING RESTORED IN THE SOUTH, THE GARRISON at Victoria on the Bay of Islands had been settling down in their camp beside the shore. The men lived in tents, seven being provided for each company, while the colour-sergeants enjoyed the greater comfort of one apiece. The officers all lodged in a large but rather dilapidated house. Apart from finding a daily guard of a sergeant, two corporals and eighteen men, and constructing a breastwork to the rear of the camp, there was not a lot to be done, and on many days Whisker could only record, 'Nothing extra'.

Towards the end of January 1846 he described an event which demonstrated the close feeling of comradeship that had developed between the soldiers and sailors during the campaign in the north, when H.M.S. *North Star* left the Bay for Sydney, en route for England.

At 30 minutes Past 6 oclock P.M. the *North [Star]* sailed for Sydney, the sailors of the *Race horse* gieving hir 3 cheers. The sailors returned it to them. The *North Star* sailors expecting to get some from us no sooner came opesite our camp than they mounted the rigging and weated. We then give them 3 cheers which they returned. We then give them 3 more. Not more than about a dozen of the old Campainers that landed first in the Bay was here to see hir start out of it for England, but every [one] regarded hir as an old friend leaveing, as hir crew both officers and men acting like brothers and being through all the campayne together.

By the end of February Bridge's leave was up, and it was time for him to depart from Auckland and return, with his wife and child, to the Bay of Islands, where he was to assume command of the garrison. Doubtless a little spoiled by his month of domestic bliss and newly-found paternity, he was a bit glum about it:

Embarked about noon, Lieut-Col Wynyard also accompanying us. Had a very delightful passage to the Bay, reached it at about 2 or 3 the following day. Found the detachment camped on a point of land opposite to Kororareka belonging to a Mr Busby named Victoria, whose house, or what remained of it, was occupied by the officers. It was in a most delapidated state, without doors or windows and the roof not watertight. However such as it was, I had to inhabit, three rooms, there being no other house in the neighbourhood nearer than the missionary settlement at Paihia. Too far for me to live away from my men, and where I was refused accomodation for my wife and child for a few nights only by the Archdeacon's wife, although there was a house belonging to the mission lying empty at the time.

On 1st April Whisker found himself in trouble, but on the same day regained the coveted post of officer's servant, which he had lost the previous May, after being charged with drunkenness:

I was Brought up before the Major and got 3 days Grog stopped for not cutting Private Wm Tanners hair according to orders, and the same day Captn Thompson sent for me to go back as servant to him Which I agreed, Private Painter being sick and uneable to perform that duty. I went to him on the same day, takeing all things over as they stood without aney inspection.

Soon after, he recorded some fun he and the other officers' servants had at the expense of a rather simple soldier:

A most laughable thing took Place. Private George Creacy came a corting to Mary Ann Johnston. He seen hir first on the Preivous night at the Millatorry theatre. He fell Desparately in love with hir, he thought she was the same with him. In the middle of the Day he come up to the kitchen. He sat down to Smoke But never Spoke to any one though he sat for an hour and then went home. In the evening he came up Drest in his Shell and white trousers With a Pocket hankerchief which he carried in his hand. He came in and sat down on my bed telling me and at the same time showing me a hankerchief he had bought for hir between his visits. As he belonged to my company I thought to be his second. I told him he should not need to be so backward as he had been in the fore Part of the [war?]. He promised to speak to hir if i would only call hir in to my room Which I done without Delay. I kept hir engaged alongside of him but the Poor fool could not find utterance for one single word but sat looking in hir face, and I did not think it Propper to detain hir aney longer so she ran off laughing at his folly. I told him he was only makeing a fool of the thing and urged him as much as posable to speak to hir at least but all in vain. We then came into the kitchen and he stood with his Back to the fire smoking his Pipe. We then thought it time to have some fun with him. We told him he had courted long enough to begin to think of marrage. He said yes. We then asked him to appoint the Wedding Day. He left it to me and the Majors orderly Hanah. We appointed Thusday the 12th giveing them 10 days to get ready. The arangements being made were as follows. The ten servants was to save a Bottle of Rum each before the wedding Day. None to be Preasant but the servants.

At this point the story becomes a little hard to follow as Whisker seems somewhat carried away by the hilarity of the situation, but the implication is that poor Creacy was to be duped at his wedding by replacing Mary Ann with 'Jerry Sullivan Drest in womans Clothes as he was slender enough to act that part in aney Place But bed'. What follows immediately is missing—perhaps Whisker cut it out later thinking the humour too broad—but in the rest of the tale, the tongue-tied Creacy still maintains his silence and, despite the teasing of the other servants and of Mary Ann, or possibly the disguised Jerry Sullivan, goes off 'in good hopes of embracing hir as his own Mary Ann on teusday week'.

To ensure the peace was kept, the officers maintained good relations with the Maoris, treating the chiefs as equals and entertaining them in their quarters. Whisker was on duty on one such occasion:

> I had the honour to attend the 2 rival Chiefs at Breakfast in my masters Room Thomathy Waka and Kowitta and there friends. My Master and 12 Maories sat Down together. Some of them would not sit down only on the floor and not one of them would use knife or fork but sat on the floor and tore it with there teeth. As soon as Breakfast was over they retired to there Respective homes.

Now that there were no field operations to keep the men busy and time hung heavy on their hands, the harsh peacetime discipline had to be enforced to deter men from crime. For an unspecified offence, Whisker records Private John Macateer being awarded 100 lashes and forty days' hard labour, a severe punishment which had an unfortunate sequel: 'After comeing out of Imprisonment his Comrades was glad to see him at Liberty once more. He had a few extra glasses of grog and after that he went to have some Dinner When he Was unfortunately choked with a small piece of Beef and Potatoes. He died about 5 oclock in the evening.' Whisker adds: 'He was opened and a corranors Inquest held on him.' On the same day Whisker himself, perhaps grieved by the wretched Macateer's untimely end, overstepped the bonds of discipline, and again lost his job as officer's servant.

> At 6 oclock PM I was attending Dinner when the Interpreter Hanson gave me some old slack jaw and I shoved my fist to his nose and though a stone weightier than Me, he had not the courage to face me like a man to take me up, But Run off and Reported me to the Major. I was then put in the guard room and lay in there to the next day.
>
> I was Brought up before the Major and Reported. Hanson like a true born Maorie come up and Prosecuted me. The Major told me that Mister Hanson was very much my supieriour and although he come to us With his hair growing through the crown of his hat and his toes growing through his Boots, he was now Mr Hansen and far a soldiers Supeariour. I was sent to my Duty but got no Punishment.

Apart from trying to maintain tactful relations between the soldiers and the local Maoris, Bridge found life at Victoria so uneventful that, from 4th March, he had nothing of interest to record in his journal except that:

> My men were getting sickly for want of proper quarters and covering since the wet weather commenced. Therefore I applied to have them removed from Victoria, and having obtained leave to do so, and made an agreement for the time of some stores at the Wahapu, I moved the detachment over, where the officers also were enabled to get comfortable quarters. Here I commenced clearing away the thick bush that surrounded the post, and to erect a field work for its proper defence.

Bridge's military sense was clearly unimpaired by Despard's derision of field defences the previous September.

The detachment moved quarters in July, but with the continued lack of activity came further acts of indiscipline. Bridge saw no reason to record these in his journal, though doubtless they caused him constant irritation and concern. Whisker, on the other hand, noted them all down, and the nature of the offences indicates the boredom and frustration felt by soldiers confined to a lonely outpost with nothing to occupy their minds.

> 2nd September. 4 of our men viz Kemp Hunt Porter and hyde Deserted from us, there being an american Whealer in the harbour. The Major had a search aboard of hir. They could not be found. He then ordered the ship to be stormed which was done. There being some Maories Women on Board, they discovered on Two of them hyde and porter. They were brought back the afternoon of the 3rd.

> 4th. Hunt and Kemp came home. They were at the sea side weating to be taken on board of the Whealer. The Whaler sailed out at ½ past ? a.m. and left them behind. They had to return to the camp at 9 oclock When they were confined.

Porter and Hyde received sentences of nine and five months' imprisonment respectively, but Hunt and Kemp got off quite lightly with twenty-eight and twenty-one days in the cells apiece.

I. Glen was tried on the 8th September for being absent and Stealing £1.4.6. from Prt Wm Tanner. [He] got 150 lashes.

On the night of the first of October Stanley was confined for striking Wm Surrey and found Drunk when going to be tried a Regtl Court Martial. He was sentenced 8 months hard labour.

2nd October. Corpl Monaghan was put under an arrest for being corpl of the guard when Stanley got Drunk under his Command when on guard. Corpl Monaghan was tried and honourably acquitted.

Patrick McKiernan got confined for going to shoot Sargant I. McConnell of No 3 Company.

Strangely Whisker does not record McKiernan's fate, which must have been severe, although next month he notes: 'Sargant McConnell was put under arrest for not confineing Privat Hallam when drinking in the canteen by orders of Mrs White' (probably the canteen manageress). Captain Thompson seems to have been unlucky in his choice of servants, for he again had to appoint a new one when Whisker's replacement, Morney, 'was confined Drunk and absent for Muster Parade, Morney got sent his Duty with 7 days [extra] Drill and 10 days [loss of] grog'.

    While the operations against the Maoris had been in train, the soldiers had remained in good spirits, despite the dangers and deprivations involved, and breaches of discipline had been few. But now the familiarity of their environment, the sense of being cut off, if not forgotten, the monotonous routine of guards and fatigues, and their rough-and-ready accommodation, all conspired to make them heartily sick of this remote garrison, and they longed to return to more congenial surroundings. It was therefore with thankfulness that, towards the end of November, they greeted the news of their relief by a detachment of the 65th, and their return to Auckland, en route for Sydney.

    On 27th November Bridge's detachment sailed into Auckland, where they found the rest of the regiment packing up and making preparations to embark. By 2nd December all was ready and that night Bridge recorded:

> A ball was given this evening by the ladies of Auckland to the Officers of the 58th Regt on their departure from the Colony. It was very well got up and attended, and dancing kept up till the hour fixed on for embarkation, when the 58th bugler sounded the assembly and officers' call in the ball room. The ladies pelted him out of the supper room with tartlets.

The next day he noted with relief, 'the Regiment made a splendid embarkation at half past 5 a.m., I hope to take their final leave of New Zealand'. Contrary winds prevented their departure, and consequently 'a large party of the Auckland people came off to dinner, after which dancing was kept up on the poop for half the night', but on the 6th the ship sailed with, said Whisker, 'a great bale of light hearts on board', Sydney was reached on 18th December, and the men were soon back in the old quarters they had quitted some twenty months before, in time to celebrate Christmas and the New Year. Whisker made the most of it. Reunited with his wife Flora, he made merry at the wedding of Corporal Sutherland and Mrs Yetts, whose husband had been killed at Okaihau, and, as the year changed, he wrote cheerfully: 'I kept on the Spree all day and Paid a man to go on guard for me. I spent a happy New year, the happiest I had spent for some time and got into no trouble.'

Not all the 58th were able to celebrate their return from the campaign. Although the area around Wellington had been pacified, the three companies of the regiment, which had been engaged against Te Rangihaeata, had been retained in garrison in the south. Now, while their comrades were sailing back to New South Wales, Captain J. H. Laye received orders to move his company, made up to 160 rank and file, together with a Royal Artillery detachment of two twelve-pounders, from Wellington to Wanganui, some 120 miles up the west coast. On 9th December he and his men embarked on H.M.S. *Calliope*.

Wanganui was a small settlement of the New Zealand

Company which had been founded in 1841, and by 1846 contained 200 settlers. Following the troubles in the north and in the Hutt Valley, they felt isolated, insecure and outnumbered by the Maoris who inhabited the surrounding countryside and the upper reaches of the Wanganui River. Some of these Maoris had assisted Te Rangihaeata in the Hutt, and, in the course of the operations there, some had been captured and put on trial for rebellion. One, Te Wareaitu, had been hanged and others sentenced to life imprisonment. The failure of their campaign in the Hutt and the treatment of their kinsmen had angered the Wanganui Maoris, whose animosity became centred more on the soldiers than on the settlers. This group looked for leadership to Topine Te Mamaku, a tall, well-built and intelligent chief, who came from the upper Wanganui, and who, with his followers, was more than ready to test his strength against the white soldiers. Thus on the one hand there was the small group of settlers, nervous for their safety and demanding military protection for their settlement, and, on the other, the warlike Te Mamaku and his followers, to whom the sight of a military garrison at Wanganui would be a provocation, and the very spark needed to set off open rebellion. In addition, there were other Maoris about Wanganui, probably the majority, who, if not actually supporting the Government as being in their best interests, had no wish to enlist with Te Mamaku. As many of them were related to Te Mamaku's followers, they were in a difficult position, running the risk of either being regarded by the Government as satellites of Te Mamaku, or inciting the wrath of the latter for reneging on his cause. The Governor was therefore faced with the choice of sending troops to protect the settlers and friendly Maoris, but thereby incurring the risk of an uprising, or leaving the settlement defenceless, which might also tempt the hostile elements to action, and allowing his authority to be defied. He decided that the settlers must have the protection they were craving, and that any dissidents at Wanganui must be brought to heel, by force if necessary. With the Hutt now pacified, troops could be spared, so Laye was ordered up to Wanganui.

Aboard the *Calliope* was Midshipman McKillop, who described the rather hit-and-miss landing of the troops:

We proceeded to look for Wanganui, which place was very

indistinctly laid down on our chart; and not having enough water to keep very close to the shore, we were rather puzzled to find the entrance to the river off which we were to anchor. Old Rauparaha, however, seeing we were at fault, pointed out the hills immediately over the town: with this landmark we stood in, and discovering a small vessel close in shore, apparently standing away from us, we fired a gun, and hoisted the pilot jack. This not being taken notice of, and the captain being particularly anxious to land the troops before dark, fired a shot, which passed so close to her that they immediately went about and stood towards us. On nearing us, we discovered her to be a colonial smack, with the police magistrate and several other of the Wanganui settlers, who had come out on purpose to meet us.

We anchored about four miles from the shore, and commenced at once disembarking the troops and guns, finding the smack of great use. I was sent in the pinnace with a party of soldiers, taking one of the colonial sailors as a pilot for crossing the bar, which is the only thing which prevents this river from being the best harbour on this coast. We entered safely—not, however, without having run considerable risk in coming through the breakers in an overloaded boat. We were told that it was highly probable that our landing might be opposed; but having a clear space on each side of the river, and seeing no one, we did not wait for the other boats, but landed our party and returned to the ship for another load, passing the smack on her way with the remainder of the soldiers. I came in a second time with provisions, and had a hard pull up the river against a strong tide, which made it very late before we reached the town; there I found Captain Laye and his party on the look-out for me, his men not having any rations that day, nor indeed himself and brother officers, who had been located in the school-house. After unloading the boat, I found it too late to return to the ship, and anchored for the night, going on shore myself to endeavour to procure a small quantity of spirits for my boat's crew, who had had a hard day's work and no grog. I found that no one was licensed to sell this luxury by retail, although there was plenty of it in the place. Thinking this rather hard, considering the mission we had come on, I pointed out the probability of the dissatisfaction such treatment would give to my captain, and succeeded at last in getting their coveted gill. I was comfortably housed myself till daylight, when I returned to the ship.

Once all were ashore, Laye took over the Commercial Hotel for his troops, and, assisted by the technical expertise of Lieutenant T. B. Collinson, Royal Engineers, began the construction of a fort overlooking the settlement. As this fort was the first of its kind to be built in New Zealand, and was to be of vital importance in the months that followed, it merits some description. The site chosen by Laye and Collinson was a sandy hill, standing some seventy feet above the Wanganui River, at the north end of the settlement. An area measuring sixty by thirty yards was marked out and enclosed by a stockade, constructed of timbers, nine inches thick, which were sunk three or four feet in the ground, leaving a wall eight feet high; the tops of the timbers were sharpened to a point. These upright logs were braced by two horizontal rails on the inside and loopholes were cut all round the perimeter. Within the stockade, two wooden blockhouses were constructed at either end, each having two storeys, the upper overhanging the lower by three feet. The larger, built to accommodate eighty soldiers, consisted of two parts, one measuring sixty by twenty feet at ground floor level, the other, at right angles to it, twenty by twenty feet. The smaller, holding twenty soldiers, measured forty by twenty feet. The lower storey of each blockhouse was ten feet high and made of twelve-inch square upright timbers, placed six feet apart, the intervals being filled with six-inch square horizontal timbers, the whole wall being lined with one-inch thick boarding. The upper storey was eight feet high, and the two storeys were divided by a floor two and a half inches thick. The projecting floor of the upper storey was hinged between the joists, so that it could be raised to enable the occupants to fire downwards in defence of the lower storey. Finally, both storeys had horizontal slits, four feet long and six inches wide, with glass frames and shutters on the outside, to serve either as windows or loopholes. At either end of the fort an embrasure was made for the twelve-pounders.

The construction work took some time to complete, and it was not until the beginning of April that the troops could move in; Laye named it 'The Rutland Stockade'. From this position and another stockade near the south end of the settlement, Lay kept a careful watch over the township and the surrounding countryside, aided by a gunboat patrolling the Wanganui River. Initially there was little to disturb the garrison, but Laye demanded a constant state of readiness from his men, and took every precaution against being surprised. Joseph Hinton, who was present, recalled that, 'whenever the men were allowed to go into town, we used to hoist a black flag with skull and cross-bones, and if we saw the natives assembling, we lowered the flag as a signal for our men to return'.

Isolated incidents showed that tension was mounting and that, sooner or later, something would happen to spark off an uprising. When it came, it was little short of ludicrous. On 16th April, a midshipman named Crozier from the gunboat was joking with a Maori, when he accidentally discharged his firearm, wounding the Maori in the cheek. The man belonged to a group which was friendly to the Europeans, and although he spread the word that it had only been an accident, others decided that this spilling of blood by a white man demanded *utu*. Two days later an outlying farm belonging to a settler, J. A. Gilfillan, was attacked by five Maoris. Gilfillan and his sixteen-year-old daughter escaped but his wife and three other children were murdered. It was believed that this attack had been carried out, not by relatives of the wounded Maori, but by others who hoped to incriminate those who were friendly with the Europeans. However the plan miscarried, for the five murderers were caught and delivered up to Laye by the very Maoris whom it was hoped to incriminate.

Laye decided to waste no time and promptly set up a court-martial composed of his four subalterns. They found the accused men guilty and sentenced four of them to be hanged and the fifth, on account of his youth, to be transported for life. On the 26th the sentence was carried out, as Hinton described:

The carpenters who belonged to us were set to work to make a scaffold, and I remember they finished it on the day before the execution was to take place, it being fitted with a cross-beam, a drop, a bolt, and all other necessaries. My old comrade, Shipley, was told off as executioner, and we were formed up into a hollow square to witness the execution. The friendly natives crowded round to see the sight, and the enemy were on the hills on the other side of the river in good numbers. We carried our loaded muskets, and the gun in the stockade was loaded with canister.

The missionary accompanied the men on to the scaffold, and Shipley pinioned their arms and legs and placed white caps over their eyes. When the commanding officer gave the signal, Shipley came down the steps and drew the bolt, and the three [sic] men went down together.

There was a lot of shouting from the enemy on the hills, and they sent in a few men with a white flag to ask for the bodies, but this was refused, and they were all buried in one grave just outside the stockade.

Looking over the walls of the stockade on the next day, Hinton saw that:

the natives had erected a flagstaff on a hill about a thousand yards from us; and our officer told one of the artillerymen, who was a wonderfully good marksman, to take careful aim at it and knock it over, which he did. Soon afterwards we saw it go up again, and the same man brought it down again with another shot. A third time it went up, and a third time it was brought down. Soon afterwards we saw a native moving about among some flax, that grew in a swamp at some considerable distance from us, watching our move-ments. Our gunner was ordered to pick him off, and some friendly natives on the following day found the man com-pletely cut in halves.

There was little doubt that further *utu* would be exacted following the execution, so Laye sensibly asked Wellington for reinforcements and enjoined even greater watchfulness on his men. All troops were now confined to the stockade, and Hinton recalled the fate of a soldier named Sculthorp, who disobeyed this order. This man

had bought a fowling-piece at Wellington, and often had permission to go into the bush when the coast was clear. When the order was that nobody was to leave the stockade,

Te Rangihaeata, nephew of Te Rauparaha, who started the Wairau Massacre and led the rebellion in the south of North Island. (Drawing by C. D. Barraud)

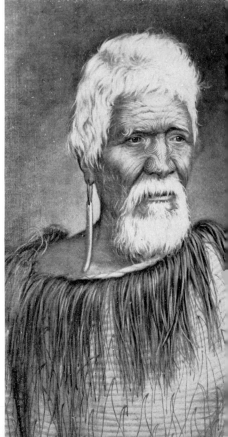

Topine Te Mamaku, who mounted the attacks against the British garrison at Wanganui. (A portrait done in later life by Gottfried Lindauer)

Captain J. H. Laye, 58th Regiment, builder of the Rutland Stockade at Wanganui, whose 'firmness' and 'gallant conduct' saved the settlement from attack on 19th May 1847.

Lt-Col W. A. McCleverty, 48th Regiment and Deputy-Quartermaster-General at Wellington, who commanded the force at Wanganui at the Battle of St John's Wood, 19th July 1847. He wears a forage cap and dark blue undress frock coat. Both drawings are by J. A. Gilfillan, the settler at Wanganui whose family were murdered by Maoris.

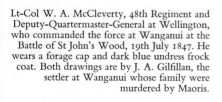

he asked me to let him out, as I was in charge of the gate, and on my refusing, he went away and got over the breast-work unperceived, and a little while after we heard from a friendly native that he had been killed. We sent out half a dozen of them with a stretcher, and when they returned, and I lifted the blanket that covered him, I was horrified to find that the blacks had cut his tongue out and scooped out his eyes.

On 3rd May Laye's anxiety was eased by the arrival of Captain J. P. Hardy and his company of the 58th. Although Laye was the senior of the two, Hardy was the older man and, with eight more years' service than his superior, the poorer. This discrepancy between their circumstances might have adversely affected their relationship, and thus the unity of the command, which devolved on Laye by right of seniority, but fortunately it does not seem to have done so, and Hardy's reinforcement of two subalterns, three sergeants and 100 rank and file brought a much-needed increase to Laye's slender resources.

Hardy's arrival was timely, for large bodies of Maoris now began assembling near Wanganui. Although they kept out of sight, the sentries on the walls of the stockade could see pillars of smoke rising from plundered homesteads, which had been hastily abandoned by their owners. In order to protect the settlers, Laye asked three of the townsfolk to fortify their houses, and gave orders that, in the event of an attack, all the civilians should assemble at these houses. To supplement his two companies of infantry, he issued firearms to some of the settlers who volunteered their services. The gunboat was on the river, sentries were posted to watch the approaches, and all troops not on duty were at immediate readiness to man their alarm posts. All they could do now was to wait.

The morning of 19th May began in the usual way. At first light, the troops were mustered to man their defences, ready to repel a sudden dawn attack. The gunners loaded and prepared their twelve-pounders for action; the infantry stood to their loopholes, peering out as the landscape took shape in the early morning light, watching for the first signs of any movement on the surrounding hills. Laye moved calmly round his command, having a word with a subaltern here and a sergeant there, and all the time wondering what was brewing in the woods of the hinterland. However, with not a sign or sound of a Maori to disturb the peaceful scene before them, the men were presently dismissed to their breakfasts, leaving only the sentries at their look-outs, and the normal daily routine of the garrison began.

Suddenly, in mid-morning, a sentry spotted Maoris in large numbers, some crowning the hill-tops, others running for the settlement. The bugles blew the urgent summons of the 'Alarm', the troops rushed to their posts, and a party of armed settlers galloped out to skirmish with the leading groups of the enemy. Down in the town the inhabitants ran to the fortified houses.

The Maoris pressed forward, forcing the mounted settlers to retire, and, covered by fire from the hills, seized some outlying houses and opened fire on the fort. The gunboat and twelve-pounders returned the fire, and as soon as groups of the enemy got within small arms range, the 58th began firing volleys from the stockade. The Maoris came on with great gallantry, but, although they got to within thirty yards of the stockade, the defenders' fire was too effective for them either to assault the defences, or to bypass the fort and attack the civilians in the settlement. Laye and Hardy kept their men to their work, and down on the river Lieutenant Holmes' gunboat provided effective flanking fire. All day the fire fight went on, but though the attack was being held, Laye could not afford to denude his defences of men to launch a counter-attack. A stalemate therefore ensued until, with the coming of darkness, the Maoris pulled back, the cease-fire was sounded, and the weary troops, grimy with powder, their arms and shoulders aching from the constant reloading and firing, were at last able to relax, cook a meal and get some rest.

During the night Laye decided to seize two of the outlying houses from which the Maoris had kept up such a heavy fire. An hour before dawn, two parties sallied out, the gunboat having moved up to cover them. They crept forward in the darkness, expecting any moment to be fired on, but when they reached the houses, they found the enemy had gone.

When day broke, the Maoris were observed still occupying the surrounding hills but making no attempt to renew the attack. Giving orders for them to be kept under observation,

Laye sat down in his quarters to recount the details of the action for the officer commanding at Wellington.

Upper Stockade, Wanganui,
20th May 1847.

Sir,

I have the honor to report, that yesterday morning 19th May, between 11 and 12 o'clock, large bodies of Natives were observed approaching the town in different directions. Some of the Armed Settlers, about 20, kept a portion in check for a short time but were obliged to retire on the town.

The Enemy had possession of all the hills, and several clayhouses about the outskirts of the town which afforded them strong natural breastworks, and kept up a fire for 5 hours at the Upper Stockade, but principally on the Town Stockade under command of Captain Hardy 58th Regiment, and the Gun-boat under Lieutenant Holmes R.N., H.M. Ship *Calliope*, which he had moved down the river to flank the Town Stockade. Several shot and shells with musketry were fired from the Upper and Town Stockades, and Gun-boat, without being able to dislodge them.

From the numerous detached parties of the Enemy, they being about 300 strong, with large parties in reserve, I was utterly unable to send a sufficient number of men to drive them out and hold my three Stockades. Some were so daring as to come and fire within 30 yards of our Guns and Stockade.

Under cover of darkness, I determined to take the two clayhouses, which I considered the Enemy were still in possession of. I therefore ordered 120 men with a proportion of Non-Commissioned-Officers from the three Stockades, and forty armed settlers, to be divided into two divisions, one under command of Captain Hardy, with Ensign Barker 58th Regiment, to attack the clayhouse belonging to Captain Campbell, the other party commanded by Lieutenant Balneavis with Lieutenant Pedder 58th Regiment, to take possession of Mr Churton's house, and a clay one adjoining, and the sand-hills; the troops being covered by the fire from the Gun-boat. On the parties reaching the houses (which I ordered to be burnt) I regret to say it was found the Enemy had decamped in the night with plunder. I should report the Troops proceeded to their work half an hour before daylight. The friendly natives reported this morning the Enemy's loss to be two Chiefs killed (one supposed to be Maketu, the Chief lately pardoned) and ten wounded.[1] I am happy to say we had no casualty on our side.

I have to thank Captain Hardy 58th Regiment (who in his report to me speaks in high terms of the assistance received by him from Ensign Middleton 58th Regiment) for the support and advice he has at all times rendered me. In fact the assistance I have received from Lieutenant Page, Acting Adjutant, Lieutenant Balneavis, Acting Assistant Engineer, to D.A.C.Gl.[2] Power for his exertions in securing supplies, and every Officer of different Services and Stockades, has afforded me the greatest satisfaction; nor can I omit to mention the exemplary and good conduct of the Non-Commissioned-Officers and Men of the force under my command. To Lieutenant Holmes I am exceedingly obliged, the efficiency of the Gun-boat under his command (which was exposed to the fire of the enemy the whole of the day), his alertness with her at all times, and cordial cooperation I am only too happy to bear testimony to.

I have the honor to be, Sir,
your obedient servant,
J. H. Laye. Captain, 58th Regiment.
Commanding Force at Wanganui.

My sincere thanks are also due to Dr Rees for the praiseworthy and active manner he fortified his house, which has been full of the inhabitants every day and night, and also to Dr Wilson who most kindly volunteered his professional services to Captain Hardy's detachment, Town Stockade.

J.H.L.

Lieutenant Colonel McCleverty,
Commanding Troops, Wellington.

This despatch, written in Laye's small office in the Rutland Stockade, was sent back to Wellington, whence it proceeded through the various military and colonial headquarters, until

[1] The following day the deaths of these chiefs were confirmed and the Maori casualties found to be more extensive than first thought.

[2] Deputy Assistant Commissary General.

Its contents eventually reached London. A year later, Laye learned from a letter written by Governor Grey, that the Secretary of State for the Colonies had received:

> The Queen's especial commands to assure me of the sense which Her Majesty entertains of the firmness with which Captain Laye of the 58th Regiment acted upon the occasion of the attack of the Natives upon the town of Wanganui in May last, as also of the Gallant Conduct of Captain Laye and the Detachment under his orders on that occasion, and I have the honor to request that Your Excellency [the major-general commanding at Auckland] would communicate this expression of Her Majesty's approbation to Captain Laye and the Officers, Non-Commissioned-Officers, and Men of the Force who were under his command on that occasion, in such manner as Your Excellency may think most fitting.

Although Laye received no order or decoration for his action, it must have been satisfying for him to know that the work of a humble captain of infantry in a small and distant outpost of the Empire was not beneath his Queen's attention.

Te Mamaku remained near Wanganui for a few more days but made no further attempt to attack. He then withdrew to a hill called Waipakura, to the east of the junction of the Wanganui River and the Makiriki stream, where he constructed a defensive position of great strength which was almost inaccessible. In the meantime Governor Grey arrived at Wanganui to see the situation for himself, bringing with him the Grenadier company of the 65th Regiment, and none other than Tamati Waaka Nene with thirty of his warriors. The day after his arrival, 25th May, a reconnaissance was made up river in search of Te Mamaku, but had to return without making any contact. Waaka offered to raise a war party to go in search of him, but Grey declined, preferring to return to Wellington and collect more reinforcements. On 4th June he was back with another company of the 65th, a further detachment of artillery and thirty-five friendly Maoris. With him was Lieutenant-Colonel W. A. McCleverty, 48th Regiment, whom Grey now appointed to command all troops at Wanganui.

McCleverty had had previous experience of colonial warfare. In 1834 his regiment formed part of a force sent to put a stop to the barbarous activities of the Rajah of Coorg in southern India. This also had been a campaign of forests and stockades, although the Rajah's followers in no way measured up to the Maoris in military terms. McCleverty, then a captain, had distinguished himself when in command of a small detachment, which was attacked in dense jungle, and had to fight its way back to camp through very difficult country when much encumbered with wounded men. After the campaign he was mentioned in despatches for his good work. He was promoted lieutenant-colonel on 19th December 1845 and, prior to being given the command at Wanganui, had been serving on the staff at Wellington as Deputy-Quartermaster-General.

His force at Wanganui was supplemented by landing parties from H.M. Ships *Calliope* and *Inflexible* (a paddle sloop) and now totalled 750 men. With his usual energy, Grey ordered a reconnaissance in force for the day after his return. Te Mamaku sent warriors down to contest the advance by sniping at the troops from the thick trees and fern which fringed the river bank. The guns were unlimbered and opened fire at likely targets, the troops deployed in skirmishing order, but the Maoris faded away into the undergrowth before their advance, and, deprived of any large body to attack, the force withdrew to Wanganui. Another expedition went out on 10th June but again no contact was made, and, after some skirmishing with scattered Maoris, the troops withdrew, once more having failed to bring Te Mamaku to battle.

Since offensive operations seemed to be achieving nothing, Grey decided to return to Wellington, leaving McCleverty in command with orders to remain on the defensive. Another stockade was put up near the river, so as to deny its use to the enemy's canoe parties, thus successfully interfering with the Maoris' fishing season and thereby depriving them of one of their major sources of food. The town's defences were strengthened, patrols still went out, but no sign of the enemy could be found in the vicinity of Wanganui.

On 1st July they reappeared near Aramaho, some four miles from the town. In the week that followed, Te Mamaku, seeing the increased strength of the fortifications, made several feints and sallies, endeavouring to induce the troops to leave the safety of their stockades, but McCleverty, mindful of his orders, held fast to his positions.

Running away from the Rutland Stockade was a low ridge which terminated about a mile off in a heavily wooded area known as St John's Wood. On 19th July a large force of Maoris came up from Aramaho and established themselves in the wood, where they threw up breastworks and sent out skirmishing parties towards the stockades. Two detachments of the 58th under Lieutenant Pedder and Ensign Middleton, and one of the 65th under Ensign Thelwall, were ordered out to counter the Maori skirmishers, but came under fire from other Maoris entrenched in the gullies that seamed the low hills. Since Te Mamaku now appeared ready to give the troops the battle he had so long avoided, the time seemed ripe to settle with him once and for all. McCleverty therefore advanced with all the troops he could muster to support his forward detachments, who were now heavily engaged. As the main force came within range, the Maoris in St John's Wood itself opened fire, and soon both sides were blazing away at each other in the trees and undergrowth. The ground in places was so overgrown that the soldiers could form no line but fought as skirmishers, each man thinking for himself and moving from cover to cover. Gradually the enemy fell back until all were safely ensconced behind the breastworks they had earlier constructed in the wood. Since little could now be achieved by musketry alone, a three-pounder gun was brought up close to the enemy position to try and effect a breach. Seeing this, a party of Maoris leaped from their barricades and made a dash for the gun. Hinton recalled: 'They came on us in such numbers and with such determination, that our gunners fell back and left the gun in their possession.' Before the Maoris could remove it however, a party of the 58th charged forward with the bayonet and sent them flying. 'We made a rush for it and recovered it in less than four minutes, and at the same time compelled the enemy to retire.' Since the Maoris seemed set on remaining behind their breastworks, McCleverty attempted a ruse to draw them out. He ordered his buglers to sound the 'Retire' and on that signal, his troops began to move slowly back towards the stockade, ready to face about in the hope of catching the pursuing Maoris in the open with volleys and a charge. But the wily Te Mamaku, perhaps remembering the levelled bayonets retaking the three-pounder, bade his men remain where they were. McCleverty therefore completed his withdrawal, realising that to renew the assault on the enemy position would incur heavy casualties, which he could not afford, and that in any case the Maoris would probably melt away before the troops could get among them.

It had been an indecisive day for both sides, but mercifully, despite an exchange of musketry lasting four hours, the British had only suffered two men killed, Privates Weller of the 58th and Spratt of the 65th; one officer, ten soldiers and a friendly Maori had been wounded. Most of the wounded were artillerymen who had had to man the three-pounder without any cover. The stoicism of the wounded under the surgeon's knife was remembered, years later, by Hinton, who had seen 'one of the artillery propped up on a table having his leg amputated. He had a rum-bottle by his side to give him courage, and during the whole operation he did not say so much as "Oh".'

Nothing occurred the next day, but on the 21st the Maoris were again seen in large numbers in St John's Wood. Expecting a further attack, the troops stood to and awaited the onset. Time passed without either side making a move. Eventually a white flag was seen coming from the wood. An interpreter escorted by some friendly Maoris went forward and shortly returned with a message from Te Mamaku, to the effect that, as the troops would not attack his position, and as they would not attack the soldiers, protected as they were by artillery, he would retire. The fighting was over.

Although the danger to Wanganui was now lifted, it was uncertain whether the farmers could return in safety to the outlying homesteads. Grey made contingency plans for further operations and let it be known that the ringleaders of the rising must be given up. McCleverty returned to Wellington, leaving Major Wyatt of the 65th in command at Wanganui. This officer believed that a policy of clemency might ensure peace, as it had in the north, and spread the word that all Maoris concerned in the rising could be pardoned, and that even the ringleaders could escape retribution, if they gave clear indications of pursuing a peaceful existence. A missionary, the Reverend Richard Taylor, went in search of Te Mamaku to persuade him of the virtues of peace. Eventually, in February 1848, Te Mamaku came down to Wanganui to see Wyatt and unreservedly declared his willingness to refrain from further hostilities. With this act all rebellion in the Wanganui area was over, and the whole of North Island was at peace.

Laye, whose firm action at the settlement in the beginning, had prevented its being overrun, was not there to see the satisfactory conclusion of the campaign. In the middle of 1847, when the Wanganui operations were at their height, the main body of the 58th returned again to New Zealand from Sydney. The plan was ultimately to deploy the whole regiment, less Russell's company still building roads in the south, at Auckland and the Bay of Islands, leaving the 65th entirely concentrated in the Wellington–Wanganui area. On 28th October 1847 Laye and his company embarked on the *Calliope* at Wellington and sailed for Auckland, rejoining the regiment there on 4th November. That they left an excellent reputation behind them can be seen from a letter written by McCleverty to Lieutenant Colonel Wynyard:

> I have seldom seen so creditable, and never a more creditable embarkation than that of the Detachment of the 58th Regiment who have this day left Wellington; not a man was Drunk, or bore even the appearance of liquour, and I take this opportunity of expressing my most favourable opinion of the conduct of the Detachment 58th Regiment while in this District, more especially for the last 9 months, during which time personal experience has taught me to rely implicitly on their cheerful and ready obedience.[3]

McCleverty's emphasis on the sobriety of Laye's men, indeed almost his astonishment, suggests that this was the exception, rather than the rule, when troops were changing quarters in those days.

In June 1848 Hardy's company rejoined the regiment at Auckland, but Russell had proved so successful a road-builder that he and his men were kept in the south, opening up the country, until March 1850. When eventually they were

---

[3] In 1884 McCleverty, by then a general, was appointed Colonel of The Northamptonshire Regiment, of which, in 1881, his former regiment, the 48th, had become the 1st Battalion, and the 58th, the 2nd Battalion, under the reforms of that year which linked the old numbered regiments of the Line in pairs, to form new, territorial regiments.

allowed to return to Auckland, the company had only three sergeants, three corporals, a drummer and twenty-nine privates; the others had all purchased their discharges and settled in the area in which they had built their roads. They must undoubtedly have had a better knowledge of the countryside than any settler. While their mundane and laborious efforts had prevented them from gaining the laurels their comrades had won in action, their work, particularly in the early stages, had not been without danger, and furthermore had made a most valuable contribution to the development of the country. Russell was commended by the Governor for his work, and subsequently received a personal commendation from the Duke of Wellington, then Commander-in-Chief of the Army and in the last years of his life.

With the conclusion of the war, the officers and men of the 58th received such rewards as were in those days considered appropriate for the part they had played in saving the colony from bloodshed. Lieutenant-Colonel Wynyard was made a Companion of the Bath,[4] and Captains Denny and Matson were granted Brevet-Majorities for gallant conduct in the field. Cyprian Bridge and practically every officer of the regiment had been 'specially named', 'commended' or 'alluded to' in orders for their conduct in the field, some of them on several occasions. Sergeant-Major Moir, five sergeants, and nine privates had also been singled out for special mention in respect of brave conduct.[5] In comparison with more recent times, such recognition seems less than generous, but, in an age before decorations for bravery were awarded, it was the most they could expect.

On behalf of the colonists, for whose safety the soldiers had marched and fought and died in the rain-swept forests and bush, Grey wrote to Wynyard to express 'the sense of the obligations the Governor and the Inhabitants of his Colony are under to yourself and the officers of your Regiment, for the Gallantry and indefatigable Zeal which you have on all occasions exhibited for the suppression of Rebellion, and the pro-

---

[4] The same award went to Colonel Despard.
[5] Okaihau and Ohaeawai: Sergeant George Brown. Okaihau: Sergeant J. Mathews, Privates J. McIvor, W. Nunnington, W. Power. Ruapekapeka: Sergeants W. Speight, T. Stevenson, D. Munro; Privates J. Gallagher, M. Munro, J. Brown, W. Mulligan, J. Russell. Wanganui: Private T. Lawrie.

tection of the lives and properties of Her Majesty's subjects, and this under Circumstances, the trying and difficult nature of which can only be fully appreciated by those acquainted with the nature of the Country, and the character of the Enemy, against which you have had to contend'. He went on to praise those who seldom attracted much favourable comment from the civil authorities, the common soldiers:

> The Lieutenant Governor and Executive Council have also placed on record the sense they entertain of the bravery which has, on every occasion been exhibited in the field, and of the discipline which has always been shewn in quarters by the Non-Commissioned-Officers and Private Soldiers of the 58th Regiment, which conduct on their part has not only had the effect of quelling insurrections, but has tended to conciliate, and gain the attachment, not only of the European population, but (particularly in the case of detached posts) that portion of the Native inhabitants of this Colony, with whom they have been brought into intercourse, many of whom were previously in open revolt against the Queen's Authority.[6]

A fine, fulsome tribute in the best mid-Victorian style of approbation but, coming from Grey who had shared many of the troops' hardships, it was probably sincerely meant and without doubt deserved.

Unsuitably clad and poorly fed, soaked to the skin or broiled by the sun, the British soldiers of the 1840s fought ferocious enemies in causes they barely understood and which no one thought necessary to explain to them. They, and their families, could expect none of the careful and extensive administrative, medical and welfare support the modern soldier is granted. They did their duty and risked their lives for a pittance, their grog, and the good name of their regiment, and if they sometimes over-indulged on the grog, who can blame them? They had precious little other consolation. Held in low esteem by their fellow-countrymen and discarded when their services were no longer required, the Hattaways, Mitchells and Whiskers of the mid-Victorian Army nevertheless carved

---

[6] Letter from the Colonial Secretary's Office, Auckland, dated 3rd December 1846, quoted 58th Regiment's Digest of Service.

out and maintained with their courage, loyalty, endurance and often their blood, a great Empire for their Queen.

At the same time as the small force in New Zealand had been struggling to put down the Maori uprisings, a much larger body of British troops had been engaged in India against another warlike race—the Sikhs. The Sikhs, like the Maoris, displayed great skill and bravery, but they had been trained and organised by Europeans on European lines; nevertheless they were ultimately defeated. In contrast, it is debateable whether the Maoris of Heke and Kawiti, of Te Rangihaeata and Te Mamaku were truly defeated, and moreover their skill-at-arms was native-born. It must also be remembered that, had it not been for the loyal aid of such as Tamati Waaka and his devoted followers, the First Maori War may well have taken a different course. The Maori was one of the most redoubtable fighting men ever encountered by the Victorian Army and, for a tribute to his prowess, whether as friend or foe, the judgment of the historian of the British Army, Sir John Fortescue, cannot be bettered:

> The Maori had his own code of war, the essence of which was a fair fight on a day and place fixed by appointment, when the best and bravest man should win. The British soldier upset his traditions, but could not touch his proud courage nor degrade his proud honour. A Maori was capable of slaughtering wounded and prisoners and perhaps eating them afterwards, but he could also leap down into the fire of both sides to save the life of a fallen foe. The British soldier, therefore, held him in the deepest respect, not resenting his own little defeats but recognizing the noble side of the Maori and forgetting his savagery.[7]

[7] Sir John Fortescue, *The History of The British Army*, Vol. XIII (London, 1930).

11

Aftermath

WITH PEACE FULLY RESTORED TO THE NORTH ISLAND BY 1848, IT would be another twelve years before warfare again threatened New Zealand. When it came, it would continue throughout the 1860s and would be fought on a larger scale, in new areas of dispute, and with new players on the scene of events. Had Heke lived to see it, he would doubtless have been in the van, but in 1848 he contracted consumption which left him too weak to withstand further illnesses, and he died at Kaikohe in August 1850, aged only forty. His confederate, Kawiti, went shortly after, in 1853, after embracing Christianity not long before his death. In January 1858 the flagstaff at Kororareka, which had not been re-erected since it was cut down in March 1845, was once again raised into position above the Bay of Islands. To prove that the quarrels of the past were done with once and for all, and as a sign of their loyalty to the Crown, 400 young men of the tribes that had been in rebellion prepared the ground on Maiki Hill and set up the new flagstaff.

A further indication of the friendly relations that existed between Maoris and whites in the region of the Bay of Islands, which was unaffected by the troubles of the 1860s, occurred in 1873. The year before, a Maori chief, Heta Te Haara of Ohaeawai, suggested that the remains of the soldiers who had fallen there in 1845 should be reburied in the cemetery of the little church, built by the Maoris on the site of Kawiti's old *pa*. Mr H. T. Clarke, the Civil Commissioner at Auckland, who had himself been wounded at Ohaeawai when acting as interpreter to Colonel Despard, wrote in a report: 'The Natives were actuated to this from a respect for our dead, and from a fear lest the remains of their former brave enemies should, by any accident, be disturbed or subjected to any indignity. The wish was a kindly one and is one of many incontestable proofs that all bitterness or soreness occasioned by the struggle, which took place in the years 1845 and 1846, had entirely passed away.'[1]

The ceremony took place on 1st July 1873, the anniversary of Despard's assault, in the same teeming rain that had been such a feature of the operations twenty-eight years before. The bones were disinterred by some old Maoris and placed in coffins, which were then carried in procession to the church, accompanied by a firing party and a large gathering of Europeans and Maoris. The burial service was conducted in Maori by Mr Clarke's brother, the Venerable Archdeacon E. B. Clarke, and the coffins buried in a large communal grave. Mr Clarke then thanked the chiefs for their gesture, and after they had all partaken of Heta Te Haara's hospitality, many of the Maoris spoke, amongst them Mohi Tawhai, who had implored Despard not to risk the soldiers' lives at Ruapekapeka.

After the last flickers of rebellion died away in 1848, the military garrison of New Zealand was fixed at two Imperial battalions. The 65th remained in the country for the extraordinarily long span of twenty years, fighting in the campaigns of the sixties until their eventual return to England in 1867. The 58th, who had borne the brunt of the war in the north, remained until 1858. When they embarked for home at Auckland in November of that year, the regiment was only sixteen officers and 194 men strong. Over 300 officers and men had elected to settle in the country where they had spent so long a time, and over the course of the thirteen years the regiment had served there, over a thousand had taken their discharges in the country and remained as settlers.

The regiment's final parade before embarkation was described by an epic piece of Victorian journalism in *The New Zealand Herald*:

As the corps formed up to the call of bugle and beat of drum, only 120 [*sic*] men gathered round the tattered and shot-riven colours. The survivors of the wars had fallen into the ranks of civilian life, and were engaged in the heroic work of colonisation, for Peace has its victories as well as War, and

[1] Letter to the Under Secretary, Native department, dated 8th August 1872, from Appendices of the Journals of the House of Representatives, 1873.

the glory of saving life is greater than that of destroying it. The women and children had embarked on the transport, and all that remained was the last parade and roll-call, and final march to the wharf.

Then I saw one of those unique incidents which no man could witness unmoved. On that parade ground were gathered grey-bearded and bronze-visaged men, whose well-knit and martial figures bespoke the old veteran, who had tramped, some of them 30 and 40 miles, through wretched bullock tracks, from the bush, to bid good-bye and 'God bless you' to old comrades who had been with them in the baptism of fire at Okaihau, at Ohaeawai, at Ruapekapeka, the Hutt, and Wanganui. Some of those veterans, in their travel-stained clothing, went up and reverently baring their heads, with tears coursing down their manly cheeks, kissed the old tattered colours under which they had fought and bled, and were prepared to die if need be. Then I understood, as I had never done before, what lay behind the colours, and the forces which made the British soldier go, as at Balaclava, 'into the jaws of death, into the mouth of hell!'

In 1860 these old colours were replaced by new ones. Cyprian Bridge, by then commanding the 58th, decided that, in view of the regiment's long association with New Zealand, the old colours should be presented to the city of Auckland. H. C. Balneavis, one of the officers of the 58th who had retired in 1855 and settled in New Zealand, was asked to arrange for the colours to be placed in the Church of St Paul in Auckland. This was duly done and, in reporting the gift, *The New Zealander* of 12th October 1860 concluded with the words: 'We can only say that they were sent out by Colonel Bridge as a courteous memorial of the kindly feeling entertained by the regiment for the people with whom they had served so long, and by whom they were so deservedly appreciated.' However, the Bishop of Auckland required their removal, on the grounds that their presence in the church would offend the Maoris. The regiment therefore asked for their return to Rutland, but Balneavis, by then a lieutenant-colonel in the Auckland Militia and Sheriff of the Supreme Court, summoned a meeting of all ex-members of the 58th living in Auckland, at which a petition was drawn up, inviting the regiment to allow the colours to remain at

Government House until a permanent resting place could be found for them. This was agreed, and the colours were housed in their temporary home until 1865, when the Government was removed to Wellington. Balneavis took charge of them and kept them in his own house until 1868, when he asked for them to be placed in the new Supreme Court at Auckland, which had just been opened. Permission having been granted, he sent a communication to the newspapers, in which he outlined the movements of the colours since their return to New Zealand, and concluded: 'The following inscription should be placed with the colours,—"First Regimental Colours unfurled in New Zealand in 1845; presented to Auckland by Colonel Bridge and the officers of the 58th Regiment". I shall be glad to see any of my old comrades of all ranks of the old "Black Cuffs" at my residence in the Alten road at half-past nine o'clock on Monday, the 2nd March, in order to escort the colours to the new Supreme Court-house.' On the day in question Balneavis and Captain Tighe, an ensign in 1846, carried the colours with due ceremony to their new home, escorted by a large number of ex-soldiers of the regiment.

In 1901 there was a move to have the colours placed on view in some place more readily accessible to the public. The vicar of St Paul's asked that they should be returned to that church, but John Mitchell, who had stayed on in New Zealand and become a captain in the Militia, also took an interest and suggested the Public Library. His view prevailed and on 10th January 1909, with an escort of ten of the last survivors of the 58th and the Auckland Militia, the colours were presented to the Mayor of Auckland for safe keeping at the Library. In 1933 they were placed in their final home, the Auckland War Memorial and Museum, where they have remained ever since. They were unveiled there by Lieutenant-Colonel Shera, a grandson of Balneavis, at a ceremony attended by over a thousand people, including 400 descendants of men of the 58th and sixty descendants of Waaka, Heke, and Kawiti.

Colonel Wynyard remained in command throughout the regiment's stay in New Zealand, and, when Grey was appointed Governor of Cape Colony in 1853, Wynyard took his place, with the title of Officer Administering the Government, until a successor was appointed. He seems to have been as well-liked by the colonists as he was by his men, and his services were recognised by a tribute to his work and character that appeared in *The New Zealand Journal* when he left for home in 1858:

> Colonel Wynyard was very handsome and soldierlike. Six feet three in height, he was so perfectly proportioned, that standing alone he did not seem a man of abnormal stature and size, yet a big powerful man of five feet ten or five feet eleven beside him looked like a boy. He had a genial kindly manner to all, military or civilian, rich or poor, which was not a mere ornament but a real engine of power. He had been in the Guards before the 58th, and was at one time A.D.C. to the Duke of Wellington. From 1854 to 1855 he introduced representative institutions into New Zealand. He was undoubtedly the most popular man who ever came to New Zealand, and yet he never laid himself out to seek anything of the kind.[2]

Wynyard gave up command of the 58th on leaving for England and was succeeded by Cyprian Bridge. Poor Bridge, now aged fifty-one, had had to wait a long time for his promotion. His wife Louisa had borne him four more children, three girls who all died in infancy, and another son Herbert Bowen, born in 1849 at the Bay of Islands. This son and the first-born, Cyprian, both settled in New Zealand in due course, married, had children, and died there. Several of Herbert's grand-children served in the New Zealand Armed Forces in the two World Wars. On 29th July 1860 Louisa died, and four months later Bridge gave up command of the regiment. In 1861 he retired by sale of his commission, and in the following year he was married, for the third time, to Mary Louisa Williamson. He died at Cheltenham on 7th July 1885, aged seventy-eight.

Several of the old 58th men who fought in the north and who have appeared in this story became worthy citizens of the land they adopted as their own. John Mitchell's journal ceased after he was wounded at Ohaeawai, but, from a letter he wrote home to his parents in 1848, it is clear that, on returning to

[2] Quoted Lieutenant-Colonel Russell Gurney, *History of The Northamptonshire Regiment, 1742–1934* (Aldershot, 1935).

New South Wales in December 1846, he had been reunited with Julia Maher, the girl he had been courting before he left England, and whom he had been prevented from seeing when he first arrived in Australia by the sudden move to New Zealand. He told his parents:

> She embarked before me for New South Wales, servant to an Officers family, and when I arrived in the Country they was a long way up the Country, and she reported to be married to some other man. But it turned out to be false. She wrote to me to show her constancy towards me, not forgetting to remind me that I must have been a blaguard or I would not have been reduced [from sergeant] but to take more care of myself, and also kept open the communication while away in New Zealand. I encouraged her by answering her letters with the intentions of marrying her when I might return. When I did so she was still about 4 hundred miles away but in about 3 months they came in to Headquarters, the match was made with the sanction of the Commanding Officer and we was married on the 26 April 1847.

He said she was 'about 22 years of age, a very nice Girl and an excellent wife such as is very hard to be met with either out of the army or in it'. On 11th March 1848 she presented him with a daughter. Marriage seems to have had a settling effect on him, for two months after the wedding he was promoted colour-sergeant of No. 3 Company under Captain Thompson. When he took his discharge is not known but, as mentioned earlier, he remained in New Zealand, achieving commissioned rank in the local militia and teaching in the native schools.

Apart from the interest he took in finding a home for the colours, he had previously, in 1890, drawn the attention of the Government to the neglected state of the graves of the men who had fallen at Okaihau on 8th May 1845. He was then living at the nearby settlement of Kaikohe, and the position of the graves was pointed out to him by some old Maoris who had fought there. The dead had been buried on the battlefield and no stone or fencing had ever been set up to mark the place. As a result of Mitchell's representations, the remains were disinterred and reburied in the churchyard of Okaihau. In

1897, when he was living at Ellerslie, Auckland, and teaching in a Maori school, he again invited Government action to repair the graves of Lieutenant Philpotts, R.N., Captain Grant 58th and Lieutenant Beatty 99th, who had all fallen at Ohaeawai and had been buried after the battle in the church-yard of Waimate North. Wooden memorial tablets and fenc-ing had been erected in 1845, but when Mitchell inspected them in the 1890s, he found the inscriptions obliterated and the wood rotten. Following his representations, the Government awarded a sum of twenty-five pounds for the graves to be put in good order. At the end of the transcription which Mitchell's daughter made of his military journal, she wrote: 'From the time he was wounded up to nearly 80 I should say his life was most interesting, true and just in all his actions, always ready to help those in distress.'

Robert Hattaway also reached the rank of colour-sergeant and after the war served some years at Wahapu on the Bay of Islands where, in addition to his military duties, he acted as clerk to the Court-house at Kororareka, then renamed Russell. He married at about that time, a son being born in 1852, and in his spare time used to assist the captains of whaling and sealing ships with their account books. Deciding to remain in New Zealand, he took his discharge in 1856 and settled in Howick as a storekeeper under the Military Settlement Regulations, with a contract for supplying troops with bread and meat. He received a commission in the militia and in 1862 was made captain, but does not seem to have been in action during the fighting of the sixties. In 1866 he gave up the store and went into farming, with sheep and wheat as the chief products, but also planting fruit orchards and nursery gardens, to which he devoted a great deal of his time, and which must must have reminded him of his boyhood in Kent. At one time he owned 600 acres at Howick and also had a town house in Auckland, where he spent most of the last years of his life. He died on 21st December 1904 and was buried at Howick, where his tombstone recorded that, 'The joy of loyal service to his Queen and Country shone through his day and lit up other lives'.

Alexander Whisker returned from Australia to New Zea-land with the 58th in July 1847, this time accompanied by his wife Flora and their two children, Mary Jane and Charles.

Another son was born in October, and in February 1848 he was employed at the household of Major-General Pitt, then commanding in New Zealand, as a farm servant, at a wage of fifteen shillings a month, in addition to his soldier's pay. The freedom this gave him from guards and fatigues did not last long, for in March he had to confess: 'I was confined for being Drunk in the Generals house. I got 7 Drill 7 grog and 7 confined to barracks.' In January 1850 he took his discharge, and, a month later, obtained work with a Mr Taylor as a labourer for twenty-four shillings a week. The closing pages of his Memorandum Book give little information about the rest of his life, although it is clear that Flora bore him two more children, and there is a suggestion that in 1852 he found himself in gaol. Most of the remaining pages are filled with songs and verses, some of which he may have composed himself or adapted from other poems.[3]

The two Irish corporals, William Free and Charles Stapp, who had charged with the forlorn hope at Ohaeawai, both achieved distinction in the New Zealand militia. After the war in the north, Stapp had been posted home to England to assist in the formation of a depot battalion in 1850. He marched in the funeral procession of the Duke of Wellington in 1852, representing the 58th, and, when the Crimean War broke out in 1854, he volunteered for service. He was granted an ensigncy in the 58th, dated 16th March 1855, and went out as a staff officer at Scutari. There he may have met one of his old officers from New Zealand, Captain Laye, the defender of Wanganui, who was serving as Assistant Military Secretary to Lord William Paulet, commanding at the Bosphorous. After the war Stapp returned to the 58th in New Zealand, as an officer in the regiment he had left as a ranker—an unusual occurrence in those days. When the regiment left for home, he retired by sale of his commission, and in 1859 was appointed captain and adjutant of the Taranaki Militia, a company of which was commanded by Major Herbert, late of the 58th who had once hid for his life up a tree in the Hutt Valley. Stapp served with distinction in the Second Maori War of 1860, receiving the personal thanks of the Governor and being mentioned several times in despatches for his coolness and judgment under fire. Promoted major in August 1865, he was

[3] For Whisker's complete 'song' of the Northern War, see Appendix 4.

appointed second-in-command of the Opotiki expedition, which was sent to capture and punish the rebels who had murdered a clergyman, the Reverend Volkner. In February 1869 he took a force of militia to recover the bodies of a number of Europeans who had been murdered at a place called White Cliffs. Subsequently he commanded the Taranaki Military District for twenty-two years, being appointed lieutenant-colonel in 1885 and colonel in 1891. In later life he contracted dropsy and although very unwell, his affliction did not prevent him travelling to Auckland to attend the funeral of another veteran of 1846, W. I. Speight. As he left to return home, he bade farewell to John Mitchell with the words: 'Goodbye, dear old comrade, I don't think we shall meet again.' He died in August 1900. In his obituary, the *Auckland Weekly News* said of him: 'During his long career he was a true soldier of the Queen, always cheerful, happy and contented, fearless and brave to a degree.'

William Free was appointed sergeant in the Taranaki Rifle Volunteers in February 1859 and took part in the 1860 campaign under Stapp's command, being wounded in the knee. He received a lieutenant's commission in the same regiment in May 1864. He lived to the great age of ninety-three, dying at New Plymouth in 1919.

William Isaac Speight, one of the heroes of Ruapekapeka whose funeral Stapp attended in 1899, attained the rank of staff-sergeant-major in the 58th. When he left the service in 1858 in order to remain in New Zealand, Colonel Wynyard wrote him a testimonial which recorded that he was 'a very good Staff Sergeant, excellent at the desk and in the field he is gallantry itself'. Speight found employment as a temporary civilian clerk in the Commissariat Department in Auckland, where he earned glowing reports for his 'high character of sobriety and respectability and his zeal, ability and industry'. He served as chief clerk in all the staff branches of the military headquarters at Auckland. It will be remembered that Wynyard's recommendation for a retrospective award of the Victoria Cross for Speight's bravery at Ruapekapeka was disallowed. However in 1876 he was granted an annuity of ten pounds and the Meritorious Service Medal, becoming the only man of the 58th, or indeed any other veteran of the First Maori War, to receive it.

Joseph Hinton returned to England in 1850 to the same depot as Stapp. He married in 1852, and, when stationed in the Channel Islands in the late fifties, aided by his wife, he taught himself to read and write. This enabled him to reach the rank of sergeant, in which he served until his discharge on 4th January 1865.

Colonel Despard never returned to New Zealand after his departure in 1846. He retained command of the 99th until he reached the age of seventy, though fortunately for his subordinates the regiment was not again engaged on active service during that time. He was then promoted major-general and died four years later in 1858. Midshipman McKillop was promoted Lieutenant in October 1847 and, on the outbreak of the Crimean War, was appointed to command H.M.S. *Snake*, a despatch gunboat with which he had numerous adventures in the Black Sea, being promoted to Commander for his gallantry in attacking three Russian ships single-handed. In 1868, as a Captain, he entered the service of the Khedive of Egypt and spent the rest of his life reorganising the Egyptian Navy and its harbours. These duties included leading an expedition to Jubaland in 1875–6 and arranging the defences of, and the free movement of shipping through, the Suez Canal during the Russo-Turkish War of 1877. He was made a Rear-Admiral and Commander of the Bath and died in 1879. Among the officers of the 58th, Lieutenant G. H. Page, the defender of Boulcott's Farm and one of the artists of the campaign, married Charlotte, daughter of Major-General Pitt, in New Zealand in 1848. He was promoted captain and brevet-major in 1855 and exchanged to the 41st Regiment in 1860. J. H. Laye received two brevet promotions to major and lieutenant-colonel during the Crimean War, went on half-pay in 1856, but was appointed to command a depot battalion at Canterbury in 1860. John M'Lerie, the adjutant, was also retrospectively recommended for the Victoria Cross for gallantry in the Maori War, but, as in Speight's case, it could not be granted. He became adjutant of the Military Mounted Police in Australia and retired from the Army in 1850. He was appointed Governor of Darlinghurst Gaol and subsequently metropolitan superintendent of police in Sydney and Inspector-General of Constabulary. He died in 1874. Ensign Middleton, who had been mentioned in despatches at Wanganui, reached high rank in the Army, serving in several regiments. He went through the Indian Mutiny, was made colonel in 1875, and in 1881 was awarded the C.B. In 1885, as a major-general, he was sent to command the Canadian Militia, in which post he conducted the campaign against Louis Riel's rebellion in that year. He retired in 1887 as Lieutenant-General Sir Frederick Middleton K.C.M.G., C.B. Richard Denny, who led the final assault at Ruapekapeka, retired as a brevet-major in 1850, and Whisker's sometime master, Charles Thompson, soldiered on with the 58th until his retirement as brevet-lieutenant-colonel in 1862. In 1857 the Auckland battalion of New Zealand militia had five ex-58th officers: Henry Matson as lieutenant-colonel, Balneavis as captain and adjutant, Philson as surgeon, Petley, and H. J. Wynyard, the son of the Colonel.

George Grey had a distinguished career as a colonial administrator. He remained as Governor of New Zealand until 1853 during which time he worked hard to make the colony more prosperous and to reform the vexed question of land purchase. He had a sincere interest in the welfare of the Maoris and a genuine wish to protect them from land speculators. He took many measures to improve their standards of living in the fields of education and medicine, and encouraged them to take up agriculture. Sadly his reforms proved to be less effective than he had hoped for, and much of what he tried to do for the Maoris was regarded by them as destructive of their own culture. He was knighted in 1848 for his services, moving on five years later to the Cape, where he enjoyed a successful governorship until 1859, when a disagreement with the Colonial Secretary led to his recall. Following a change of government, he was almost immediately re-appointed and sailed again for the Cape. During the voyage, however, his still-beautiful wife attracted the attentions of Rear-Admiral Sir Henry Keppel, recently appointed to the chief naval command in South Africa. Grey was furious and had his wife put ashore at Rio de Janeiro; Keppel's appointment was cancelled, and Grey returned to the Cape alone. In 1861, during the Second Maori War, he again became Governor of New Zealand, a post he held for another seven years until he returned to England. Since no further employment was offered to him, he decided to go back to New Zealand as a private citizen, where he remained until 1892, serving as the country's Prime Minister from 1877–9. At the age of eighty-two he sailed for England in order to live out his last few years at home. This proved to be a sad mistake, for his return was marred by the re-appearance of Lady Grey, who chose to rejoin him after a separation lasting thirty-six years, primarily, it seems, to make financial demands upon him. Worn out by her insistence and suffering from failing memory, he died at the age of eighty-eight on 19th September 1898 and was buried at St Paul's Cathedral.

With one exception, the regiments that provided the first garrisons of New Zealand live on to this day, though under different and somewhat attenuated guises. The exception, the 65th, became in 1881 the first battalion of The York and Lancaster Regiment, which was itself disbanded in 1968. The 80th, later 2nd Battalion The South Staffordshire Regiment, is now, after amalgamation with the North Staffords in 1959, The Staffordshire Regiment. The 96th, 2nd Battalion The Manchester Regiment, now stands as The King's Regiment, following the union in 1958 between the Manchesters and the King's Liverpools. The 99th, though titled Lanarkshire, lost all links with Scotland when it became 2nd Battalion The Wilt-shire Regiment, which was joined in 1959 to the Royal Berk-shires, thus forming The Duke of Edinburgh's Royal Regiment.

The chief actors of the Northern War, the 58th, faced a comparable foe to the Maoris in the Zulu War of 1879, as did the 80th and 99th, and, shortly after, fought their last campaign under the old designation, against the Boers in the Transvaal War of 1881, before becoming 2nd Battalion The Northamptonshire Regiment later the same year. After the amalgamation in 1960 of the Northamptons and the Royal Lincolns, the new regiment so formed was converted, in 1964, to the second of four battalions of The Royal Anglian Regiment, an organisation embracing seven former county regiments. Despite these changes of identity, links with the Maori War remained. For many years the Northamptons' sergeants held a Ruapekapeka Ball. A piece of puriri wood from the remains of Kawiti's old *pa*, mounted with a silver plaque and presented by the allied New Zealand regiment, the North Auckland, graced the Officers' Mess dining table. The commanding officer's bugler could read on his silver bugle, if he had a mind to, the words commemorating the act of Drummer Allen at Boulcott's Farm. The colours of the Royal Anglians bear the battle honour 'New Zealand', and the khaki uniforms of their second battalion are distinguished by lanyards of the same colour as the facings of the 'Old Black Cuffs'.

Appendix 1

58th Regiment—Extract from the Army List, 1845

"GIBRALTAR"—with the Castle and Key, "Montis Insignia Calpe."—The Sphinx, with the words "EGYPT"—"MAIDA"—"SALAMANCA"—"VITTORIA"—"PYRENEES"—"NIVELLE"—"ORTHES"—PENINSULA."

Years' Serv.			
Full Pay.	Half Pay.		
66		**Colonel.**	
		Frederick Maitland,[1] Ens. 1 Sept. 1779; Lieut. 19 Sept. 82; Capt. 2 Dec. 89; Major, 21 Aug. 93; Lieut.-Col. 2 July, 94; Col. 1 Jan. 1800; Major-Gen. 30 Oct. 05; Lieut.-Gen. 4 June, 11; Gen. 25 May, 25; Col. 58th Regiment, 11 Dec. 33.	
		Lieut.-Colonel.	
26	0	Robert Henry Wynyard, Ens. 25 Feb. 19; Lieut. P 17 July 23; Capt. P 90 May 20; Major, 25 July 41; Lieut.-Col. P 30 Dec. 42.	
20	0	**Majors.**—Cyprian Bridge, Ens. 8 April, 25; Lieut. P 31 Jan. 28; Capt. P 16 Dec. 30; Major, P 30 Dec. 42.	
19	11/12	Charles Augustus Arney, Ens. P 5 Nov. 25; Lieut. P 9 Aug. 31; Capt. P 1 July, 37; Major, P 12 May, 43.	

Full Pay.	Half Pay.	CAPTAINS.	ENSIGN.	LIEUT.	CAPTAIN.	BREV.-MAJ.
14	0	Wm. Edward Grant	P 23 Dec. 31	P 13 May 36	P 23 Apr. 39	
12	0	Geo. Ponsonby Hume	P 28 June 33	P 16 Dec. 36	P 20 Sept. 39	
27	5	Henry Matson	16 Sept. 13	2 June 14	30 Nov. 38	
11	0	Joseph Henry Laye	P 2 May 34	1 Dec. 37	25 June 41	
19	5/12	Jonas Pasley Hardy	29 Sept. 25	3 Nov. 26	25 June 41	
10	0	Cha. Lavallin Nugent	P 21 Aug. 35	4 Feb. 38	P 16 Nov. 41	
17	0	Andrew Hamilton Russell	18 Jan. 28	23 July 34	P 31 Dec. 41	
9	0	Richard Denny	P 13 May 36	P 12 Oct. 38	P 30 Dec. 42	
20	0	Wm. Wild Jos. Cockcraft	8 Apr. 25	P 22 Apr. 26	20 July 39	
9	0	Charles Wm. Thompson	P 23 Dec. 36	P 3 May 39	P 12 May 43	
		LIEUTENANTS.				
9	0	Charles Dresing	P 19 Feb. 36	2 June 38		
9	0	Alexander Macleod Hay	P 22 July 36	19 Oct. 38		
7	0	Cha. Chester Master	P 6 July 38	P 2 Oct. 40		
7	0	Henry Colin Balneavis	7 July 38	P 26 Mar. 41		
7	0	John Alex. Cha. Petley	P 12 Oct. 38	P 26 June 41		
7	0	John M'Lerie, adj.	28 Dec. 38	27 June 41		
9	0	Alfred Rush	P 15 July 36	13 July 41		
6	0	Isaac Rhodes Cooper	P 23 Apr. 39	P 16 Nov. 41		
6	0	Michael Lionel Westropp	P 20 Sept. 39	29 Dec. 42		
8	0	Wm. Henry More Simmons	10 Mar. 37	30 June 39		
4	0	Cha. St. John S. Herbert	P 26 Mar. 41	P 27 Jan. 43		
4	0	George Hyde Page	P 23 Apr. 41	P 12 May 43		
4	0	J. D. M. Bidwell Edwards	30 Apr. 41	P 23 June 43		
		ENSIGNS.				
4	0	Thomas Pedder	P 16 Apr. 41			
4	0	Robert Main	P 26 June 41			
4	0	Leslie Jenkins Thompson	17 Sept. 41			
3	0	Fra. Robert Chester Master	P 22 Nov. 42			
3	0	Fred. Dobson Middleton	30 Dec. 42			
3	0	Edward Oliver Barker	P 31 Dec. 42			
2	0	Christophilus Garstin	P 27 Jan. 43			
1	0	George Henry Wynyard	3 May 44			

Full Pay.	Half Pay.	
15	0	**Paymaster.**—Tho. Richardson Timbrell,[4] 25 Oct. 42; Qr.-Master, 19 Nov. 30.
7	0	**Adjutant.**—Lieut. John M'Lerie, 28 Dec. 38.
3	0	**Quarter-Master.**—Edward Kirby, 25 Oct. 42; Ens. 25 Oct. 42.
12	0	**Surgeon.**—Chilley Pine,[5] 5 Dec. 43; Assist.-Surg. 2 Aug. 33.
6	0	**Assist.-Surgeons.**—Richard Bannatine, 17 Sept. 30.
2	0	Thomas Moore Philson, M.D., 6 Oct. 43.

Facings Black.—Agents, Messrs. Cox & Co.

[Returned from Ceylon, 23 June, 1839.]

1 Gen. Maitland served at the relief of Gibraltar in 1781; and was subsequently for many years Military Secretary to Sir Ralph Abercrombie in the West Indies; and during about 30 years' service in that climate, he was at the reduction of every Island taken by the British arms; and commanded at the Saints. In 1811, he was removed, by orders from home, from the Government of Granada in the Mediterranean, where he commanded the British army until the arrival of Lord W. Bentinck and subsequently took a force of ten thousand men from Sicily to the eastern coast of Spain. Medal for Martinique.

4 Paymaster Timbrell was present, as a volunteer, with the old 94th, at battles of the Nive on the 9th, 10th, 11th and 13th Dec. 1813; and at the action at Sauveterre, battles of Orthes and Toulouse, and other minor affairs in the South of France, as an Ensign, with the 87th Regiment.

5 Mr. Pine served with the 26th on the China expedition, and was present at the first capture of Chusan, attack on Canton attack and capture of Amoy, repulse of the night attack on Ningpo, attack and capture of Tseke, Chapoo, Shanghai and Woosung, and Chin Kiang Foo.

Appendix 2

Despatches written by Colonel Henry Despard after the assault on Ohaeawai, 1st July 1845

Camp before Heke's *Pah,*
2nd July 1845.

Sir,

It is with much more regret than I can express, that I have to acquaint Your Excellency, that an attempt was yesterday made by the Troops under my Command in the afternoon to carry the fortified position or *Pah* of Heke without success and we were repulsed with heavy loss; the particulars shall be forwarded to you with as little delay as possible.

I enclose herewith a list of Killed and Wounded, many of the latter I am sorry to say, are severe and dangerous.

It is impossible to say too much in praise of the bravery and good conduct of both Officers and Men.

I have etc, etc,

(Signed) H. Despard,
Colonel Commanding the Troops.

His Excellency,
Governor Fitzroy,
Auckland.
Return of Killed and Wounded of the Force under command of Colonel Despard, 99th Regiment, from the 30th June to 1st July 1845.
Her Majesty's Ship *Hazard*:
  Lieutenant Phillpotts Killed.
  1 Seaman Killed.
  2 Seamen Wounded.
  1 Private of the R. Marines Killed.

Her Majesty's 58th Regiment:
   Captain Grant Killed.
   3 Serjeants, 11 Rank & File Killed.
   2   "   33   "   Wounded.
   2 Privates since dead.

Her Majesty's 96th Regiment:
   Three Rank & File Killed.
   3 Rank & File Wounded.

Her Majesty's 99th Regiment:
   1 Serjeant, 14 Rank & File Killed.
   Bt. Major Macpherson severely wounded.
   Lieutenant Beatty   do.
   Lieutenant Johnston slightly wounded.
   Ensign O'Reilly severely wounded.
   1 Serjeant & 21 Rank & File Wounded.
   2 Privates since dead.

Volunteers (Pioneers):
   4 Rank & File wounded.
   Mr Henry Clarke, Interpreter to the Forces severely wounded.

Camp before Heke's *Pah,*
July 2nd 1845.

Sir,
    Annexed is a detailed account of the action that took place between the Troops under my Command and the rebels in the early part of the fore-noon of yesterday, as also of our assault on the *Pah*, and our repulse which took place in the afternoon afterwards.
    Finding the Guns which I had brought with me from Auckland quite inefficient for breaching, from their very defective Carriages, as they frequently upset from their own firing, I requested Captain Johnson of H.M.S. *Hazard* to send me one of his heavy Guns, which was accordingly brought up to camp, a distance of 15 miles land carriage, over most execrable roads with great labour and difficulty on the 30th, and during that day a platform was erected on the side of a hill on the right

of our position, the top of which hill was occupied by our Ally Nene and his Tribe; a Serjeant's Guard of the 58th Regiment was also there to protect a six-pounder that had been placed there with a view to raking the Enemy's position. The *Hazard*'s Gun opened its fire about 10 o'clock A.M., and while the attention of everybody was occupied observing its effects, a sudden attack was made on this position from a very thick wood close in its rear, and Waka's people were driven from it. I was in the battery halfway down the hill when this attack was made, when I instantly ordered up a party of the 58th Regiment under Major Bridge, who gallantly charged up the hill so as to turn the Enemy's left flank, and regained the position with the loss of only one Man.

This attack shewed me the necessity of coming to an immediate decision, and I accordingly determined on attacking the *Pah* by assault, in the afternoon, as soon as the few shot brought up from the *Hazard* (26 in number) were expended; which I expected would so loosen the Stockades, as to enable the men attacking them to cut and pull them down. In pursuance of this resolution, a storming party was ordered to parade at 3 o'clock P.M. for this purpose, and I issued instructions for its guidance as detailed in the accompanying Memorandum.* The parties for the attack were enabled to advance to within 60 to 100 yards of the point of attack, and there remain unperceived by the Enemy, in a ravine under cover. When the advance was sounded, they rushed forward in the most gallant and daring manner, and every endeavour was made to pull the Stockade down. They partially succeeded in opening the outer one, but the inward one resisted all their efforts, and being lined with men firing through loop-holes on a level with the ground, and from others halfway up, our men were falling so fast, that notwithstanding the most daring acts of bravery, and the greatest perseverance, they were obliged to retire, this could not be effected without additional loss in the endeavour to bring off the wounded men in which they were generally successful. The retreat was covered by the party under Lieut-Colonel Hulme of the 96th Regiment, and too much praise cannot be given to that officer for the coolness and steadiness with which he conducted it under heavy fire.

* See page 100.

I must here remark that the hatchets and axes, as well as the ropes for pulling down the Stockade, and the ladders, were all thrown away or left behind by those appointed to carry them; and to this circumstance I attribute the main cause of the failure.

I trust that it will not be thought that the character of the British has been tarnished on this occasion. One third of the men actually engaged fell in the attack, and during the eight days that we have been engaged carrying on operations against this place, one fourth of the whole strength of the British soldiers under my Command (originally not exceeding 490) have been either Killed or Wounded.

From Lieutenant-Colonel Hulme I have received every assistance during the whole time of these operations, independent of his gallant conduct in covering the retreat. Major Macpherson of the 99th Regiment, who led the principal attack and was severely wounded also deserves every praise for the daring manner in which he led his men to the assault, and though slightly struck on the left breast at the commencement, he gallantly persevered until struck down by a serious wound. Equal praise is also due to Major Bridge of the 58th Regiment for the coolness and steadiness with which he led his men to the attack, and his perseverance until called off. Where every individual has behaved equally well it seems invidious to particularize names, but I cannot avoid mentioning the unwearied toil, zeal and energy displayed by Lieutenant Willmott of the Royal Artillery in conducting that department with the most inefficient means. Captain Marlow, Royal Engineers, and his Department gave me every assistance in their power while labouring with the same inefficiency of means as the Royal Artillery. I must not omit either to mention the able assistance and the active zeal displayed by Lieutenant and Adjutant Deering of the 99th Regiment (acting as Major of Brigade) whether under fire of the enemy or in conducting the necessary details.

The three officers with Major Macpherson's party were all either killed or wounded, Captain Grant, Lieutenant Beatty (who volunteered the forlorn hope) and Ensign O'Reilly.

The Volunteers from the New Zealand Militia, acting as Pioneers under Lieutenant Figg deserve to be mentioned, and that officer himself has undergone increasing toil of the most harassing nature with zeal and energy. Lieutenant Wood and the Volunteers for the Artillery deserve to be included in this commendation. Captain Johnson of H.M.S. *Hazard* has given me the most unwearied assistance in every possible way from the commencement of our operations, by sending up supplies of all sorts, even from his own ship when our public stores were deficient. The Seamen and Marines of H.M. Navy have always borne the same character for bravery and intrepidity whereever they have been employed, and the few 13 in number that joined this expedition from H.M.S. *Hazard* have notably supported the same character. Lieutenant Phillpotts R.N. fell while endeavouring to force his way through the Stockade.

I have the honor etc, etc,
(Signed) H. Despard, Lt-Col 99th Regt, and
Colonel on the Staff in N.Z.

His Excellency Robert Fitzroy,
Governor,
Auckland.
P.S. The wounded are doing well under the able care and constant attention bestowed on them by Dr Pine of the 58th, and Dr Galbraith of the 99th Regiment.

Camp, Heke's *Pah*,
3 A.M. July 11th
1845.

Sir,
    I have the honor to acquaint you that the *Pah* is in our possession. Offensive operations against it were resumed yesterday, and continued until night, and would have been again resumed this morning, but the Enemy vacated the Fortress during the night fearing to stand another assault; I was made acquainted with the circumstance around midnight, but pursuit was then useless, and from the nature of the country through which the retreat lay, thick wood and no road, an attempt at it would probably have been attended with an unnecessary waste of human life.

I now anxiously await Your Excellency's further instructions, and am very desirous to get the troops under better cover before the rainy weather again commences.

I have etc, etc,

(Signed) H. Despard, Colonel Commanding
the Troops in New Zealand.

His Excellency Governor Fitzroy,
Auckland.

P.S. The body of Captain Grant of the 58th Regiment which was missing has been found; it had been buried outside the *Pah* where he fell and was not mutilated.

Camp before Heke's *Pah*,
11th July 1845.

Sir,

In my letter of this morning 4 o'clock A.M. I had the honor to acquaint you that the *Pah* was in our possession, and that the Enemy had retreated to fastnesses among the hills about 10 miles distant, where it is I believe impossible to follow them.

The Enemy was unable to carry off his Guns, and we have taken three Iron ones on Ship Carriages, and one more was found disabled in the Fortress.

There is no doubt that it was the fear of another assault being made after the renewal of Offensive Operations yesterday, that caused this retreat.

In consequence of the alteration in the state of affairs here since my letter by the *Velocity* I have taken upon myself to suspend the sailing of that vessel, until your further instructions are received.

The quantity of provisions stored in the captured fortress (potatoes) exceeds anything I could have formed an idea of.

One report in Camp is, that the principal part of the Enemy have dispersed in different directions, but I have so little opportunity of gaining correct information, that I scarcely give credit to any.

I shall proceed as rapidly as possible to pull down and burn every part of the *Pah*.

I have etc, etc,

(Signed) H. Despard, Colonel Commanding the Troops.

His Excellency Governor Fitzroy,
Auckland.

Camp at Hone Heke's *Pah*,
12th July 1845.

Sir,

   I have the honor to acquaint you that the total destruction of Heke's fortress was commenced yesterday and will be completed this evening, fire having been applied to every part of the Stockading and all the wood work burned down.

The strength of this place has struck me with astonishment, and I feel convinced that some European has had the direction of it.

Independent of the double Stockade many of the timbers of which were twelve inches broad, by four and six inches thick, and sunk three feet in the ground, there was a ditch within the inner Stockade about five feet deep and the same broad, which was crossed by traverses every five or six feet with a narrow communication between each, that would admit of only one man passing at a time. Deep holes were sunk in various parts of the interior of the place, and thick embankments of earth were thrown up round them, and some of them were strongly blockaded besides with heavy timbers which enabled the Garrison to remain in them without being endangered from our shot, and it was only after the Guns were raised to a considerable elevation on a hill, about 350 yards distant, that we were enabled to seriously molest them by a plunging fire which entered those under-ground habitations.

I cannot venture following the enemy into the interior, as the season of the year is so very unfavourable, and there would scarcely be a possibility of my obtaining supplies. I shall therefore break up from this camp on Monday next the 14th inst. and return to Waimate.

The Guns taken consisted of 2 iron 9 pounders, 1 iron 4 pounder, and 1 iron 2 pounder swivel.

I have etc, etc,

(Signed) H. Despard, Colonel

Commanding the Troops.

His Excellency Governor Fitzroy,

Auckland.

P.S. As I had no means of carrying the captured Guns with me, I have given orders that they should be blown up.

Appendix 3

Despatches written by Colonel Henry Despard concerning the taking of Ruapekapeka *Pa* January 1846

Camp before the Ruapekapeka,
Kawiti's *Pah*, Jan. 5, 1846.

Sir,

In my letter dated the 28th ultimo, addressed to your Excellency, I had the honour of detailing the proceedings of the force under my command up to that time; and I now proceed with the detail of what has taken place since. Before daylight on the morning of the 29th, a party of our native allies penetrated the wood immediately in our front in a most praiseworthy manner, and took possession of an open piece of ground on the opposite side, sending me immediate intelligence of what they had done. I directly moved forward with 200 men to their support, and secured the position.

The 30th and 31st were principally occupied in bringing up the guns and ammunition through the woods; a work of great labour and time, as it required between fifty and sixty men to each gun to get them through, on account of the heavy trees it was necessary to cut down in making the road, and the steepness of the hills they had to pass over.

Several rockets and shells have been thrown into the *pah* on the 31st, and each day since, with the utmost accuracy, doing great credit to the officers of her Majesty's navy who directed them—namely, Lieut. Egerton, *North Star,* who had charge of the rockets, and Lieut. Bland of the *Racehorse*, and Lieut. Leeds of the H.E.I.C. ship *Elphinstone,* who directed the shells.

On the morning of the 1st instant, I pushed forward a strong party into the only wood that now divided us from the enemy, and taking up a position in the centre of it, on an open piece of ground about 400 yards from the *pah*, a strong stockade was immediately commenced for the purpose of covering a battery; and the work was sufficiently advanced before night to hinder any attempt of the enemy to drive us away: the work was carried on under cover of a very thick part of the wood, which completely concealed it from the enemy. On the afternoon of the following day, the enemy made a strong sally from the *pah*, with a view, it is supposed, of turning the flank of this advanced party of ours in the stockade, which was not yet finished; but they were most gallantly opposed by our native allies, under the direction of chiefs Tomati Waka Nene, Noble or Nopera, Mohai Tawai and others, who instantly dashed out and attacked them, driving them back with some loss, supposed to amount to eight or ten killed and between fifteen and twenty wounded. On our side five were wounded on this occasion; and one of our most active chiefs, Rippa, was severely wounded the previous day in a skirmish with a small party of the enemy, who, it appeared, had come out of the *pah* for the purpose of picking off any stragglers from our camp, and who had succeeded in killing one of the volunteer pioneers, who had gone an unnecessary distance for water, and was shot in the act of taking it. Up to this date, no casualty, with the above exceptions, has taken place in the European part of the force.

It may be proper for me to observe, that in the action of the afternoon of the 2nd, the European troops acted only as a reserve, at the particular desire of the Native chiefs, who were fearful that their own people might be mistaken for the enemy and fired upon.

> I have the honour to be,
> H. Despard, Acting Colonel on the Staff, commanding the Troops in New Zealand.

To his Excellency Governor Grey.

> Camp before the Ruapekapeka,
> Kawiti's *Pah*, Jan. 9, 1846.

Sir,

In continuation of my despatch of the 5th instant, I have the honour to acquaint your Excellency that, the stockade and battery mentioned therein as being commenced within about 400 yards of the *pah* being nearly completed, I determined on throwing up another, but much smaller, on its right flank, and considerably in advance, so as effectually to put a stop to any attempt on the part of the enemy at making a sally, such as took place on the 2nd inst.; as also entirely to cut his communication with the country on the side of our camp. This second work was completed this day, and two guns (one 18-pounder and one 12-pound howitzer), placed in battery within it. The larger stockade is also now completed, and contains two 32-pounders and four 5½-inch mortars. Our present position before the *pah* is as follows. The main camp is placed on an open piece of ground, or rather ridge, with deep wooded valleys on either side, and thick woods both in front and rear; the distance from the *pah* suposed to be about 750 yards. In our front are three guns (one 32-pounder, one 12-pound howitzer, and one light 6-pounder), with an apparatus for throwing rockets. From this position several shells have been thrown into the *pah,* as well as rockets; and much execution must have been done by them, as they were well directed. Within the larger stockade, which, at the utmost, cannot be more than 400 yards from the *pah*, there are two 32-pounders, and four small 5½-inch mortars; and the wood in front of these guns has been so completely cut down, that nearly the whole face of the *pah* is now open to their fire. The small advanced stockade contains one 18-pounder, and one 12-pound howitzer, and commands a range not only along the same face (the western) that is exposed to our other batteries, but will also range along the southern face, and, I expect, destroy the defences on the south-west angle. Our progress up to this period may have been considered slow, but great difficulties have been encountered, as your Excellency, who has been an eye-witness to all our movements, will, I am sure, admit; and the decided advantage that will arise to the colony at large, if we succeed in carrying this with little or no loss, has decided me in proceeding with so much caution.

I have the honour to be,
H. Despard, Acting Colonel on the Staff,
commanding the Troops.

To his Excellency Governor Grey.

Extract from Brigade Orders

Camp before Ruapekapeka
Jan. 11, 1846.

The officer commanding the forces against the rebel chiefs Heki and Kawiti has the greatest satisfaction in congratulating the whole of the force at the brilliant success that has attended their operations of the last two days. The capture of a fortress of such extraordinary strength by assault, and nobly defended by a brave and determined enemy, is of itself sufficient to prove the intrepidity and gallantry displayed by all concerned, whether seamen, marines, troops of the line, artillery of the H.E.I.C. service, or the volunteer pioneers; and it will be a most pleasing part of his duty to bring such conduct to the notice of his Excellency the Governor of New Zealand, and through him to that of her Majesty, and his Grace the Commander-in-Chief.

The colonel cannot conclude this order without expressing his admiration at the brave and intrepid conduct displayed by our native allies on every occasion since these operations commenced; and more particularly since the assault of the *pah*, on which occasion their bravery was fully equal to what might have been expected from her Majesty's bravest troops.

The colonel commanding feels the greatest regret at the loss of so many brave men as have been killed and wounded on this occasion; but it will be considered an alleviation by their friends, that they have fallen while nobly performing their duty to their Queen and country.

Camp at Ruapekapeka,
Kawiti's *Pah*, Jan. 11, 1846.

Sir,

It is with extreme satisfaction that I have the honour of acquainting your Excellency, that Kawiti's stronghold or *pah*, at the Ruapekapeka, was this day carried by assault by the force under my command, after a bold and most determined resistance on the part of the enemy, who continued the action long after he had been driven from the fortress; but the ardour and intrepidity displayed by the British force of every description, as well as by our native allies, overcame every obstacle, and after three hours' hard fighting the enemy was obliged to fly, and dispersed in different directions. The detail of this attack, as well as that of the preceding day's cannonade, shall be laid before your Excellency with the least possible delay. I greatly regret to add, that our loss on this occasion has been heavy, as will be seen by the enclosed list of killed and wounded; but when the extraordinary strength of the place assaulted is taken into consideration, I am only surprised it has been so small.

> I have the honour to be,
> H. Despard, Acting Colonel on the Staff,
> commanding the Troops.

To his Excellency Governor Grey.

Return of killed and wounded during the assault on Kawiti's *Pah* on January 11th, 1846

H.M.S. *Castor*.
    Killed. 7 Seamen.
    Wounded. 10 Seamen
                    2 Marines.

H.M.S. *North Star*.
    Killed. 1 Marine.
    Wounded. 2 Seamen, including Mr Murray, Midshipman.

H.M.S. *Calliope*.
    Killed. 1 Marine.
    Wounded. 1 Marine.

H.M.S. *Racehorse*.
    Wounded. 1 Seaman.

H.E.I.C.S. *Elphinstone*.
    Wounded. 1 Seaman.

H.M. 58th Regiment.
    Killed. 2 Privates.
    Wounded. 10 Privates.

H.M. 99th Regiment.
    Killed. 1 Private.
    Wounded. 1 Private.

Volunteer Pioneers.
    Wounded. 1 Private, also 2 wounded during the previous
                    operations, one since dead.

Mr Murray, H.M.S. *North Star*, the only officer wounded, severely not dangerously.

Camp before the Ruapekapeka,
January 12th, 1846.

Sir,

In my letter of yesterday, I had the satisfaction of acquainting your Excellency of the fall of Kawiti's *pah* by assault on that day. I now proceed to communicate the detail. On the morning of the 10th instant, our advanced batteries being completed (one within 350 yards, and the second about 160 yards off the *pah*), a general fire was commenced from all the guns, with a view of opening a breach into the place, and several rockets were thrown into it at the same time, for the purpose of driving the enemy out. The fire was kept up with little intermission during the greater part of the day; and towards evening it was evident that the outer works on those parts against which the fire was directed were nearly all giving way, but the numerous stockades inside crossing the place in different directions, and composed of much stronger timbers were scarcely touched. Towards evening our fire slackened, and was only continued occasionally during the night to prevent the enemy attempting to repair the breaches that had been made. On the following morning, the 11th instant, no person being observed moving within the *pah*, a few of our native allies, under a chief named William Waka, a brother of Tomati Waka Nene, went up to the place for the purpose of observing whether or not the enemy had evacuated it. This party entered the breach unopposed; which being perceived from the first battery, a party of 100 men of the troops under Captain Denny was pushed up rapidly, and together with the natives gained the inside of the stockades before they were perceived by the enemy, who, at the time, were sheltering themselves from the fire of the guns on a sloping piece of ground in one of their outworks. Our parties had scarcely gained the inside when they were noticed by the enemy, and a heavy fire of musketry instantly poured in upon them. The stockades, however, now became our protection; and strong reinforcements being immediately brought up from the camp, possession of the place was secured in spite of all the efforts of the enemy to drive us back, being obliged to retreat and shelter himself in a wood opposite the east face of the *pah*; where the trees being extremely large, and forming complete breastworks—many of them having been cut down previously, and evidently purposely placed in a defensive position—he was enabled to maintain a heavy fire against us for a considerable time, until a doorway in that face having been broken, the seamen and troops rushed out and disloged him from his position. He, however, still continued to keep up a fire from the woods, but more with a view to cover his retreat, and enable him to carry away his wounded men, than with any expectation of renewing the contest. The attack commenced about ten o'clock A.M., and all firing had ceased about two P.M. The extraordinary strength of this place, particularly in its interior defences, far exceeded any idea I could have formed of it. Every hut was a complete fortress in itself, being strongly stockaded all round with heavy timbers sunk deep in the ground and placed close to each other—few of them being less than one foot in diameter, and many considerably more—besides having a strong embankment thrown up behind them. Each hut had also a deep excavation close to it, forming a complete bomb-proof, and sufficiently large to contain several people, where at night they were completely sheltered from both shot and shell. The enemy's loss has been severe, and several chiefs on their side have fallen. The numbers I have not been able to ascertain, as they invariably carry off both killed and wounded when possible. Several of the former were, however, left behind; and it has been decidedly ascertained from a wounded prisoner that the chief Heki had joined Kawiti in the *pah* on the afternoon preceding the attack.

As your Excellency has been an eye-witness to our operations, and, I may say, actually engaged in the assault, it may be thought unnecessary to draw your attention to those persons who had a greater opportunity than others of distinguishing themselves; but the satisfaction I feel in recording the obligation I am under to those persons, makes me persevere in doing so. To the officers, seamen, and marines from her Majesty's ships, for their extraordinary exertions in dragging the guns over steep hills and through difficult and thick woods, as well as for their distinguished bravery in action, the service on this occasion is greatly indebted. To Captain Graham, of H.M.S. *Castor,* for his co-operation, and the readiness with which he afforded every possible aid and assistance since his arrival;—to Captain Sir E. Home, who had previously been the senior naval officer, and who, not only upon the present occasion but

on all former ones, has used the most strenuous exertions to
forward all the objects of the expedition;—to Commander
Hay, of H.M.S. *Racehorse,* who commanded the whole of the
seamen attached to the force, and who so greatly aided our
operations by his personal exertions and example, not only
during the assault, but in all the previous difficulties we had to
encounter;—to Lieutenant Otway, of H.M.S. *Castor,* commanding the small-armed seamen;—to Lieutenant Falcon, of
H.M.S. *Castor*; Lieutenant Bland, and Mr Nopps, master of
H.M.S. *Racehorse*; and Lieutenant Leeds, H.E.I.C.S. *Elphinstone,* who all directed the fire of the guns with such precision
and excellence; and to Lieutenant Egerton, of H.M.S. *North
Star,* who directed the rockets, much of our success is to be
attributed. To Lieutenant-Colonel Wynyard, commanding
the 58th Regiment, I feel the greatest obligation. His advice
was of the utmost use to me on many occasions; and his
personal exertions, whenever an opportunity offered, as well
as his gallantry during the assault, were most conspicuous. To
the Captain commanding the flank companies of the 99th
Regiment, and Captain Langford, Royal Marines (attached),
much praise is due. To Captain Marlow, Royal Engineers,
for his exertions in constructing the batteries; Captain Matson, 58th Regiment, who acted as Deputy Assistant
Quartermaster-General; and Lieutenant Wilmot, Royal Artillery, who directed the mortar battery, great praise is also due. I
have also derived great assistance from the services of Lieutenant O'Connell, Aide-de-Camp to Lieutenant-General Sir
Maurice O'Connell, and Acting Major of Brigade to this
force. And I must not omit to notice in very strong terms the
indefatigable exertions of Captain Atkins and his small corps
of Volunteer Pioneers, whose conduct and services during the
whole operations have been of the greatest advantage. Every
kindness has been shown to the wounded men by Doctors
Kidd and Pine, the Senior Medical Officers, and all the medical
officers, both naval and military. And I have reason to be
satisfied with the exertions of the Commissariat Department,
under D.A.C.G. Turner. The wounded men are generally
doing well, and the only officer amongst them, a young midshipman of the *North Star*, Mr Murray, whose ardour carried
him too far when the enemy were driven from the woods. I
have now only to express the peculiar satisfaction I feel, that

your Excellency has had an opportunity of personally witnessing the toils and difficulties that were encountered, and the cheerfulness with which every part of the force exerted itself to overcome them; and I beg to express my own sincere thanks for the advice and observations that you have occasionally been kind enough to favour me with during that period. I should also wish to draw your Excellency's attention to Mr Edward Shortland, who was prevailed upon to act as my interpreter, and who has rendered me many important services while acting in that capacity.

I have the honour to be,
Your Excellency's most obedient servant,
H. Despard, Acting Colonel on the Staff,
commanding the Troops.

To his Excellency Governor Grey.

Appendix 4

Alexander Whisker's Song

It was the tenth of April from Sydney we set sail
And Fortune did us favour—with a sweet and pleasant gale
We Landed in New Zealand upon that very day
And at Auckland we got orders to sail straight for the Bay
When first we landed on that shore to fight we went straight-
  way
to face the dareing Maories all on the 8th of May

2nd

At 6 oclock the 3rd of May we mustered for the war
the 58th and 96th Likewise some gallant tars
To face Bold Honi Heke—that Dareing Maorie Chiefe
And Likewise Bold Kowitta that came to his Reliefe
We fought on the 8th of May. although we were not beat
At 5 oclock that evening we were forced for to Retreat

3rd

When at the hour of 5 oclock we were forced for to yield
There was 7 of our comrades lay dead upon the field
But Heke Buried them next day and quickly left the Pah
For he found the British soldiers was nobly taught to war
We marched to Keri Keri for hopes to get away
And we Burned the Waicaro Pah on the 16th of May

4th

Upon the 26th of May for Auckland we set sail
and fortune did us favour with a sweet and Pleasant gale
We had not got our anchor cast When our orders came
that we were quickly to return to face our foes again
two hundred of the 99th came in on the next day
and there Colonel takeing the command we sailed down to the
  Bay

5th

It was on the first Day of July the year of forty five
When lieing in our encampment the order did arrive
to go and storm Kowitas Pah without aney Delay
It was our Determination to take it on that Day
the 32s being fireing for maney Days before
the Pah was strong no breach was made which grieved our
  hearts full sore

6th

At 3 oclock that evening 2 hundred of our men
the 58th the 99th the sailors and marines
they all like men did muster upon that fatal Day
to fight for Queen and country and show them British Play
But men been few the Pah was strong we could not Rightly
  stand
For in 7 minutes and a half we lost one hundred men

7th

Upon that Day I am grieved to say 3 officers was slain
And maney a gallant soldier lay Dead upon the Plain
We Buryed them in 2 Days time which grieved our hearts full
  sore
to see so maney heroes all Buried in there gore
We had no coffins made for them but all was silant Round
We Rolled them in there Blankets and gently laid them
  Down

8th

It was on the 10th of January to fight we next did go
We had large guns and mortars and Rocket tubes also
they being in there strongest Pah and well secured all Round
We fired on all sides of them in hopes to Break it Down
We made 3 Breaches in the Pah and scattered it about
We kept the fire up all night but could not get them out

9th

When early the next morning to Breakfast they did go
Into the huts outside the Pah not thinking we would know

When 50 men from each stockade they strove with might and
    main
they kept them all outside the Pah to more assistance came
We fought from 8 that morning to it was nearly 3
When with maney killed and Wounded they were forced to
    run away

10th

Upon our side but 12 were killed and wounded very few
On the next day we burned the Pah before that we withdrew
We Buried our comrades upon that very day
And we planted willows on there greaves before we came
    away
So now the war is over and we have saved our lives
So let us join in Drinking to our sweethearts and our Wives

Finis

Composed by Alexr. Whisker 58th Regt Camp victoria
24th March 1846

List of Sources

Manuscripts:

BRIDGE, Major Cyprian, 'Journal of Events on Expedition to New Zealand, Commencing 4th April 1845' (Alexander Turnbull Library, Wellington, New Zealand).

MITCHELL, Corporal John, Diary kept in New Zealand; Letter dated 19th March 1848 (Museum of The Northamptonshire Regiment). Letter dated 14th June 1897 (Mr J. Kitt, Auckland, New Zealand).

WHISKER, Private Alexander, 'Memorandum Book' (Auckland War Memorial and Museum).

SPEIGHT, Sergeant-Major W. I., Various documents relating to his service (The Speight family, Auckland, New Zealand).

Digest of Service, 58th Regiment (Museum of The Northamptonshire Regiment).

Muster Rolls, 58th Regiment (Public Record Office, W.O. 12-6745).

Published Works:

ANGLESEY, The Marquess of, *A History of the British Cavalry, Vol. 1, 1816–1850* (London, 1973).

BARTHORP, Michael, *The Northamptonshire Regiment* (London, 1974).

BLACKMORE, Howard L., *British Military Firearms, 1650–1850* (London, 1961).

BRIDGE, John S. C., *The Family of Bridge of Harwich* (privately published, 1959).

BUICK, T. Lindsay, *New Zealand's First War* (Wellington, 1926).

CHICHESTER, H. M. and BURGES-SHORT, G., *The Records and Badges of the British Army* (London, 1900).

COLLEDGE, J. J., *Ships of the Royal Navy: An Historical Index*, two volumes (David & Charles, 1969).

COWAN, James, *The New Zealand Wars and the Pioneering Period*, Vol. 1 (Wellington, 1923).

FORTESCUE, Hon. J. W. *History of the British Army*, Vol. XIII (London, 1927).

GIBSON, Tom, *The Maori Wars* (London, 1974).

GUDGEON, Thomas W., *Heroes of New Zealand and Maori History of the Wars* (1887).

GURNEY, Lieut-Colonel Russell, *History of The Northamptonshire Regiment, 1742–1934* (Aldershot, 1935).

HAIGH, J. Bryant, 'The 80th Foot in New Zealand', *Bulletin of the Military Historical Society*, Vol. XXVI (1976).

HATTAWAY, Robert, late Colour-Sergeant, *Reminiscences of the Northern War* (Auckland, 1899).

HOLT, Edgar, *The Strangest War* (London, 1962).

Journal of the Society for Army Historical Research, 1922–77.

KENRICK, N. C. E., *The Story of The Wiltshire Regiment* (London, 1963).

KNOX, Ray (Editor), *The Maori–European Wars* (Wellington, 1973).

LEWIS, Michael, *The Navy and Britain* (London, 1948).

LLOYD, Christopher, *The Nation and the Navy* (London, 1961).

MCKILLOP, R.N., Lieutenant H. F., *Reminiscences of Twelve Months Service in New Zealand* (London, 1849).

OLIVER, W. H., *The Story of New Zealand* (London, 1960).

SINCLAIR, Keith, *The British Empire—New Zealand, (Time Life/*B.B.C. publications, 1972).

SMALL, E. Milton, *Told from the Ranks* (London, 1898).

SOMERVILLE, A., *The Autobiography of a Working Man* (London, 1848).

THOMSON, A. S., *The Story of New Zealand* (London, 1859).

TURNER, E. S., *Gallant Gentlemen* (London, 1956).

WATTEVILLE, Colonel H. de, *The British Soldier* (London, 1954).

Military Manuals, Regulations, etc:
  Field Exercises and Movements of Infantry, 1833.
  The Manual and Platoon Exercises, 1834.
  Queen's Regulations, 1844.
  Army Lists, 1845, 1846.
  Regulations for the Dress of General, Staff, and Regimental Officers of the Army, 1846.
  Royal Warrant and Regulations regarding Army Services, 1848.

Newspapers:
  Illustrated London News.
  New Zealand Herald.
  New Zealand Spectator.
  Auckland Weekly News.
  Daily Southern Cross.
  The New Zealander.

Index

Index

Regiments, 58th—*cont*

Colours, 21, 118, 191, 192; recruiting areas, 26; uniform, 17, 34, 64, 95, 116, 122, 128, 167; in Australia, 13; to New Zealand, 13, 49, 50, 54; to Bay of Islands, 56; band, 21, 54, 56, 115, 118; at Pomare's *pa*, 58–60; at Puketutu, 67–70; at Kapotai *pa* (Waikare), 76–9; at Ohaeawai, 91–5, 98, 100, 101, 105, 204–6; reinforced from N.S.W., 116; at Ruapekapeka, 126, 134, 137, 215, 218; at Wellington, 147; at Porirua, 151, 158; at Boulcott's Farm, 152–4; at Victoria, 165–70; to Sydney, 171; at Wanganui, 171–85; awards to, 186; tribute from Grey, 186–7; later service, 190, 200

65th, 159, 190; arrives New Zealand, 158; relieves 58th, 170; at Wanganui, 181, 185; later service, 190, 200

80th; first garrison in New Zealand, 45, 46; at Bay of Plenty, 45; leaves New Zealand, 47, 49; later service, 200

83rd, 117

87th, 20

94th, 20

96th, 40, 56, 61, 64, 76, 86, 87, 112, 115, 137; to New Zealand, 47; in Australia, 49; to Bay of Islands, 47, 49, 55, 82; at Pomare's *pa*, 60; indiscipline, 60, 83; at Puketutu, 67–70; at Ohaeawai, 100, 204; at Wellington, 147, 150; later service, 200

99th, 85, 86, 87, 112, 120, 146, 154; to New Zealand, 46, 48; in Australia, 49; at Ohaeawai, 98, 100, 101, 104–6, 115, 204, 206; at Ruapekapeka, 137, 215, 218; at Wellington, 147; at Porirua, 151, 158; at Horokiwi, 161; later service, 200

Duke of Edinburgh's Royal, 200

King's, 200

Manchester, 200

North Auckland, 200

Northamptonshire, 14, 185 fn, 200

Royal Anglian, 200, 201

Royal Berkshire, 200

Royal Lincolnshire, 200

Royal Marines, 12, 61, 62, 64, 72, 76, 87, 120; at Kororareka, 39; at Puketutu, 67; at Ohaeawai, 203, 207; at Ruapekapeka, 128, 217, 218

South Staffordshire, 200

Staffordshire, 200

Wiltshire, 200

York and Lancaster, 200

Rewa (Manu), chief, 145

Richmond, Fort, 150

Riel, Louis, rebellion in Canada, 199

Rio de Janiero, 199

Ripa, chief, 76–8, 80, 82, 88, 120, 124, 125, 212

Robertson, Acting Commander, R.N., 39, 40

Ross, Asst Surgeon, R.N., 161

Royal Commission on Military Punishments, 31

Royal Navy (see Navy)

Ruapekapeka (The Bat's Nest), 119, 121–123, 141, 146, 190, 191, 197, 199, 200; operations at, 123, 139; casualties at, 137, 215; Despard's despatches on, 143, 211–19

Rumburgh, Suffolk, 115

Rush, Lieut A., 58th, 202

Russell, Bay of Islands (see Kororareka)

Russell, Capt A. H., 58th, 54, 150, 202; at Wellington, 147; road building, 151, 185; commended by Duke of Wellington, 186

Russell, Pte J., 58th, 186 fn

Rutland Bay, 64

Rutland, county, 17, 26, 191

Rutland Stockade, 174, 175, 180, 183

S

St Paul's Church, Auckland, 51, 52, 191, 192

St John's Wood, Wanganui, 183, 184

Sandhurst, Royal Military College, 22

Sculthorp, Pte, 58th, 176

Scutari, 196

Selwyn, Bishop, 39, 40, 46

Shera, Lt-Col, 192

Shipley, Pte, 58th, 175, 176

Ships (see also Warships)
Prince of Orange, 18
Hyderabad, 36
Lord George Seymour, 37